Devotions

January

Eileen H. Wilmoth, editor
photo by Chuck Perry
Volume 45

©2001 STANDARD PUBLISHING, 8121 Hamilton Avenue, Cincinnati, Ohio, 45231, a division of STANDEX INTERNATIONAL Corp. Topics based on Home Daily Bible Readings, International Sunday School Lessons, © 2000 by the Committee on the Uniform Series. Printed in U.S.A.

I Love a Parade!

Nations will come to your light, and kings to the brightness of your dawn
(Isaiah 60:3, *New International Version*).

Scripture: Isaiah 60:4-9
Song: "We're Marching to Zion"

Who can resist the thrill of a parade? In anticipation crowds line both sides of the street, straining to see the first signs of the parade. Soon marching bands fill the air with their brass blare and the *thump, thump, thump* of bass drums that reverberate in every chest. Best of all are the parade's surprises: jugglers, animals doing tricks, miniature cars, horse-drawn wagons, and beautiful floats.

Today's Scripture describes a remarkable parade to the holy city of God. Her scattered children are coming home, carrying the wealth of the world with them. The purpose of it all is to praise God and to honor the Lord.

To some, straining to see the glory of the Lord amid the problems of this world, these sentences may seem surprising. Where is this city honoring God above all and by all? When will the whole world, like the watchers at a parade, focus on the unparalleled spectacle of God's goodness and grace?

We do not know, but weary with our world, we can rejoice: someday everyone will march to bring glory to our God. That will be a parade like none other!

Dear God, Creator of all, in anticipation of that day, help us to bring You the glory that You deserve. Help us to remember that You are the only worthwhile one to receive praise. May we offer it with abandon. In Jesus' name, we pray. Amen.

January 1-6. **Mark A. Taylor** is vice president and publisher with Standard Publishing. He and his wife, Evelyn, have two grown children, Jennifer and Geoffrey.

No Enemies

All who despise you will bow down at your feet and will call you the City of the Lord (Isaiah 60:14, *New International Version*).

Scripture: Isaiah 60:10-15
Song: "When We All Get to Heaven"

Many young people have trouble applying Christ's command to "love your enemies" (see Matthew 5:43-48). "I don't have any enemies," they say.

Unfortunately, as we grow, we may acquire a few enemies. We realize that every day we confront a spiritual enemy, our "adversary the devil" (1 Peter 5:8), who seeks our downfall at every turn.

We see our fight with the devil in the doctor's office, the hospital, and the funeral home. The apostle Paul calls death the "last enemy that shall be destroyed" (1 Corinthians 15:26), and many of us yearn to experience that victory. We lose someone close to us, and we become sensitized to the losses of those all around us. We realize that death is life's constant companion, the tool of our enemy to weaken and discourage someone we know week after week after week.

The Scripture reminds that someday Christ will "put all enemies under his feet" (1 Corinthians 15:25). This is the promise implied in today's Scripture reading. Ancient cities kept their gates firmly shut, in order to protect themselves against enemy attackers. But at the end of time, the gates of God's city "shall be open continually; they shall not be shut day nor night" (see Isaiah 60:11). What a day of rejoicing that will be!

Dear God, help us to live with confidence that the devil's victories are only temporary, that Your power will overcome his every weapon, and that Your dwelling place waits to offer rest from the battle for eternity. Amen.

Give Me the Best!

Instead of bronze I will bring you gold, and silver in place of iron. Instead of wood I will bring you bronze, and iron in place of stones (Isaiah 60:17, *New International Version*).

Scripture: Isaiah 60:17-22
Song: "Blessed Be the Name"

Some may say, "I don't need a lot of stuff, but I want what I have to be the best!" This wry comment of a suburban housewife reflected her frustration with years of making do. Compact cars, bargain-basement furniture, discount-store clothes, and weekly menus created from grocery store specials—these had been her lot. And although she realized that no one can buy everything he wants, she was ready to have a few things that were the best. She was tired of settling for "just good enough to get by."

Anyone who's been forced to live on a budget—and that includes most of us!—can sympathize with her point-of-view. That's one of the reasons that today's Scripture is so appealing. God promises His people that the holy city of the future will be outfitted with nothing but the best. Although bronze is beautiful, it will never be as dazzling as gold. Although iron tools may be functional, those made of silver are lovely to display. Although wooden rafters can support a house, those made of metal are stronger. It's a promise to hold onto today. God wants the best for us, not just the "good enough." We worship God and He gives salvation—the very best thing of all.

O Father, we desire the best instead of the mediocrity that characterizes the world's enticements. We will accustom ourselves to the spiritual excellence that comes only from You. In the name of Jesus, we pray. Amen.

The Promise of the Prophet

The Spirit of the Lord is on me, because he has anointed me to preach good news to the poor. He has sent me to proclaim freedom for the prisoners and recovery of sight for the blind, to release the oppressed, to proclaim the year of the Lord's favor (Luke 4:18, 19, *New International Version*).

Scripture: Isaiah 61:1-7
Song: "I Must Tell Jesus"

Several centuries after the prophet penned this passage, Jesus read it in His hometown synagogue (see Luke 4:14-30). He told the spellbound crowd that He is the fulfillment of Isaiah's prophecy. Today Christians take comfort in His claim, but those who first heard Him reacted by trying to kill Him.

Comfort and controversy have accompanied these words from that time until now. The poor, the prisoner, the blind, and the burdened have found peace in Jesus. But many in the world have depended on the world's wisdom to solve problems. Some have rejected and some have opposed Christ's solutions.

But their protests have not diminished the appeal of His claim. Even today, as we ponder these verses, we know people who need the ministry that Jesus outlines here. We can be His agents; He will work through us to touch others with His offer of freedom, release, and recovery. We can rely on His assurance to help us see our way, too. For the promise of the prophet so many centuries ago offers hope to Christ's followers in this moment as well.

Heavenly Father, help us to extend the ministry of Jesus to brokenhearted people we will meet today. Help us to show them that You still offer grace and hope, no matter what their situation. And, God, no matter what our burden, help us to see how Christ can lighten our load, too. In the name of Jesus, we pray. Amen.

A Shirtsleeve Faith

Put ye on the Lord Jesus Christ (Romans 13:14).

Scripture: Isaiah 61:8-11
Song: "Fairest Lord Jesus"

What we wear may tell who we are and what we're doing.

Young couples dressed in tuxedoes and formal gowns are probably on the way to the school prom. A woman wearing a hard hat and jeans is probably employed at a construction site. A man in a dark suit with a white shirt and tie is likely at work as a businessman. A family wearing swim suits and T-shirts is probably on the way to the beach.

Today's Scripture, and passages throughout the Bible, recognize this common truth from everyday life. We choose our clothes to indicate attitude or mood or profession or social standing. God uses the everyday issue of clothing to challenge us to live for Him (see Ephesians 4:22-24). In today's reading, the prophet, speaking with the voice of the redeemed city of God, rejoices because God has given garments of salvation. Just as a bride and groom's outfits signify the hope and joy they have in each other, God arrays us in a robe of righteousness to prove that we belong to Him.

Without realizing it, we may make judgments about a person by looking at his or her clothing. And we may not realize how the world is judging us by the actions and attitudes we "wear." God wants us to "put on Christ," and to demonstrate His ways day-by-day to the watching world.

Heavenly Father, help our relationship with You to be as evident as the color of our clothing. Help our commitment to You to be as clear to those around us as the style we wear. In the name of Jesus Christ, the Savior of the world, we pray. Amen.

Seeking Jesus

When they saw the star, they were overjoyed
(Matthew 2:10, *New International Version*).

Scripture: Matthew 2:1-12
Song: "More Like the Master"

Like many seekers today, the wise men journeyed a long way before they found the true God. They did not let time or distance stop them, because they believed that nothing was more important than finding the One they were seeking. God has promised that those who sincerely seek Him will find Him (see Proverbs 8:17 and Jeremiah 29:13). Do you remember your own quest to uncover the truth about God? Can you recall the joy you felt when you finally discovered how to find Him?

Of course, some "seekers" aren't looking for God at all. Some want only to feel good. Some seek justification for a lifestyle they do not want to give up. Some who say they're looking for God are really focusing on themselves.

So it was for the wicked King Herod. He said he sought to worship the toddler King. But he really wanted to eliminate any possible threat to his own power and position.

The wise men, accustomed to receiving honor, bowed in humility before Jesus. They proved their motives by worshiping Him with their hearts and with their wealth. Herod did not find Jesus, and in spite of his murderous rampage, he could not eliminate Him either (see verses 13-17). This Jesus is still alive, promising peace to all who find Him today.

Dear heavenly Father, we want the presence and power of Jesus in our lives more than anything else. Help us to find Him and to show Him to others, too. In the holy name of Jesus, our Savior, we pray. Amen.

Seek God to Relieve Fears

O taste and see that the Lord is good: blessed is the man that trusteth in him
(Psalm 34:8).

Scripture: Psalm 34:1-10
Song: "God Will Take Care of You"

On a gloomy summer day, I visited a Christian friend in the hospital. He had been sick for quite some time and wanted to see me. Somehow, he believed that unless he confessed his sins and received forgiveness, either from God, or me he would not be content to die. I assured this friend that when one repents, God forgives. It is God who gives both forgiveness and salvation. After a prayer, a smile and a sigh of relief, he rested peacefully those last few days of his life.

This man was seeking the Lord and His forgiveness even though God had already forgiven him when he became a Christian. My friend knew that God would take away fear and give him the peace he wanted. What joy he experienced!

This is what David is reminding us of in his song. He will extol the Lord, he will boast in the Lord, he will glorify the Lord, and he will seek the Lord. And when we, like David, do these things, we will "lack no good thing." Our God will give us what we need.

Almighty and everliving God, we thank You for the freedom to seek You and to find You. It is through You that we are delivered from our fears and saved from worldly troubles. We trust You and celebrate our freedom in You. We give You praise! May we always celebrate life in You. In the name of Your Son, Jesus, we pray. Amen.

January 7-13. **Don Stowell** and his wife, Sharlene, minister to a church in Cincinnati, Ohio. They have three teenage daughters.

He Is All I Need

Because thy loving-kindness is better than life, my lips shall praise thee
(Psalm 63:3).

Scripture: Psalm 63:1-8
Song: "Savior, Like a Shepherd Lead Us"

In the darkest days of life, we need comfort. When we cry out in anguish, we need someone to speak and draw us close. God's servants throughout history have looked to God for the comfort that only He can give. One may want that comfort from a friend or family member, but only God can give the comfort the soul really needs. Job heard no good advice from his friends. Moses was disillusioned by the idolatry of the nation. Elijah felt he was the only one left in Israel to serve God. David, the writer of Psalms, was alone many times in his grief.

We often feel as if we travel alone in a wasteland of despair. It is sometimes difficult to summon the strength to offer praise in our darkness.

The Scripture in today's text reveals the heart of a faithful man. David would not give in to the emptiness of life. He chose to follow the Lord in spite of the troubles he faced.

Some children want a night light in their dark rooms when they go to bed. They feel that the light will give them comfort; and if they need to see, the small light will help them. David's walk in the dark times of his life was soothed by his knowledge that God was always present.

Almighty and everfaithful God, You are our God. In our darkest hours, may we never fail to seek You. We praise Your holy name and worship You this day. Help us to know that indeed You are all that we need. In the name of Jesus Christ, our Savior and Lord, we pray. Amen.

My Father Can Do Anything!

The works of the Lord are great, sought out of all them that have pleasure therein (Psalm 111:2).

Scripture: Psalm 105:1-7
Song: "I Sing the Mighty Power of God"

Award programs, introductions of famous people, newspaper articles, and interviews all use a long list of credentials or descriptions about those who are being promoted. These lists are testimonials of people who desire fame, fortune, or simply the opportunity to serve.

Perhaps you've heard the story of the two little boys arguing over whose father was the best, the biggest, the strongest, and the smartest. The story isn't necessarily about trying to prove which child can out-argue the other, but it is the testimony of how great dad really is.

We sing praise songs to God to tell Him that He is the best, the biggest, the strongest, and the smartest. Our expressions of faith are found in a host of anthems, hymns, songs and choruses such as the hymn, "How Great Thou Art" or the contemporary chorus, "I Could Sing of Your Love Forever."

Someone once said, "If you bring a thimble to God, He'll fill it. If you bring a bucket to God, He'll fill it. If you bring a 50-gallon barrel to God, He'll fill that too. Which describes the faith we have in God? The thimble, the bucket, or the barrel?" What do we bring to God?

Heavenly Father, we give You thanks not just for what You have done, but for who You are. We worship You. To You we lift our praises and our songs. To You we give glory. We bow before You and praise Your holy name. For You alone can do everything! In the name of Jesus, our Savior, we pray. Amen.

The Comfort of God

"Never will I leave you; never will I forsake you"
(Hebrews 13:5b, *New International Version*).

Scripture: Isaiah 54:4-8
Song: "It's Just Like His Great Love"

Many of us remember the days when we were younger. We can now see that we sometimes made unwise decisions. We may have spoken harsh and tasteless words. Perhaps we were cruel to classmates, rebellious to our parents, or at odds with our siblings.

We became young adults and perhaps we continued to make unwise choices. Maybe our words did not improve. Perhaps we are still cruel and rebellious.

God is calling us out of our childish behavior and into child-like innocence. He tells the penitent believer that the days gone by can be forgiven and forgotten. He says that when we leave our sins behind, we will have an entirely new life, and we can forget the foolishness that we participated in during our younger years. When God redeems us, He helps us to move forward.

The Apostle Paul knew this when he wrote, " . . . Forgetting what is behind and straining toward what is ahead, I press on toward the goal to win the prize for which God has called me heavenward in Christ Jesus" (Philippians 3:13b-14, *New International Version).*

Thank You, almighty and ever loving God, that You remain faithful to us. Even in our foolish ways, You call us to come to You. We know that You will always be there for us. Help us to move forward in lives filled with righteousness. We bow before You this day. In the name of Jesus, our Savior and Lord, we pray. Amen.

January 11

Love Never Fails

O give thanks unto the Lord; for he is good: for his mercy endureth forever
(Psalm 136:1).

Scripture: Isaiah 54:9-17
Song: "All Creatures of Our God and King"

Children learn early in life to trust their parents. They want to be cuddled and cared for by their parents. They soon recognize the provider of food and diaper changes. When the walking and talking begin, they realize who it is that will say "No," or "Stay away from that." In later years, children bear with parental instruction. When they disobey, they know that there will be punishment.

God nurtures us. He also punishes us when we disobey (Hebrews 12:5, 6). It is because of His love for us that He disciplines us. His love always goes beyond punishment. God desires us to have a pure relationship with Him and therefore, provides terms of reconciliation for us. In Isaiah's prophecy, he reveals God's promises of restoration.

In spite of what we have done in the past, God still has an unfailing love for us. He promises strength and prosperity, safety from enemies and His constant compassion. Our loving Father will do this for His children.

When we endure punishment, let us never forget the words of the One who continues to nurture us: ". . . my unfailing love for you will not be shaken nor my covenant of peace be removed" (see Isaiah 54:10b, *New International Version*).

Almighty Father, thank You for reminding us that You will not push us aside when we've sinned. You have promised a renewal and a restoration. May we remember the good that comes from discipline. In Jesus' name, we pray. Amen.

A Balanced Diet

Blessed are those who hunger and thirst for righteousness, for they will be filled (Matthew 5:6, *New International Version*).

Scripture: Isaiah 55:1-5
Song: "Praise Ye the Lord, the Almighty"

Physical well-being is important to all of us. Conversations concerning our health become a part of our daily routine. Almost every week, there are new magazines on the market that contain articles about dieting and good health. One magazine reveals how certain foods are bad for the human body, while another magazine tells how we can eat what we want and as much as we want and still lose weight and stay healthy. There are articles about healthy eating and exercise and books about how to avoid such sicknesses as high blood pressure, cancer, or a heart attack. Often it seems that we never learn just what is the best diet for us. We are interested in each new idea.

When we read the Word of God, we see that God invites His people to come to His table to drink and eat what is good. He isn't talking about the new fad diets. He is talking about spiritual food, the food that will last and fill us properly. His food is the food that gives security, peace and joy. If we are willing to come to His table, we will be fed. If we choose to listen and obey, we will be satisfied with what God offers. What God provides will make us complete. Eating the food of righteousness gives peace, joy and fulfillment in life.

Dear God and Creator of all, we know that what You have to offer is all we need for life. Thank You for giving us spiritual food that is free, no strings attached. Help us always to be filled with Your goodness. In the name of Jesus we pray. Amen.

The Value of God's Word

The grass withers and the flowers fall, but the word of our God stands forever
(Isaiah 40:8, *New International Version*).

Scripture: Isaiah 55:6-13
Song: "Thy Word Have I Hid in My Heart"

In the United States courtrooms, witnesses are asked to promise to tell the "truth, the whole truth, and nothing but the truth." Why all those truths? First, the truth must be told. Secondly, nothing is to be left out, and thirdly, no lies are to be included in the testimony. This is very important for the judge to get the whole story in order to make a sound and rightful judgment.

When we are faced with the promises of God, we can be assured that God has told us the truth, the whole truth, and nothing but the truth. When He says that His ways are higher than our ways, then we can be sure that God is trustworthy in all that He says and does. He does not contradict Himself, nor does He speak lies, nor deceive His people.

The Scripture reminds us that God's Word goes out and does not return empty. When this truth is revealed, then we will reap the rewards of God's promises. God's Word will turn the hearts of men to Himself. His truth, will reveal the deceitful schemes of the devil's work.

Isaiah reminds us in his writings that we will "go out in joy and be led forth in peace. . ." (see Isaiah 55:12a). How great and wonderful it is that God's Truth will bring us joy and peace!

Almighty heavenly Father, we bow before You as humble servants. We take Your Word as truth. Help us to allow Your Word to direct our ways for Your glory. In Jesus' name, we pray. Amen.

Not the Where But the How of Worship

God is spirit, and his worshipers must worship in spirit and in truth
(John 4:24, *New International Version*).

Scripture: John 4:19-26
Song: "Praise Him! Praise Him!"

We ask, "Where do we worship God? Is it in the buildings where people come on the first day of the week to worship and praise God, or is it in the land where the Bible tells us that Jesus lived while here on earth?" We want to know how we can get near to Him.

When the Samaritan woman at the well of Sychar sensed that Jesus knew more about her than she was comfortable with (John 4:16-18), she turned the conversation to the issue of the place of worship. The Samaritans had their place of worship, Mount Gerizim, just above the well where they spoke. Jews had theirs, Mount Moriah (2 Chronicles 3:1), in Jerusalem. "Which", she asked, "is correct?"

Jesus turned the conversation from the place of worship to the how of worship. God is interested in the way we worship. He wants our worship of Him to be seen in our hearts and in our lives. Jesus asserted that God seeks people who worship Him in spirit and truth. His emphasis was on the inner nature of worship, the heart and mind of worshipers.

Great and wonderful God, help us to worship You as You desire, in spirit and in truth. May our faith be expressed in a hunger after Your presence and a thirst for Your blessing. Help us to look to You and Your Word for help in true worship of You. In the name of Your Son, our Savior, Jesus Christ, we pray. Amen.

January 14-20. **Dr. Ward Patterson**, is a Christian educator and author of numerous books and articles. He lives in Cincinnati, Ohio.

Great Among the Nations

My name will be great among the nations, from the rising to the setting of the sun. In every place incense and pure offerings will be brought to my name, . . . says the LORD Almighty (Malachi 1:11, *New International Version*).

Scripture: Malachi 1:6-14
Song: "Give of Your Best to the Master"

My mother loved missionaries. She packed countless boxes to be sent around the world. She wanted us to send some of our best to the mission field. She felt that workers for Jesus in foreign lands deserved the very best that we could send to them. We often sent new items as well as our best used items to them.

We have much to learn about our homage to God from an understanding of Old Testament sacrifice. For burnt offerings, people were to bring an animal without defect (see Leviticus 1:3). But many times, people would not bring their best but would bring their worst, those that were imperfect and diseased. By so doing, the prophet pointed out, they showed contempt and disrespect for God and debased His name.

How do we look at our offerings to God? Do we give as little as we can? Do we give of our overflow? Do we give the best we have or the most inconsequential? Do we honor the name of God by our faithful generosity or tarnish the name of God by our selfish hoarding?

We serve a great and wonderful God. He is worthy of our very best. Let us strive this day to give Him our very best. He alone can save us.

Dear God, we know that all things are Yours. Often we act as if we can fool You with our insincere generosity. Help us to render our best to You, Great King and Lord of all. In Jesus' holy name, we pray. Amen.

Let Justice Roll On

But let justice roll on like a river, righteousness like a never-failing stream!
(Amos 5:24, *New International Version*).

Scripture: Amos 5:18-24
Song: "Living for Jesus"

Often when a nation has a good economy, plenty of high-paying jobs, and easy availability to material things, little else matters. This sounds much like the people in the days of Amos. It was a prosperous time in both the northern and southern kingdoms. Their neighbors, Egypt and Assyria, were unusually weak and the Jewish nations were experiencing a boom.

The future looked bright. The idea was going around that the "day of the Lord" was coming with the destruction of the enemy. Amos knew otherwise. The "day of the Lord" would be darkness because of their oppression of the poor, their injustice, pride, and greed.

The people felt comfortable with their prosperity and their religious rituals, but God was not pleased. God said, "I will not listen to the music of your harps. But let justice roll on like a river, righteousness like a never-failing stream!" (Amos 5:23, 24, *New International Version*).

Prosperity is not necessarily evidence of righteousness. God calls His people to humbly fear Him and have compassion for the needy. When we show love and compassion to others, we obey Him. In this we please God.

Almighty Father, help us not to be complacent in our love and service to You and others. We often close our eyes to the injustice to those in need around us. Help us to live a life of compassion and righteousness. In the name of Jesus, we pray. Amen.

Do What Is Right

The LORD says: "Maintain justice and do what is right, for my salvation is close at hand and my righteousness will soon be revealed"
(Isaiah 56:1, *New International Version*).

Scripture: Isaiah 56:1-5
Song: "To God Be the Glory"

Isaiah 55 is one of the great chapters in the Old Testament. It reminds us of the transforming power of the Word of God. "As the rain and the snow come down from heaven, and do not return to it without watering the earth and making it bud and flourish, so that it yields seed for the sower and bread for the eater, so is my word that goes out from my mouth: It will not return to me empty, but will accomplish what I desire and achieve the purpose for which I sent it" (see Isaiah 55:10, 11). The chapter closes with joy and hope.

In the Scripture reading for today, Isaiah turns his attention to foreigners and eunuchs. He reminds his people that these have a special place in God's heart, if they keep the Sabbath, choose what pleases God, and hold fast to His covenant. The foreigners and outcast are welcome in the temple, for it is a "house of prayer for all nations" (see Isaiah 56:7).

It is God's desire that all the world bow down and worship Him. "Inclusiveness" is important to God. This is what He expects for us to do. God reaches out in love and calls all people to share in His blessings.

Loving and everliving Father, You call us to follow You in a spirit of obedience and love. Your blessings surround us when we walk in Your ways. Thank You for Your transforming Word and Your heart of compassion. Teach us, O Father, to bow before You and to worship You. Thank You for the joy we find in Your house of prayer. In the name of Jesus, our Savior, we pray. Amen.

Joy In the House of Prayer

These I will bring to my holy mountain and give them joy in my house of prayer (Isaiah 56:7, *New International Version*).

Scripture: Isaiah 56:3-8
Song: "In Christ There Is No East or West"

We have all, at one time or another, experienced what it means to be an outsider. We move to a new town and enter a new school. We go to a new church and no one makes any effort to get to know us. We travel to another country where no one knows us, speaks our language, or dresses as we do. Such experiences can be very painful.

The Jews had a special covenant relationship with God, yet He had concern for other peoples and nations. His love overarched cultural and ethnic divisions. The key factors in receiving God's blessing is keeping God's commandments and doing what pleases Him.

Our Scripture text for today mentions several things that will come to those who are faithful, no matter what their national origins. They will receive an everlasting name (Isaiah 56:5), they will receive joy in the house of prayer (Isaiah 56:7), and they will receive acceptance of their offerings and sacrifices (Isaiah 56:7). These all imply God's favor and acceptance of all who follow Him.

We may occasionally experience what it means to be an outsider in human relationships here on earth, but in our relationship with God, we are welcomed and accepted when we seek Him with sincerity and truth.

God of all nations and peoples, we thank You for the joy of prayer. Sovereign Lord, help us to find our place, our strength, and our peace in You. In the name of Christ, we pray. Amen.

No Peace for the Wicked

"There is no peace," says my God, "for the wicked"
(Isaiah 57:21, *New International Version*).

Scripture: Isaiah 57:14-21
Song: "It Is Well with My Soul"

Have you ever been at a seashore on a stormy day? The waves break on the shore with great force, churning up the sea bottom with a swirling undertow. Breakers pound against the shore with a sound like that of cannons.

This is the word picture Isaiah paints for the lives of wicked people. They are restless, driven, filthy, and troubled. "There is no peace," says God, "for the wicked." When we choose the path of wickedness we poison ourselves and those around us.

What, then, of the path of peace? Isaiah records the words of God: He lives with those who are contrite and lowly of spirit. Contrition is grief and repentance for sin. A lowly spirit is an attitude of humility. Both recognize our dependence on God and our own unworthiness.

John Pasatour was on a plane from Zurich to Beirut when he suddenly cried out that he was suffocating. The plane made an emergency landing in Athens, where Mr. Pasatour died. As the medical attendants undressed him, they found he was wearing a corset hiding 1,500 valuable Swiss watches he was smuggling to Beirut. It was the watches that had caused his death.

How like those watches is the wickedness of life.

Dear Father, thank You for reviving the spirit of the lowly and reviving the heart of the contrite. Please bring peace to our troubled lives. In the name of the Prince of Peace. Amen.

The Lord will Satisfy your Needs

The LORD will guide you always; he will satisfy your needs in a sun-scorched land and will strengthen your frame. You will be like a well-watered garden, like a spring whose waters never fail (Isaiah 58:11, *New International Version*).

Scripture: Isaiah 58:9b-14
Song: "Wonderful Peace"

We were lost. We were hot and thirsty and did not know where we were. The hot sun beat down upon my friend and me as we moved through the *wadis* and studied the terrain.

We had started early in the morning, walking along the sandy paths of the wondrous city of Petra. We walked past multi-colored tombs, cut from red mountains. We were heading for a small, white dot on the pinnacle of a mountain to the west, the place tradition has established as Aaron's tomb.

The climb seemed endless. We had no map or guide. We inched our way up to the fantastic view from the peak where the small, whitewashed, domed tomb stood.

Coming down should have been easy, but we got disoriented. I began to think that we might spend the night wandering endlessly in the hills and dry steam beds.

Finally, we stumbled into a Bedouin camp where generous strangers gave us water and bread. They were like a gift from Heaven. We ate, rested, and, with sign language, learned the way back to familiar territory.

I think of that day in Jordan when I read that the LORD will satisfy my needs in a sun-scorched land. How wonderful is our God who does not abandon us.

O Lord, our Guide, lead us in the way of safety and hope. Strengthen and renew our spirits when we come to the end of our resources. May we find joy and strength in Your care. In the name of Jesus, we pray. Amen.

Wait, Watch and Work

Wherefore, beloved, seeing that ye look for such things, be diligent that ye may be found of him in peace, without spot, and blameless (2 Peter 3:14).

Scripture: 2 Peter 3:11-18
Song: "A Charge to Keep I Have"

I don't like to wait for a bus, a taxi, a plane, a doctor or a special event. Often I prepare for a wait by cramming stationery, a Spanish textbook or some yarn into a big purse.

Many times, though, I have become too distracted to accomplish much. One time I became so absorbed in the historical novel I was reading that I missed the arrival of a special friend I had gone to the bus station to meet.

I do not know if my time on earth will be long or short, but I do want to spend time listening to God speak to me. I want to keep my attention focused on Him. I want to learn to wait upon the Lord.

I try to listen to God as He speaks to me through His Word. I want to hear Him as He leads me day by day. What I do for Him is of uppermost importance. I may find that sometimes I have set too many goals for myself that are focused only on myself. Today, I resolve to do what I can to keep my life in balance with what God has in store for me. I want to live a life of victory in Him.

Dear Lord and Father of all, help us neither to sit with folded hands nor to rush pell-mell into everything we see that needs to be done. And whatever we do, dear Father, help us to keep looking upward. Let our lives be a witness for You to those around us. In the name of Jesus Christ, the Savior of the world, we pray. Amen.

January 21-27. **Margaret Primrose** is a retired teacher and former missionary to Bolivia. She lives in Kansas City, Missouri.

No More Stormy Seas

I saw a new heaven and a new earth, for the first heaven and the first earth had passed away, and there was no longer any sea (Revelation 21:1, *New International Version*).

Scripture: Revelation 21:1-8
Song: "Jesus, Savior, Pilot Me"

Catalina was obviously overwhelmed by her first glimpse of the ocean. "It can't be that big," she said. She had probably never seen a globe, a world map or a picture of any part of the world. She knew only of the Andes where she grew up. Little did she know that a pinprick on the map could easily have represented all she could see from the window of a train descending the foothills.

A day or two later Catalina and a friend were standing spellbound on the beach near high tide. Suddenly a swelling wave slapped a rock and sprayed the unsuspecting girls. In fear they turned and ran.

In some ways life and the sea are alike. They entice us and offer smooth sailing at times. Then a sudden storm and an encounter with thunderous waves come that could capsize us or shipwreck us on hidden rocks.

How good it is to know that the turmoil will end! In the new Heaven and the new earth there will be no more boisterous waves and no more tempestuous sea. We long to see the new Heaven and the new earth.

O Lord and Father of all mankind, thank You for telling us that You are making everything new. We look forward to the day when the old order of things will have passed away and there will be no more death, mourning, crying or pain. We praise You for the salvation we have in Your Son, Jesus Christ. In His holy name, we pray. Amen.

God Can Transplant Hearts

And I will give them one heart, and I will put a new spirit within you; and I will take the stony heart out of their flesh, and will give them a heart of flesh (Ezekiel: 11:19).

Scripture: Ezekiel 11:14-20
Song: "Let Jesus Come into Your Heart"

One day I began teaching my grade-school science class by asking a question. I asked the class, "How many hard blows would it take to break this rock I am holding?"

The children and I took the rock outdoors, put it on a cement step and began to hit the rock, and we counted as we pounded . . . 1 . . . 3 . . . 20 . . . 45 . . . 75 . . . 96 . . . Just before we reached the number of 100, the rock split. There was certainly nothing pliable about that rock!

My friend who is a "rock hound" tells of another story. Her story also told of how hard rocks can be. She has found it necessary to leave stones in an electric rock tumbler 24 hours a day for six weeks just to get the luster she wants.

How much worse it is for a heart to be stony! Polished or broken, an individual can still be "as hard as a rock." What can change the heart that is a hard as a stone?

Only God can take a stony heart and replace it with a heart full of love and compassion. God can change the heart to be full of love. His promise is for us today just as it was for those of Ezekiel's day. The promise is for anyone in all times who will allow Him to work in them.

All powerful Lord, we are glad, that You can do what man can not do. You can transform a heart of stone into a heart filled with love. Help us allow You to take away the stone in our hearts and give us a love for all mankind. In the name of Jesus, we pray. Amen.

Clean and New

Then will I sprinkle clean water upon you, and ye shall be clean: from all your filthiness, and from all your idols, will I cleanse you (Ezekiel 36:25).

Scripture: Ezekiel 36:22-28
Song: "Jesus, I Come"

Can you imagine a boy wading into the slime and stench of a hog wallow to retrieve his "fish," which was really just a little stick? I can. I saw my brother do it. And surely he must have known that Mother would punish him.

A few years later, though, mud ceased to magnetize him, and there always seemed to be a lot of his hard-to-iron white shirts in the wash. None of them showed much soil. It would not be difficult to guess what happened. He had grown up and had fallen in love.

The Israelites had passed through a somewhat parallel experience. Once bound to the idol worship God abhors, they had experienced a change of heart. They knew that only God, not grave images, could cleanse them and give them new hearts.

God has not changed. He is always the same—yesterday, today, and forever. He can cleanse the heart of anyone—even those who have made idols of things, people, status or anything else. He can change your heart and my heart to be filled with compassion and love. We just need to allow Him to be the Lord of our lives.

Dear Lord and Creator, we know that falling deeply in love with You brings about the change of heart needed to serve You. Thank You also that maintaining our focus on You helps us to keep our hearts pure. We want You to be the Master of our lives this day. In the name of Jesus Christ, our Savior and Lord, we pray. Amen.

Get Up! You're Going Home!

Arise, shine; for thy light is come, and the glory of the Lord is risen upon thee
(Isaiah 60:1).

Scripture: Isaiah 52:7-12
Song: "The Light of the World Is Jesus"

Our farm neighbors' house was dark after a summer storm. Familiar with power outages caused by lightning, they found candles, flashlights or whatever else they had to help them through the night.

Though they had seen no linemen in the area the next day, the family began to notice that other farms had light. It seemed odd until one youngster told his brother he had wondered what would happen if he pushed "that thing" on the windmill. He had, in fact, moved it, and that move had switched off the electricity. They indeed were the only farm house without electricity!

Israel, too, had caused herself to cut off from the power and light that she should have had from God. Because of her idolatry, God had allowed her to be taken into Babylonian captivity. Then after 70 long years of captivity, there was exciting news for God's people. "Get up. Light has come. You're going home."

It was not that Israel deserved to be redeemed. We can look at her record and know this. But then none of us do. But God has provided forgiveness, redemption, and light for all who will act upon His offer.

Heavenly Father and Lord of all, thank You that You still love us when we must suffer the consequences of cutting ourselves off from Your blessings. We praise You for the redemption You provide. In the name of Jesus, we pray. Amen.

Seeing God's Glory

It shall come, that I will gather all nations and tongues; and they shall come, and see my glory (Isaiah 66:18).

Scripture: Isaiah 66:18-23
Song: "O Zion, Haste"

Louis does not come to our church community on a mule or camel. He drives a car with quite a bit of horse power. Ana's litter for baby Brenda is actually a car seat, and Ebony would not call our old church bus a chariot.

It does not matter that our Hispanic and Oriental neighbors do not travel the same way we do, or the way the Greeks, Libyans and other nations of Isaiah's day did. What is important, however is that we all are coming to worship our Creator, the one true and living God.

Today, as in the past, God sends those who know Him to invite others to learn of Him. Like Jesus' disciples we may begin by visiting the sick, weeping with the bereaved and feeding the poor. It does not seem likely, though, that St. Peter taught any English-as-a-second-language classes.

Our numbers are increasing, and I believe that at least Juan and his brother Josh caught a glimpse of God's love when they heard of The Prodigal Son in their English class. We appreciate the gifts some of our new people have been bringing, but our prayer is that all of us will give our hearts to Jesus.

O Lord and Father of all mankind, this is a big world that You have created, and our impact on it seems so small. Nevertheless, there is an important place for us to fill. Help us to live a life of peace and to point the way for others to declare Your glory. In the name of Jesus Christ, our Savior and Lord, we pray. Amen.

God's Plans for Us

And it shall come to pass, that before they call, I will answer; and while they are yet speaking, I will hear (Isaiah 65:24).

Scripture: Isaiah 65:17-25
Song: "Just When I Need Him Most"

Something that looked to me like smoke was spewing from the front of my car. I slammed on the brakes, pulled to the shoulder of the two-lane road and jumped out. Why wait for an explosion?

I barely had time to think about hiking the two or three miles to the little town where my cousin lives when both a northbound and a southbound pickup truck stopped. The drivers soon discovered the problem—just a leaky hose. One headed back to town, returned with a new hose and soon installed it. He also had a jug of water for the radiator. When the job was completed, he left quickly without accepting payment.

Later in the day, I remembered that my prayer for the problem was answered while I was still speaking. If God would use a stranger on a lightly traveled road to help me, why shouldn't I believe that He would hear us before we call in the new Heaven and new earth? Hasn't He given us parents, family, friends, air, sunlight, water, food, shelter, clothing and even birds and flowers long before we were old enough to ask for them?

Dear Lord and Father of all mankind, You are awesome in Your provision and love for us. Your care for us is wonderful. We look forward to even greater wonders in the new Heaven and the new earth. Thank You for giving us glimpses of them. In the name of Jesus Christ, the Savior of the world, we pray. Amen.

Love as We are Loved

And you are to love those who are aliens, for you yourselves were aliens in Egypt (Deuteronomy 10:19, *New International Version*).

Scripture: Deuteronomy 10:12-22
Song: "Bring Them In"

A school had a fire drill and the principal was pleased that the five hundred students emptied the building in less than three minutes. Later the bell rang to dismiss school for the day. Out of curiosity the principal looked at his watch. The building was cleared in one and one half minutes. Now that's what we call sufficient motivation!

The greatest motivation for sharing the message of God's love, forgiveness, and hope to those who are alien to the Kingdom of God is that we ourselves were once aliens without the love of God

When we read Matthew 18:23-35, this passage is relevant to more than the question of forgiveness. The one who had risen in society and was prosperous forgot or even despised the one who was less fortunate.

It is sad to think that a recipient of someone's compassion may never share that compassion with others. They have forgotten that at one time they were strangers and someone cared about them.

Almighty God and Lord of all, help us to share with others what has been shared with us. We have received Your salvation because another servant of Yours witnessed of Your love to us. We are what we are because others showed compassion for us. Thank You, dear Father, for all things. In the name of Jesus Christ, our Savior, we pray. Amen.

January 28 - February 3. **E. Ray Jones** is a retired minister and now is active in leading seminars for churches across the United States. He and his wife, Betsy, reside in Clearwater, Florida.

Make Us a Blessing

And you and the Levites and the aliens among you shall rejoice in all the good things the Lord your God has given to you and your household (Deuteronomy 26:11, *New International Version*).

Scripture: Deuteronomy 26:1-15
Song: "All for Jesus"

The youth at First Christian in Clearwater spend two weeks in our community making minor home repairs for the elderly, not only in our congregation but also in the community as a whole. One of the men of the church gave his labor free to single women and widows who could not afford to have their cars repaired. Other leaders took money from their own pockets to save a house, while others sent students to college.

It is inspirational to learn of the generosity of some Christians. I know of a church family that funded money for the surgery of a child. The chairman of the benevolent committee spoke of the joy experienced by the entire church family because they were able to meet this special need. Others churches have mentoring programs, food pantries and clothing rooms.

To care for those in need is the modern day equivalent of bringing our offerings to the Lord. We set the offering before the Lord our God, we worship our God and we rejoice in all the good our Lord has given to us. What He gives—our homes, our lives, and all that we have—we share with the strangers among us.

O Lord, thank You for all the blessings that You have given to us. May we be willing to use these blessings to the glory of Your name. We pray in the name of Jesus, our Savior. Amen.

Genuine Religion

Do not trust in deceptive words and say, "This is the temple of the Lord, the temple of the Lord, the temple of the Lord!"
(Jeremiah 7:4, *New International Version*).

Scripture: Jeremiah 7:1-7
Song: "Trust and Obey"

Jeremiah prophesied and wrote his book during a period of Israel's spiritual decline. The nation still had the external signs of religion, but their prophets lied and their priests lived lives that were both empty and scandalous.

Jeremiah teaches us how dangerous it is to speak unpopular truth. The prophet spoke plainly about the futility of Israel's reliance on the gods they had recreated. He pleaded for them to change their ways—both as a nation and as individuals. The price Jeremiah paid was rejection, ridicule and imprisonment.

Truth is no more popular today. To confront us with our idols and sins is still a dangerous business. Often times, because we are regular church members, read the Scriptures, and feel that the church we attend interprets the Word of God correctly, we think we are exempt from wrong.

Let us take note that a worship service, no matter how meticulous and correct, is useless unless it leads to true worship of God and a change in our moral and spiritual life. It is not difficult to talk of our commitment and to praise God with our mouths, but it is in the connection of worship with life that we express genuine faith.

Heavenly Father, may the meditation of our hearts and the words we speak be consistent with the life we lead. Help us to give all that we are to You as we bow in complete worship of You. We know that You can change us. Through the name of Christ, our Savior, we pray. Amen.

The Bible and Social Justice

Do what is just and right. Rescue from the hand of his oppressor the one who has been robbed (Jeremiah 22:3, *New International Version*).

Scripture: Jeremiah 22:1-8
Song: "Help Somebody Today"

God, in order to show how serious He is about social justice swears by Himself—the most solemn of all oaths. Unless His people give praise, justice and protection to those who are beaten down and robbed, they will ultimately face His wrath. The picture is of a beautiful forest that without irrigation turns into a desert. So those hearts are not refreshed by their love and sacrifice for the needy will become dry arid and useless.

The emphasis on the widows is deliberate. God did not lead us to believe that we have to choose between spending our time in proclaiming the Gospel or in ministering to the widows—the most vulnerable of all the needy. Unless a widow could be part of a Levirate marriage or have a family to support her, she could literally starve to death.

The example of the early church teaches us to properly divide our task. The preaching ministry must not neglect the Word of God. The church must help those who need assistance for food, clothing, shelter, or medicine. In fact the preaching should be a powerful motivating force to cause us to care about those for whom Christ gave His life.

When we care for the needy, we are blessed.

Lord, help us to understand that love for You and love for those whom You love cannot be separated. Through the name of Jesus Christ, the Savior of the world, we pray. Amen.

Devotions

February

photo by Chuck Perry

Helping the Underprivileged

Remember that you were slaves in Egypt and the Lord your God redeemed you from there. That is why I command you to do this (Deuteronomy 24:18, *New International Version*).

Scripture: Deuteronomy 24:14-21
Song: "The Bond of Love"

In the Scripture lesson for today, Moses is concerned with the protection of the underprivileged. In an agricultural society in which the Israelites lived, the death of the husband and father was tragic. The widow and the children were thrown into poverty. The fatherless families, foreigners and immigrants were ready targets for prejudice, ill treatment and general social injustice. God's people were told to care for them on a daily basis.

The Israelites were told to give their first fruit. This means that they gave out of the first fruits of the season. The amount of the fruits determined the gift.

Christians receive blessings of peace and joy when they respond to our responsibility to treat in a Christ-like manner those who cannot fight back. We are responsible for helping the vulnerable people hurt by irresponsibility. This is why it is vital that the church family help those in need by providing shelters for battered women and children. Those who are privileged with material wealth are under the compulsion of love to care for and to deal with the physically underprivileged.

Almighty God and Lord of all, help us to remember that none of us are exempt from the possibility of becoming one of the needy. Help us to remember that God meets our needs and, we have the responsibility to meet the needs of those whom He loves. In Jesus' name, we pray. Amen.

February 1-3. **E. Ray Jones** is a retired minister and now is active in leading seminars for churches across the United States. He and his wife, Betsy, reside in Clearwater, Florida.

Hold On to Hope

Would you wait until they grew up? Would you remain unmarried for them? No, my daughters. It is more bitter for me than for you, because the Lord's hand has gone out against me!" (Ruth 1:13, *New International Version*).

Scripture: Ruth 1:1-14
Song: "O God, Our Help in Ages Past"

The book of Ruth is the account of disasters that hit an obscure family. A family searching for a better life goes to a heathen country. They are reduced to three childless widows—Naomi, whose husband and two sons are dead, and her two daughter-in-laws, Ruth and Orpah. It seemed as if tragedy will never stop.

I believe God works powerfully in lives. At the age of fourteen our family moved to Florida for a better life. Two months later my father was killed in a train wreck. We moved back to Eastern Kentucky and my life changed radically. I was able to go back to school. My high school coach who was also an elder in the church came into my life. What at the time seemed a disaster turned into a life changing decision. "God works in everything to the end that good is accomplished" (see Romans 8:28).

Ruth was determined to go with her mother-in-law. Once home in Israel, Naomi set about to find Ruth a husband. God works effectively when He is aided by our work. God gives opportunities and when we put forth the effort to make use of the opportunities, we are blessed.

Ruth did not know she was being used of God to prepare a lineage through which the Savior of the world would come.

Father, almighty, and Creator of all, help us to know that You are working even when we can not see the results. In the name of Jesus, we pray. Amen.

Watching Love At Work

Ruth replied "Don't urge me to leave you or to turn back from you. Where you go I will go, and where you stay I will stay. Your people will be my people and your God my God" (Ruth 1:16, *New International Version*).

Scripture: Ruth 1:15-22
Song: "O Master, Let Me Walk with Thee"

These words in Ruth 1:16 have been read at a marriage ceremony. The words of Ruth in this verse reflect more than the attitude of marriage. This Scripture is much broader.

Love does not always act in a practical manner. It was not practical for Ruth to leave her land, her family, a possible future husband and security. But love caused her to follow a woman, whom she loved and who loved her, to a strange land.

Love has sent people to the far corners of the earth to take the message of God's love. Some give their lives for the message. Love causes a mother to sacrifice sleep, pleasure and her own physical health to stay with a disabled child when she can do nothing but love. Love causes a spouse to stay close to a long-loved companion. Love causes a father to refuse a promotion because it will expose his children to an environment that is dangerous to their souls

Genuine love gives. Ruth gave Naomi her future. The God of Israel became her God. She would be with Naomi through her life and her death.

Genuine love is lasting. Paul as an old man said, "I've kept the faith and finished the course." God requires the same kind of loyalty from His people today.

Compassionate Lord, help us to love not in word only but also in deed. May our daily lives be a witness to a deep love for You. In the name of Jesus, we pray. Amen.

Living for God

Finally, brothers, we instructed you how to live in order to please God, as in fact you are living. Now we ask you and urge you in the Lord Jesus to do this more and more (I Thessalonians 4:1, *New International Version*).

Scripture: Ruth 2:1-7
Song: "Make Me a Blessing"

In October of 1999 Gordon Elwood died in his hometown of Medford, Oregon. He was known as an eccentric man who frequently peddled through town on a bicycle with a cat that he had trained to ride in a basket. After retiring as a TV repairman, he read day old newspapers, ate free meals, made phone calls from a pay phone, and stuffed his pockets with cookies on special days at the local bank. When his estate was settled, it was discovered Mr. Elwood was worth nine million dollars! Sadly, before he died, he told his broker, "I'm a miser, and this money hasn't done me or my family any good."

Ruth possessed little but the clothes on her back, her faith in God and a willingness to work. She gleaned grain in a local field as was the custom of the poor and destitute. God rewarded her persistence by giving her favor in the eyes of Boaz, and enough food for Naomi and herself to survive. What began, as an act of desperation became a life-changing adventure.

God takes our limited resources and multiplies them when we allow Him to direct us. When we practice wise stewardship of the resources God gives, our hearts are satisfied.

Dear God, open our eyes to the opportunities we have to serve You. Teach us to be faithful. In Jesus name, we pray. Amen.

February 4-10. **Larry Ray Jones**, ministers at a church in Newport News, Virginia. He and his wife, Jane, have two children, Nathan and Laura.

February 5

Safe In His Presence

I will both lay me down in peace, and sleep: for thou, Lord, only makest me dwell in safety (Psalms 4:8).

Scripture: Ruth 2:8-13
Song: "A Shelter in the Time of Storm"

Twenty-five years after the end of the Vietnam War, Tammy and Jarred Gasel left their home in North Dakota and traveled to Vietnam to take custody of their adopted child. They kept the adoption a secret from Tammy's father until just days before leaving. He was a Vietnam veteran and they feared bringing a Vietnamese child into their home would cause too many painful memories. When they told him, his immediate response was, "When are you bringing her home?"

It was easy for Ruth to feel unloved. Not only were there few career opportunities for her, but there were plenty of unkind people waiting to take advantage of her vulnerable circumstances. Ruth found love and safety in the fields of Boaz.

The world longs for a secure place. Such a place exists in the presence of God. God can heal our hearts and make us clean with the blood of His Son Jesus. The psalmist says, "He makes me lie down in green pastures, he leads me beside quiet waters, he restores my soul. He guides me in paths of righteousness for his name's sake" (see Psalm 23).

Let us walk with Him today. Let us share our deepest, darkest secrets with Him and ask for forgiveness. He stands ready to listen. Let us run into His loving arms for safety.

Almighty Father, direct our steps, and draw us into a closer relationship with You. In the name of Jesus, we pray. Amen.

A Part of the Family

The Son of Man came eating and drinking, and they say, 'Here is a glutton and a drunkard, a friend of tax collectors and "sinners"' (Matthew 11:19, *New International Version*).

Scripture: Ruth 2:14-23
Song: "'Tis So Sweet to Trust in Jesus"

A relative of diva Mariah Carey battled addiction to drugs and alcohol. Several years ago, when she lost custody of her children, Mariah came forward to take care of the children, and had them placed in a loving home. One of the children later said, "Mariah took on the role of caretaker of our family at an extremely young age. I reached a certain point in my life when I realized that for my own sanity I could not maintain a relationship with my mother. Without Mariah and my birth father in my life, I can honesty say I don't know where I would be today. Mariah has been a source of stability in my life. Her financial support has allowed me to pursue my academic goals."

Aside from any feelings Boaz had toward Ruth, he also had a family obligation. As a near relative of her deceased husband, he was responsible for her safety and survival. He told his field hands to leave extra grain on the ground so Ruth and her mother-in-law Naomi would have food to eat.

God redeems us through the blood of His Son Jesus. Our inheritance is not due to anything we have done, but a result of Jesus' great love and sacrifice for us.

Jesus cares for us and wants us to thrive spiritually and to experience the abundance of His Father's blessings.

Almighty God, open our eyes to the friendless and help us to lead others to You. In the name of Jesus, we pray. Amen.

Whatever You Say Lord

Submit yourselves, then, to God. Resist the devil, and he will flee from you
(James 4:7, *New International Version*).

Scripture: Ruth 3:1-5
Song: "He Leadeth Me"

The DeLasalle High School football team in Concord California was playing for its 100th win in a row, the longest winning streak in high school history. Still, they remained humble about their record and attributed their success to old-fashioned hard work and commitment. In a media interview coach Bob Ladouceur said, "It's not about the streak. The wins are outcomes. The way we accumulated so many wins is that we lived day to day. We try to figure out what we can take care of and figure out what we can do to get better."

A godly lifestyle is also a process. It begins when we offer our lives to Him in humble submission. Through reflection and prayer, we learn to make right decisions on a daily basis. God's Word is our guide and the church our spiritual family where we are nurtured and encouraged. Soon we experience victories over temptation and learn the joy of pleasing God.

Ruth obeyed Naomi because she trusted Naomi. She said, "I will do whatever you say," and Ruth was not disappointed.

"I will do whatever you say!" What an appropriate phrase to describe the attitude we should have toward God. Sometimes the vision of where He wants us is incomplete. At other times His commands demand personal sacrifice. When we remain committed to His will, we begin to see His plan.

Dear God, give us wisdom and strength to do the right thing. Help us to trust You in all that we do. In the name of Jesus, our Savior, we pray. Amen.

Strength of Character

Blessed is the man who perseveres under trial, because when he has stood the test, he will receive the crown of life that God has promised to those who love him (James 1:12, *New International Version*).

Scripture: Ruth 3:6-18
Song: "I Would Be True"

In the spring of *2000,* Brooke Ellison graduated from Harvard University. She received the highest possible grade for her thesis titled "The Element of Hope and Resiliency in People Who Have Been through Major Life Difficulties." Brooke knew something about major life difficulties. At eleven years of age she was hit by a car, and left paralyzed from the neck down. Her mother, a school teacher, left her job to be by Brooke's side. Her mother attended college with her daughter, feeding her, holding her books, helping her study, and wheeling her to and from class. When asked how she felt about what she had done, her mother replied, "A lot of people think I made a big sacrifice. I don't feel that it is. I think the word 'sacrifice' has negative connotations. It's a privilege to do it."

Ruth left the land of Moab to follow the true God, slaved in the grain fields to provide food for Naomi and herself. The Lord blessed her decisions and rewarded her for her faithfulness. The sacrifices Ruth made were overshadowed by the joy she experienced serving God.

Jesus Christ demonstrated an attitude of love when He gave His life for us on the cross of Calvary. He endured a painful death to free us from sin.

Heavenly Father, give us the wisdom to recognize how You are working in our lives. In the name of Jesus, we pray. Amen.

February 9

Duty and Honor

Live such good lives among the pagans that, though they accuse you of doing wrong, they may see your good deeds and glorify God on the day he visits us (1 Peter 2:12, *New International Version*).

Scripture: Ruth 4:1-12
Song: "My Soul, Be on Thy Guard"

April 21, 2000, Col. Robert Malcolm Elliot was laid to rest in Arlington National Cemetery. His plane was shot down over North Vietnam in 1968, but his remains were not found and identified until 1998. Two years later, Col. Elliot's family met at Arlington to honor him with a final tribute to his life and faithful service to his country.

In Boaz' culture, one way for a relative to honor the memory of a dead husband was to marry his wife, buy the family inheritance and produce children in the name of the deceased. Family possessions were then passed along to the children in the name of the first husband. Since Boaz was related to Ruth's husband, he was a candidate for this family tradition. However, there was one closer relative, and Boaz needed his permission before proceeding. When the closer relative passed on the opportunity, Boaz claimed Ruth as his wife. Boaz acted honorably to Ruth, to tradition, and his respect for the dead.

Duty and honor permeated Jesus' life and ministry. He had countless opportunities to abandon His mission, but His love for us and His obedience to His Father pushed Him forward to the cross of Calvary.

O Lord, God of all, teach us patience and help us to preserve the convictions that are necessary for our Christian witness. In the name of Jesus Christ, our Savior, we pray. Amen.

The Final Chapter

The Lord bringeth the counsel of the heathen to nought: he maketh the devices of the people of none effect. The counsel of the Lord standeth forever, the thoughts of his heart to all generations (Psalm 33: 10, 11).

Scripture: Ruth 4:13-22
Song: "All the Way My Savior Leads Me"

A few years ago Charles Schultz' last *Peanuts* comic strip appeared in newspapers around the world. On that very weekend Schultz lost his battle with cancer. In anticipation of the final run, *Today* had asked its readers how they thought *Peanuts* should conclude. One reader wrote, "All of the Peanuts gang is watching as Charlie Brown attempts one last kick. You see him running really fast. And he boots Lucy skyward." Another wrote, "For all the Charlie Browns in the world, Charlie Brown and the little red-haired girl should walk off into the sunset holding hands, with Snoopy and Woodstock at their side." Still another, "The last scene should be everybody doing the Snoopy dance, celebrating life in our minds for all eternity." However, in the final analysis it did not matter how others thought *Peanuts* should end. That decision was up to its creator.

Who could have guessed that Ruth would be married to a successful land owner and her mother-in-law Naomi would be holding Ruth's new baby. Only God, the Creator could have written such an ending.

We get into trouble when we try to write others' conclusions for them. Nowhere is this more true than with God. His only limitation is our reluctance to trust Him.

Dear God, give us the courage to glorify You with the life You give. In the name of Jesus Christ, the Savior of the world, we pray. Amen.

Ask Someone Who Knows

Then Philip opened his mouth, and began at the same Scripture, and preached unto him Jesus (Acts 8:35).

Scripture: Acts 8:26-40
Song: "Open My Eyes, That I May See"

When I was a boy, I lived with my family on a farm six miles from town, and we didn't have a car. When Dad went to town, he rode in a buggy pulled by a horse. That was slower than a car, but Dad liked it. When he started home, he didn't have to pay attention to his driving. The horse knew the way. Dad could sit back and read a book.

Our Scripture for today tells about another traveler who read a book on the way home. It was one of the books of the Bible which told about someone who gave his life as meekly as a lamb. The traveler wondered who that could be.

Then the traveler met someone who knew. Philip explained that it was Jesus who gave His life for all of us. When the traveler learned that, he wanted to become a Christian that day.

When we read the Bible, do we sometimes find a part we don't understand? Then we need to ask someone, but we want to be sure that we ask a good Christian who knows. By asking someone else to help us learn more about the Bible, we will learn more about God, Jesus, and the Holy Spirit.

Dear Father and God of all, thank You for the Bible that tells us what we ought to do. Help us to be strong in keeping Your promises. May we always read Your Word. Thank You, dear God for the people who help us understand Your teachings. In the name of Jesus, we pray. Amen.

February 11-17. **Orrin Root** is a former editor at Standard Publishing. He resides in Cincinnati, Ohio, where he enjoys gardening and writing.

God Loves Everybody

What God hath cleansed, that call not thou common (Acts 10: 15b).

Scripture: Acts 10:1-16
Song: "All People That on Earth Do Dwell"

Race prejudice was serious in ancient Israel. God had chosen the Jewish people to have His law and His help, so the Jews tried to be separate from everybody else. The first Christians were all Jews, and they thought nobody but Jews would ever be Christians.

God had a different plan. He loved the whole world. He wanted everybody to hear about Jesus. Today and the next two days we will be seeing a continued story that tells how God got the Jewish Christians to take the good news of Jesus to people who were not Jews.

First, God sent an angel to Cornelius, one of the best of the Gentiles. Cornelius believed in God and tried to obey Him. The angel told him to send for Peter, a Jewish Christian who would tell him something he ought to do.

Then God had to get a message to Peter, for Peter was a strict Jew who would not even go into the house of a Gentile. In a vision, God told Peter to eat some kinds of meat that were forbidden to Jews.

Tune in tomorrow to see how Peter learned that the vision was about people as well as meat. In the meantime, let us think about ourselves. Do we look down on anyone because he is from another country or belongs to a different race?

Almighty God, thank You for loving us, and for loving everybody in the world. Thank You for Jesus, and for the Bible that tells us about Jesus. Teach us to continue daily in Your ways. In the name of Jesus Christ, we pray. Amen.

Reaching Out

God hath showed me that I should not call any man common or unclean
(Acts 10:28).

Scripture: Acts 10:19-33
Song: "We've a Story to Tell to the Nations"

Yesterday we read that Peter saw a vision of animals that the law said were not fit for food, but a voice told him to eat them. Peter protested. He had never eaten such things, and he was not about to start now. They were unclean! But the voice spoke again. Peter must not call anything unclean when God had cleansed it.

How did Peter know that meant people as well as food? He knew because some men were waiting for him. They were Gentiles, people would have called them unclean; but God said to go with them.

People who make no claims of being Christians are the very people we need to reach with the message of Jesus. He can help them do right.

Whom do you avoid at school or at work or in social life? Foreigners? People who use unclean language? African Americans or Whites? Hispanics? Of course, if there is a gang that really does bad things, you will not join it. But what if Christians would all make friends with someone who does not know Jesus? Could we perhaps steer them into knowing Christ and accepting Him as the Savior of the world?

O God, **Creator of the universe,** we thank You for people like Peter who took the good news of Jesus beyond the Jewish nation and shared it with all kinds of people. Thank You for the church that encourages us in doing right. Help us to tell the world about Your love. In the name of Jesus Christ, we pray. Amen.

Tell Everybody Jesus Saves

He commanded us to preach unto the people, and to testify that it is he which was ordained of God to be the Judge of quick and dead (Acts 10:42).

Scripture: Acts 10:34-48
Song: "Jesus Saves"

The first Christians were Jews, and they did not know the message of Christ was for Gentiles until God gave Peter a special vision to let him know. The Gentiles did not know that message was for them until God sent an angel to let Cornelius know. Then Cornelius got his relatives and friends together, and Peter went and told them about Jesus.

Then God did one more wonderful thing to let everybody know He wanted Gentiles to be Christians along with Jews. He sent the Holy Spirit to Cornelius and other Gentiles in a special miraculous way. The Holy Spirit led those Gentiles to talk in languages they had never known before. That was what He had done for Jesus' apostles when they first told a crowd that Jesus had risen from the dead. So now everybody in the house knew God wanted Gentiles to be Christians.

Now everyone who reads the book of Acts knows God wants all the people in the world to be Christians. Who will teach about Jesus? Will it be you and me? Perhaps we can find a friend who will help us to tell others about the salvation that comes only from Jesus.

Heavenly Father and God of all, thank You for letting the early Christians know the Gospel is for everybody. Thank You for all the Christians who have been telling it through the centuries, and especially for the ones who told of Your salvation to us. In the name of Jesus Christ, we pray. Amen.

You Can't Hide From God

Trust in the LORD with all thine heart; and lean not unto thine own understanding (Proverbs 3:5).

Scripture: Jonah 1:1-6
Song: "I'll Go Where You Want Me to Go"

This week we have seen how the early Christians learned that God wanted them to tell everybody about Jesus. Let's think about a time before Christ came to the earth to bring salvation to all the world. Even before Christ came, God wanted a man to take a message for Him.

God wanted Jonah to warn the city of Nineveh that it would be destroyed if it would not stop doing wrong. Jonah didn't want to do that. Nineveh was the enemy of Jonah's people, and he wanted Nineveh destroyed. So Jonah tried to run away by sea. The trip ended in a storm, and the ship was about to sink.

We know we can't run away from God, but some still try to hide from Him. One hid in his work, twelve or fourteen hours a day. He had no time for God, or the Bible, or his family. The storm that stopped him was a nervous breakdown. Another hid in play–parties, casinos, basketball games, or just sitting in a bar. The storm that stopped him was alcoholism. A third man is trying to hide by pretending there is no God. No storm has stopped him yet, but he's getting old. What will happen when he dies?

Who wants to hide? It's better to stand up in the sunlight, worshiping God and doing what He wants us to do.

Heavenly Father, thank You for being honest with us and letting us know what You want us to do. We promise to strive to be honest with You, not trying to hide anything from You because we know that You see all. Please forgive us for our sins. In the name of Jesus Christ, we pray. Amen.

Time to Think

Look upon mine affliction and my pain; and forgive all my sins (Psalm 25:18).

Scripture: Jonah 1:7-17
Song: "Nearer, Still Nearer"

Nineveh was a city with thousands of people. God didn't want all of them to be destroyed. He wanted Jonah to go and tell them to do right so God would not have to destroy them. But instead of going northeast to Nineveh, Jonah got on a ship going west to Tarshish.

God sent a big storm. The ship was about to sink. Jonah knew it was his fault. He told the sailors to throw him overboard. They did, and the storm stopped.

Of course Jonah expected to drown, but the Lord did not want that. He wanted Jonah to have another chance. So He prepared a very big fish to swallow Jonah alive.

How do you think Jonah felt inside the fish? It was cold in there and darker than midnight. There was so much water that he couldn't lie down and sleep, but the water was not fit to drink. There was nothing to eat. Jonah felt very bad indeed, and he had three days to think about it.

Did you ever want to do something wrong? Did you go ahead and do it, even though you knew it was wrong? Then when it was done, did you feel bad, even if there was no big fish to swallow you, and the storm was only in your mind and conscience? Tune in tomorrow to see what Jonah did when he felt bad after doing wrong.

Dear God, thank You for Your Word, which is a lamp to our feet and a light to our path (Psalm 119:105). Please forgive us for the wrongs we have done today. In the name of Jesus Christ, the Savior of all mankind, we pray. Amen.

God Is Merciful

The LORD is merciful and gracious, slow to anger, and plenteous in mercy
(Psalm 103:8).

Scripture: Jonah 2:1-10
Song: "Trusting Jesus"

Have you thought about what you would do if a big fish swallowed you? You would be cold and hungry and thirsty and tired, of course. You would be totally blind in the darkness. But what would you do by choice, by your free will? Jonah prayed.

Jonah prayed with a wonderful faith. Already God had saved him from being drowned, and now he felt sure God would not let him be digested by that fish. He prayed as if he were free from the fish already. So the Lord gave the fish another order, and it vomited Jonah out on dry land.

What do you think Jonah did then? He did what God had told him to do. He went straight to Nineveh and warned the people that the city would be destroyed if they didn't straighten up and do right. He was so convincing that the people stopped sinning and went into mourning because they had been so bad. That was what God wanted, so He didn't destroy Nineveh after all. It was more than a century and a half before that town became so wicked that it was destroyed.

God will forgive us, too, if we are honestly sorry for the wrongs we have done and if we ask Him to forgive us. Let's not forget what to do after we are forgiven. Let's strive to always do right. This is what God wants us to do.

Almighty God, teach us to walk in the way of the Lord. We want to uphold Your ways. Give us the wisdom to follow Your guidance that we find in Your Word. In the name of Jesus, our Savior, we pray. Amen.

A Gospel for All People

Being justified freely by his grace through the redemption that is in Christ Jesus (Romans 3:24).

Scripture: Acts 15:1-11
Song: "Just As I Am "

A little girl sat with her legs folded under her body listening intently. One student brought it to the teacher's attention. "She's not sitting right, her feet aren't on the floor." The teacher replied, "But she's listening."

Now as a teacher, she remembers that day when she is tempted to insist that everyone sit up straight with their feet on the floor, and reminds herself, "But they're learning." They are learning. So it was in the Jerusalem church. The missionaries excitedly shared the wonderful stories of conversion among the Gentiles. Some of the church rejoiced, but others were disturbed. The converts were not circumcised. But God saved them as they were and used them to reach others.

Today's missionaries are frequently unconventional in appearance and style, witnessing to drug addicts, the homeless and runaways wherever they find them. Could it be that God uses us, not in spite of but because of our differences? Christ does not take away who we are. He takes who we are and puts it in harmony with God's will for our lives.

Gracious God, thank You for Your wonderful gift of salvation and for the uniqueness of every person. Help us to rejoice in all who love You and share with all who need You. Grant us strength to love and accept others even as You have loved and accepted us. In the name of Jesus, we pray. Amen.

February 18-24. **Essie M. Johnson** is a Christian educator and consultant and freelance writer. She lives in Columbus, Ohio.

Our Diverse Christian Family

There is neither Jew nor Greek, there is neither bond nor free, there is neither male nor female: for ye are all one in Christ Jesus (Galatians 3:28).

Scripture: Acts 15:12-21
Song: "Blest Be the Tie"

Separated by language and age, they were, nevertheless, friends. One woman spoke no English and the other spoke no Spanish. Yet when one spoke of a grandson playing outside and her love for him, the other smiled with equal pride in her bilingual student. They understood each other. What they shared was so much greater than what separated them.

The new converts were different from those who came from the Jewish tradition. The Gentile Christians didn't observe all the right traditions and holidays, creating some questions for earlier converts. They were, however, all in agreement. The church believed in the deity of Jesus Christ. The converts believed that He rose from the dead, and they were anxious to learn more about His teachings. The Jerusalem Church made an important decision. They decided to focus not on what divided these two groups but what unified them. They would remind everyone of particular teachings of Moses taught to all and continue to encourage the converts in the ways of Christ.

How easy it is to focus on problems and differences in our homes and churches. Let us take time to think of what binds us together and makes us one family. These are the gifts that matter most.

Dear Father, help us to find common ground and unity in Your Word today. Help us to plant words of peace instead of discord and hope instead of discouragement. In the name of Jesus, we pray. Amen.

Share the Good News

Teaching them to observe all things whatsoever I have commanded you: and, lo, I am with you alway, even unto the end of the world (Matthew 28:20).

Scripture: Acts 15:22-35
Song: "If Jesus Goes with Me"

In discussing one of the missionary journeys with a group of preschoolers, I shared with them the importance of telling others about Christ. "Now," I said, "They are about to go, do you have any advice for them." One thoughtful student brightened and said, "Look both ways before you cross the street!" He was correct. Make sure you're in the safety zone, living in obedience to the Master before attempting a task for Him. Make sure you have looked both ways, counted the cost and are willing to go.

The entire church at Jerusalem prayed and was directed by the Holy Spirit to lay hands on selected missionaries and send them forth. Living in the will of God and following His direction, they went forth. They were joyfully received, and their journey and work were blessed.

Christians are called to serve God. The task may vary, the conditions may be different, but every task should be saturated in prayer and true to the teaching of His Word. The missionaries taught even as they were directed and served in a spirit of love and obedience. Do we know our task in God's family?

Dear God, thank You for the missionaries who share with others all over the world. Grant them safety and success in their task. Thank You for the work You have given us. Guide and direct us so that we might fulfill our mission today as we go about our daily lives. In the name of our Savior, Jesus Christ, we pray. Amen.

The Wisdom to See

Though he fall, he shall not be utterly cast down: for the Lord upholdeth him with his hand (Psalms 37:24).

Scripture: Jonah 3:1-5
Song: "I Surrender All"

Mirrors are heartless. They show us not only what we want to see but also what we need to see and want to ignore. Once aware of the ill fitting garment or added pounds, we can change it. God put a mirror before the city of Nineveh.

God commissioned Jonah to confront the people of Nineveh with the reality of their sins. Sin in the harsh, bright light of day is a horrible sight indeed. The city of Nineveh saw them in the mirror and knew they had to change.

Like a parent who has reasoned with a child long enough or a teacher who has given second chances long enough or an employer who had counseled long enough, God too has limits. Disobedience brings judgment. The people of Nineveh understood the words of judgment, humbled themselves and sought God's forgiveness. Our sins may not be as the sins of Nineveh but let us ask ourselves, "Are we tempting God by living in willful disobedience in some areas of our lives?" He has pleaded with us to change. Are we listening? We too must kneel in humble obedience in all areas, or we too must face the penalty for our disobedience. When we look in the mirror, what do we see?

Gracious Savior, we humbly submit every area of our lives, every thought, every act and deed to Your will. We want to live in obedience to You. Please forgive our failures and grant us the strength and wisdom to reflect not our will and desire but Yours. In the name of Jesus Christ, we pray. Amen.

The Power of Repentance

If we confess our sins, he is faithful and just to forgive us our sins, and to cleanse us from all unrighteousness (I John 1:9).

Scripture Jonah 3:6-10
Song: "Lord, I'm Coming Home"

What tears at a parent's heart more than a tiny son or daughter admitting their wrongdoing and asking for forgiveness? "I'm sorry" are two of the most powerful words in the world when sincerely uttered. These words cannot undo wrong but can melt away anger. There is always a price to pay for wrongdoing but that price frequently becomes bearable when the person seeks forgiveness. The harsh word, the broken toy, the cookie taken without permission provide a lesson learned and the memory of a behavior not to be repeated. Forgiveness holds its own mystery.

The people of Nineveh realized what they had done. God reprimanded them and promised destruction. They saw themselves as they were and were driven to their knees. The king willingly led the country in fasting and prayer seeking God's forgiveness. As the leader, he had to assume responsibility and lead the country in repentance. God heard their prayers and, when He saw the sincerity of the people, He changed His mind. He gave the people a second chance. A country that admits its failure and has leaders that will lead the way in prayer and fasting can make a difference.

Forgiving Savior, grant us another chance. Draw us together in a season of prayer to seek Your forgiveness and direction. Guide those in government and positions of authority to please You. Give them purpose and wisdom. Help us to be found within Your will. In the name of Jesus, we pray. Amen.

Justice Balanced with Mercy

And God saw their works, that they turned from their evil way; and God repented of the evil, that he had said that he would do unto them; and he did it not (Jonah 3:10).

Scripture: Jonah 4:1-5
Song: "Surely Goodness and Mercy"

While some will undergird someone caught in wrongdoing with prayer, there are others who choose to celebrate the fact that the guilty have finally been revealed. "Told you so," they may say. Some love to say and feel justified that they were right all along.

Jonah knew what was coming, the destruction of Nineveh, a destruction the city richly deserved. God commissioned him to tell them. Jonah, after some persuasion, faithfully fulfilled his responsibility and waited to see God's words come to pass, but something happened. The city was not destroyed. Jonah was angry but God asked him a simple question, "Do you do well to be angry?" Anger is understandable, but mercy and compassion are desirable.

Jonah's anger grew out of his own righteous indignation. How often do we observe others and condemn their sins either silently or openly? Sin should never be justified or excused. When God forgives others we too must forgive. We cannot rejoice at the misfortune of others. It's a hard lesson but a lesson that can help us become more like Him.

Loving Father, sometimes forgiveness is hard, and we can't do it without You. Touch our hearts and minds and help us to do with You what we cannot do by ourselves. Help us to forgive the unforgivable acts and love the unlovable. Help us to reflect Your mercy and Your love. In the name of Jesus, we pray. Amen.

The Gift of Compassion

Blessed are the merciful: for they shall obtain mercy (Matthew 5:7).

Scripture: Jonah 4:6-11
Song: "My Savior's Love"

I watched as a friend cleared out a terrarium. She pulled up and threw out the plants that were dead. One plant caught my attention; it was still struggling to live. I pulled it out of the trash and decided to nurse it back. It responded to care and quickly flourished. After a few months it was a beautiful, full plant, so unlike its former. Self-forgiveness and mercy are that way. They give us a new beginning.

Jonah was angry. God forgave Nineveh. What was the point of his personal suffering, bringing the message to the people if God was going to let them off? They deserved to die. Why wouldn't God just give them what they deserved? Jonah considered it all as he sat under the shade of a castor-oil plant. The plant died and exposed him to the hot sun. Jonah missed the comfort and shade of the plant. He was sorry it was gone. That loss, that pity for the plant helped him understand God's pity. God cared for the many people, including young children, who lived in the city of Nineveh. God even pitied the animals. Being merciful, Jonah discovered, can sometimes be better than being right.

God of mercy, You have given us so much even when we don't deserve it. Melt again the angry negativity in our lives and relationships and help us to extend to others the same compassion and love You extend to us. In the name of Jesus, we pray. Amen.

February 25

The Enticement of False Doctrine

Guard the good deposit that was entrusted to you—guard it with the help of the Holy Spirit who lives in us (2 Timothy 1:14, *New International Version*).

Scripture: 2 Timothy 1:8-14
Song: "The Way of the Cross Leads Home"

Americans love yard sales. We find bargains. For very little money, we can buy what we may or may not need from someone who doesn't need or want it anymore. Looking for a yard sale also allows us to get out and drive around and meet new people. Here in Hawaii where I live, these sales are called *lanai* sales, and driving down the road, especially on Saturdays, there are a number of these enticements along the way, calling to me to pull over and either interrupt my trip or make me forget where I am supposed to go. The road goes to town, but I might turn off and end up doing something else and getting totally distracted from where I was supposed to go.

Our lives are on the highway of life daily. God tells us, "This is the way, walk in it, stay on the right track." We learn to follow His teachings, in order to arrive where we want to go and to be in God's will and purpose for our lives. If we are enticed away from His righteous ways and get off track, there may be tragic results, both in this life and in the next. The better we know and follow God's Word, the better our journey through life will be.

Dear Father in Heaven, teach us to follow. Show us the truth in Your Word as we walk through this world. We commit to being faithful to You. In the name of Jesus, our Savior, we pray. Amen.

February 25-March 3. **Donnie Mings** and his wife, Charlotte, have ministered in Hauula, Hawaii for many years. They have two grown children and five grandchildren.

Perseverance in Witnessing

Endure hardship with us like a good soldier of Christ Jesus
(2 Timothy 2:3, *New International Version*).

Scripture: 2 Timothy 2:1-13
Song: "Heaven Came Down and Glory Filled My Soul"

People who are seeking Christ will sometimes ask us, "Who taught you to know the Lord?" What would have happened if that person had gotten discouraged and given up before you heard the gospel? Teaching people the way of God is not always easy, and sometimes people don't want to listen, but everyone needs to know about Jesus and the righteousness of God that He brings.

In today's Scripture, Paul gives Timothy three illustrations of persevering in teaching others about God and His ways. There is the soldier, there is the athlete, and there is the farmer. All three of these endure hardship, for a purpose. All three work hard and stay focused on what they are supposed to be doing. And they are rewarded for their efforts.

Let us think about our Savior, Jesus, as we persevere in teaching. His teaching was often rejected. His position as the Messiah was denied by many. He was called names, spit upon and finally suffered the ultimate cruelty for His work. But He did not get distracted. He did not give up. He was victorious. He set the example, not only for His servant, Timothy, but also for us today.

Almighty and everloving heavenly Father, thank You for those who have witnessed faithfully for You throughout the years. Thank You for those who have kept Your Word that we might learn of You. Help us all to follow their example to witness with love and wisdom. May we never give up. In the name of Jesus, our Savior, we pray. Amen.

God's Family Scripture

I am the good shepherd; I know my sheep and my sheep know me
(John 10:14, *New International Version*).

Scripture: 2 Timothy 2:14-22
Song: "Now I Belong to Jesus"

Recently some children came to church that I really did not know. When I saw their faces I knew whose children they were because they looked so much like their mother, whom I did know. We usually identify people by their physical looks, but God has other ways of knowing people. He looks at the hearts of people, and their natures.

In the Scripture text for today, there are some people who were teaching heresy and leading people astray. Paul warns that God knows who are following His teachings, and conversely, God also knows who are not following Him. Those who belong to God are known for their faithfulness to Him. Those who follow Him can be known by their commitment to God and His Son, Jesus. They avoid godless chatter and foolish doctrines. They stand firm in the love and compassion that comes only through Jesus Christ, the Savior of the world.

God's children have a love of the truth and a commitment to righteous living. God has a family, a race of people through which He can show His love and His power to the world. We who have committed our lives to Jesus Christ are part of that great family that God recognizes as His very own.

Father, thank You for this day. Thank You for loving and accepting us into Your family. Help us to speak and to act today and every day consistent with being a precious child of God. In the name of Jesus Christ, the Savior of all mankind, we pray. Amen.

Powerful Words

For the message of the cross is foolishness to those who are perishing, but to us who are being saved it is the power of God (I Corinthians 1:18, *New International Version*).

Scripture: Romans 1:11-17
Song: "Wonderful Words of Life"

The jury spent two days in deliberation. Finally they arrived at a verdict. As they filed back into the courtroom and took their seats, all eyes were on them. The judge waited, the crowd was still, and the defendant sat nervously in his chair. "How do you find the defendant?" the judge asked. One juror stood up and declared the verdict solemnly. "Guilty," he said. That one word sent shock waves through the crowd and struck terror in the heart of the defendant. Just one word.

If man's word can carry so much weight, how much more weighty and powerful are God's words. The divine message has the backing of God's awesome power and presence behind it and the working of His Holy Spirit with it and through it.

The Gospel message is of salvation through Jesus Christ. It is for all people of the earth. It is a message of salvation and love to all mankind. Instead of condemnation of the world, it is the good news of salvation that we are declared "not guilty" when we are in Jesus Christ. Christ's blood cleanses us from the sins of the world and gives us the opportunity to spend all eternity with the Creator of the universe. It is a message of joy and celebration for all mankind. It is a message in which God has invested tremendous power to change lives and nations.

Dear Father, thank You so much for the good news of salvation through Your Son Jesus. Thank You for the powerful message of the Gospel. Help us to share Your message. In the precious name of Jesus Christ, we pray. Amen.

My Prayer Notes

Devotions

March

photo by Chuck Perry

The Righteous Judge

For the Lord your God is God of gods and Lord of lords, the great God, mighty and awesome, who shows no partiality and accepts no bribes (Deuteronomy 10:17, *New International Version*).

Scripture: Acts 17:22-31
Song: "At the Cross"

If you have ever stood before a judge, even if for something like a traffic ticket, you will have seen the seriousness of the courtroom. Even if you spend a day in a courtroom hearing the cases brought before the judge, you will see the effect that the decision of the law and the interpretation of the judge of that law has on a person's life. However, it is still a human attempt at justice with recognizable human frailty and certain inadequacies. Caring, informed societies build into their judicial systems ways of helping correct and account for the human factor in courtrooms and judgments.

God is our eternal Judge. He is the ruler of all of the universe. The Scripture tells us that He will judge the world through His Son, Jesus Christ, and that judgment is uniquely just and impartial, as only God can be. But God is also merciful. He has compassion for His creation. To both satisfy His moral requirements and rescue us from condemnation, a unique plan was devised. God Himself paid our fine by allowing His Son, Jesus to take our place.

Almighty and ever living God and heavenly Father, thank You for everlasting life we can have through Jesus Christ, Your Son and our Savior and Lord. We can not adequately express our gratitude to You for the opportunity to live with You forever. Though we were not deserving of it, Your love sent Jesus to pay for all our wrongs. Thank You for this unfailing love. In His name, we pray. Amen.

March 1-3. **Donnie Mings** and his wife, Charlotte, have ministered in Hauula, Hawaii. They have two children and five grandchildren.

The Problem with Being Critical

There is only one Lawgiver and Judge, the one who is able to save and destroy. But you—who are you to judge your neighbor?
(James 4:12, *New International Version*).

Scripture: Romans 2:1-11
Song: "There's a Wideness in God's Mercy"

Psychology tells us that criticizing others often reveals a sense of inadequacy or low self-esteem in ourselves. By judging others, our flesh tries to build itself up. We seem somehow justified, or we look better when we can point out the mistakes of others. Some people in the secular world gleefully point out and loudly proclaim the failures of Christian leaders. Maybe when one criticizes another, it makes the person doing the criticizing feel less guilty of his own shortcomings.

We learn to criticize when we are young children, and unless we allow God to help us to correct this behavior, we carry this practice over into adulthood. We will find ourselves finding fault in our fellow Christians and family members.

But God says in this passage that bringing judgment on others for their failures actually serves to bring us under judgment too. When we judge others, we do not look better, instead we end up condemned too, because we have made the same mistakes that we are now condemning. When we condemn sin in others, we condemn sin in ourselves. We need to leave the judging to God.

Father, we confess that we have sinned, and yet we criticize others, whether spoken or unspoken. Help us not to participate in Satan's deception of justifying ourselves and yet judge others around us. You alone are worthy to be the Judge, O God. In Jesus' name, we pray. Amen.

Obedience From the Inside Out

"This is the covenant I will make with them after that time, says the Lord. I will put my laws in their hearts, and I will write them on their minds"
(Hebrews 10:16, *New International Version*).

Scripture: Romans 2:12-16
Song: "True-Hearted, Whole-Hearted"

As children, most of us were told by a parent, grandparents, teacher, or another adult, "Don't touch that!" "Remember to look both ways before crossing the street." A child has to be told what to do and what not to do. As the child grows, he or she will know what to do without being told. When we are children, there are corrections and warnings from outside oneself, from a guardian or parent. When we mature to adulthood and the lesson is learned, the knowledge is on the inside, in the mind and heart of the person. Now we see that we do not have to be instructed to follow the simple instructions that we learned while we were children.

In the Mosaic Law, external rules and regulations abounded. But under the new covenant, we have both the knowledge and the desire to do right, inside of us, in our hearts. We have the love of God, and even the presence of God within us, motivating us as well as giving us wisdom. We therefore do the right thing, without someone else making us do it. Then it can be said that God's laws are written in our hearts. As Christians we have received a part of God's nature, the nature to do what is right.

Heavenly Father, thank You for Your presence in the world and in our lives today. Thank You for Your indwelling Holy Spirit. Help us to follow Your Word and Your will. Help us to stay close to You. In the name of Jesus, our Savior, we pray. Amen.

God Reveals His Grace

But God commandeth his love toward us, in that, while we were yet sinners, Christ died for us (Romans 5:8).

Scripture: Ephesians 1:3-14
Song: "Wonderful Grace of Jesus"

It all began in the Garden of Eden. God created and placed two innocent people in the garden to dress and to keep it. God told them, "Of every tree of the garden thou mayest freely eat: but of the tree of the knowledge of good and evil, thou shalt not eat of it: for in the day that thou eatest thereof thou shalt surely die" (Genesis 2:16, 17).

As God walked in the Garden one evening, he said, "Adam, where are you?"

Adam confessed, "I heard you in the garden and I was afraid." Until then Adam never knew fear. Adam had never been a baby, a child, where he would have grown up realizing fear. He had been formed by the hands of God from the dust of the ground, and then God breathed the breath of life into the nostrils of Adam. God created man in His image. Adam was to care for the Garden of Eden. Can you imagine Adam's heart when God said, "Adam, have you eaten of the tree?"

Here God introduces His marvelous grace to mankind. In Genesis 3:15 God promises a Messiah. Jesus Christ is the fulfillment of that promise. What a wonderful God we have!

Lord, open our hearts this day that we may come to know the love You expressed on Calvary, as You commended Your love toward us. May we all come to the realization of Your all-sufficient grace. In the name of Jesus Christ, the salvation of the world, we pray. Amen.

March 4-10. **Betty Sweeney**, is a retired nurse and mother of three grown children. She resides in Jersey Shore, Pennsylvania.

Hope, Seeing Beyond All Obstacles

Now faith is the substance of things hoped for, the evidence of things not seen
(Hebrews 11:1).

Scripture: Ephesians 1:15-22
Song: "Under His Wings"

The hope of a child is pure. Shortly after my husband died, my youngest daughter searched for her father. He worked from 11:00 p.m. till 7:00 a.m. When he got home he would put her on his shoulders, and they would walk down the railroad tracks. He often would stop and show her the beauty of nature. In the evenings he would read to her and her siblings before putting them to bed, and he always said, "I'll see you in the morning." Every morning there he was. It was a daily ritual.

Following his death, my little daughter continued to wake in the morning looking for her father. Even after we moved closer to my family, she was always looking for him.

When we deal with heartbreaking circumstances, our heavenly Father promises hope. When Jesus left His disciples and returned to His father in Heaven, they remembered that He said, "In my Father's house are many mansions: . . . I go to prepare a place for you. And if I go and prepare a place for you, I will come again, . . . that where I am, there ye may be also" (John 14:2, 3).

Today, let's celebrate the hope He left with us. Our hope is built on the Eternal Word of God. In His time He will return. What a blessing—this day hope is ours!

Almighty God and Lord of all, thank You for the hope we have in You. We look to You for hope and assurance that one day we will live with You for all eternity. Teach us to rise above our circumstances. In the name of Jesus Christ, our Savior, we pray. Amen.

By Grace Alone

For by grace are ye saved through faith; and that not of yourselves: it is the gift of God: not of works, lest any man should boast (Ephesians 2:8,9).

Scripture: Ephesians 2:1-10
Song: "Grace Greater Than Our Sin"

What is Grace? Ordinarily speaking it is the gift of love that one gives to another for no reason at all. A child drops a cup of juice on his mother's rug. She cleans it up because she realizes this little fellow is in the grace period of his life. In other words a mother's love is given without some merit on the part of a child. It's his birthright. He has not done anything to merit it.

When Adam sinned in the Garden of Eden, God in His infinite wisdom demonstrated His unmerited mercy and grace for mankind. God promised the seed of woman, (Genesis 3:15) who would die for man's sin. In Matthew 1:21 we find the arrival of that seed. He lived, loved, died and arose again—for all mankind.

So no matter where we live today or where we are spiritually, Christ is available to meet our every need. He wants us to know the love and compassion that only He can give to us. When we receive Him and obey Him as Savior and Lord of our lives, He places us in the family of God. There is no need too great, no sorrow too painful, that He cannot heal. His grace is sufficient for all.

O Lord, thank You for Your great love and the grace that You give to us. Thank You for Your unmerited mercy. The thought that You took on the form of man so You could die for man's sin overwhelms us. Raise us above every stumbling block that Satan might place in our way today. We want to live victoriously in You. In the name of Jesus Christ, we pray. Amen.

Part of a Family

But as many as received him, to them gave he power to become the sons of God, even to them that believe on his name (John 1:12).

Scripture: Ephesians 2:13-22
Song: "The Family of God"

Today people travel far away from their hometowns, and often live away from their parents and grandparents. People who have lived in a foreign country far away from family and friends often talk about their feelings when they return to their hometowns or to their home country. If you have been asked by your country or your church to serve far away from home or if your work has required for you to live out of the country, you know the feelings of leaving home. It is then that one feels the need to touch the land of home.

In the United States, we learn about servicemen and women who express great joy upon returning home. As a serviceman returning home, my husband said tears began to flow as he got a glimpse of the Statue of Liberty in the New York harbor. His first action when he touched American soil was to kiss the ground. Connecting to our past and to family and tradition is important for us.

When we accept Jesus Christ as Savior, we are accepted into a new family. In John 1:12 we find that we can be transformed into the family of God. As Christians, God is conforming us into the image of His Son.

O Lord, open our eyes to see new things from Your Word. Give us understanding of Your Word. May our attitudes be a revelation of what You are doing in our hearts. Help us to reach out to all those that You put in our paths. Help us to live by Your Word. In the name of Jesus Christ, the Savior of the world, we pray. Amen.

The Justness of God

For what if some did not believe? shall their unbelief make the faith of God without effect? God forbid: yea, let God be true, but every man a liar; as it is written, That thou mightest be justified in thy sayings, and mightest overcome when thou art judged (Romans 3:3,4).

Scripture: Romans 3:1-9
Song: "Great Is Thy Faithfulness"

In the center of a turning wheel is a stationary point. At the center of a whirlwind is a stillness. Regardless of the commotion man creates, God stands firm in His statues.

God will do what is right no matter what men do. His justice may not come immediately, but it will come ultimately. And His decision is final!

"How can a just God condemn anyone to hell?" has often been asked. By the same token, one may respond, "How can a just God allow cancerous sin into His unspotted paradise?" Paul asks in 2 Corinthians 6:14, "What fellowship (intimate relationship) hath righteousness with unrighteousness?" Thanks be to God that the forces of good are more powerful than the forces of evil. He will set the record straight in His good time.

> Pardon for sin and a peace that endureth,
> Thy own dear presence to cheer and to guide:
> Strength for today and bright hope for tomorrow,
> Blessings all mine, with ten thousand beside!
> T. O. Chisholm

Thank You, Lord, for being that "solid rock" on which I can anchor my life. I know that in You alone I have salvation. Help me to follow Your teachings that I might have everlasting life with You. In the name of Jesus, we pray. Amen.

All Mankind has Sinned

As it is written: There is no one righteous, not even one (Romans 3:10, *New International Version*).

Scripture: Romans 3:10-20
Song: "Love Divine, All Love Excelling"

In this chapter of Romans, Paul declares that the only "advantage" in being a Jew is that the Jew has been entrusted with God's message of salvation for the world. It is through the Israelites—the Jews that the Messiah, Jesus Christ, the Savior of the world will come. However, when it comes to sin, the Jews are granted no loopholes. The Scripture states that all of mankind have sinned and come short of what God wants of us. Paul paints a bleak picture of mankind in today's Scripture passage.

I've been working to say the right thing at the right time—to build up rather than to offend. I've been trying to break bad habits and to discipline myself to accept problems which can't be solved right away. While I'd be the first to believe that God doesn't sit in Heaven pulling my string to do His bidding, I sense the difference between accomplishing something primarily to exalt myself and accomplishing something primarily to exalt God's power. Everyone has sin blocking His relationship with God. That point of impasse can only be broken by God's intervention.

Yes, all of mankind has sinned. But both Gentiles and Jews are equal candidates for God's grace and salvation.

Thank You, Creator and God of all, that in Your love and mercy You had a plan to rescue us from sin and that there is a way that all who would come to You can receive salvation. Motivate us as individuals and as churches to reach out lovingly with this urgent message. In the name of Your Son, we pray. Amen.

God's Grace Justifies All

For all have sinned and fall short of the glory of God, and are justified freely by his grace through the redemption that came by Christ Jesus (Romans 3:23, 24, *New International Version*).

Scripture: Romans 3:21-31
Song: "Love Lifted Me"

Have you ever known someone who gives, gives, and gives—seeming never to tire and is especially generous when another is in need of help? The passage for today pictures God as the giver of a gift no person can attain for himself—the gift of a clean slate, a life free of sin's grip, a relationship with Him. No matter how hard we try, in and of ourselves we cannot rid ourselves of sin.

As with the beauty of a national park, the resources of the earth, and the expanse of space, what one group can lay exclusive claim to God's infinite love? He sets the standards for receiving His love. Those standards are that any man, woman, or child who comes to Him with a penitent heart shall be welcomed.

The story is told of the brothers and sisters who argued about whom their mother loved most. Disturbed by their bickering, the mother called to them and as she stretched forth her arms to encompass them all, she said, "My love is big enough for all of you!" Christ's arms are always outstretched to us, ready to take us in and warm us with His love.

Gracious Father and Lord of all, giver of my salvation and the salvation for all mankind, we thank You that we need not comprehend Your love and compassion but merely accept it. Help us this day to follow Your teaching and to live by faith in You. In the name of Your Son and our Savior, Jesus Christ, through whom we all can come to salvation and live life eternal with You in Heaven. Amen.

Seeing Stars

He took him outside and said, "Look up at the heavens and count the stars—if indeed you can count them." Then he said to him, "So shall your offspring be" (Genesis 15:5, *New International Version*).

Scripture: Genesis 15:1-5
Song: "My Faith Looks Up to Thee"

Abraham's encounter with God was a dramatic one. He also had to learn that God's delays are not God's denials. Abraham had been promised that he would have a son. More than that, he was promised that he would be the father of a great nation. So far that son had not arrived.

In a vision the Lord had Abraham look to the sky and the countless stars. Abraham was promised that so would his offspring be. This seemed to satisfy him to a great extent and that is why we call him the Father of the Faithful. Only a man of faith could trust that this great promise would come to pass. When you don't have a single heir, it's hard to imagine offspring as plenteous as the stars. But God does fulfill His promises in His own time and His own way.

It has been wisely said that God often shows trust in His people by forcing them to wait. That's a hard thing to do in this culture where we desire instant everything and even the computer starts to seem slow to us. When there is something that we have been waiting for from God, let's not give up. God keeps His promises. Let's see the stars.

Dear **Lord**, we confess that we often doubt Your faithfulness. Help us to hold fast to Your promises. Even in the waiting, may we ever draw closer to You. In the name of our gracious Savior, Jesus Christ, we pray. Amen.

March 11-17. **J. Michael Shannon** is the senior minister of First Christian Church in Johnson City, Tennessee.

I Never Promised You a Rose Garden

Then the Lord said to him, "Know for certain that your descendants will be strangers in a country not their own, and they will be enslaved and mistreated four hundred years" (Genesis 15:13, *New International Version*).

Scripture: Genesis 15:12-18
Song: "I Know Who Holds Tomorrow"

Sometimes God's promises lead us down difficult roads. One evening, when a deep sleep came upon Abraham, the Lord warned him about what would happen to his descendents. He was warned that they would be considered strangers; they would be enslaved and mistreated. That's not the news Abraham wanted to hear. We think we would like to know the future, but maybe it would distress us. Abraham was given a view of the future and it was not all good news. When it comes to the future we know nearly nothing. We know this for sure: there will be trouble.

Sometimes we assume that if we are right with God everything will go right with us. God's promise to Abraham was that in the end there would be justice and peace and that God's purposes would be accomplished. Let's apply that to our problems. God's promises in Scripture do not guarantee us a trouble-free life, but they do guarantee us a life filled with God's presence and His ultimate blessing.

It was Warren Wiersbe who told the story of a brother and sister climbing a hill. The little girl complained to her brother about the bumps along the way. The boy replied, "Don't you know, the bumps are what you climb on."

Dear Father, forgive us when we want an easy life. Help us to realize that our great privilege is to help conform the world to Your will. In the name of Jesus, our Savior, we pray. Amen.

I Want You

The God of the people of Israel chose our fathers; he made the people prosper during their stay in Egypt, with mighty power he led them out of that county (Acts 13:17, *New International Version*).

Scripture: Acts 13:13-25
Song: "Faith of Our Fathers"

Is it good or bad to be chosen? Is it pleasant or unpleasant? In some ways it is both. The Israelites were God's chosen people. Yet, they faced many challenges. In the midst of challenges, they knew that they were in partnership with God.

The Apostle Paul says that God was both patient with them and concerned over their suffering. Most of us would like to be chosen if we were chosen only for an honor, but what kind of honor comes without some kind of sacrifice? To be chosen of God means both privilege and responsibility.

Paul was speaking to a Jewish audience when he reminded them of their privilege and responsibility. Israel was chosen to be a nation God could work through and uniquely bless. This did not mean immunity from trouble. Israel still had to endure slavery for several hundred years. Yet, in the exodus, occupation and development of a nation, God was exalted before the people of the world. There was one supremely important mission for the Jewish nation. They would produce the Messiah. For that, all of us give thanks.

God chose the children of Israel and out of that nation came our Savior Jesus. His sacrifice was our salvation. Now we have been chosen to share that message.

Dear Lord, thank You for wanting us and for sacrificing for us. While we enjoy that fact, we know it was not because we were lovable, but because You love. In the name of Jesus, who embodied that love. Amen.

It All Comes Down to Jesus

We tell you the good news: What God promised our fathers he has fulfilled for us, their children, by raising up Jesus (Acts 13:32, 33a, *New International Version*).

Scripture: Acts 13:26-39
Song: "Jesus, Name Above All Names"

The great Apostle Paul was going one direction in life when Jesus turned him around. It was a vision of Jesus that transformed the persecutor into the missionary. Paul had always loved God in his own way, but Jesus changed everything. To Paul, it all comes down to Jesus. That was the message he shared with some worshippers in a synagogue in Antioch of Pisidia.

The plan of God all comes down to Jesus. Jesus is the Messiah, the prophesied anointed one. All of God's redemptive work is bound up in Him. Jesus is the cornerstone of Christian doctrine. He is the most prominent figure in human history. Yet, when He came there were those who tried to silence Him. They thought He was too dangerous to live, but the Father had the final word. In raising Jesus from the dead, He was testifying to Jesus' identity.

When it comes to our personal lives, it all comes down to Jesus. It is Jesus who gives us hope and life everlasting. It is Jesus who makes it possible for us to live again. His resurrection is the precursor to our own resurrection.

Dear Father and almighty God of the universe, thank You for sending Jesus to give us salvation. We know that He was longed for in the past, is dearly loved in the present and will be celebrated as long as there is a future. It is our desire to appreciate Him and to forever live for Him. Give us the power to make Him our all in all. In the name of Jesus Christ, our joy and hope, we pray. Amen.

It's In the Book

All Scripture is God-breathed and is useful for teaching, rebuking, correcting and training in righteousness, so that the man of God may be thoroughly equipped for every good work (2 Timothy 3:16,17, *New International Version*).

Scripture: 2 Timothy 3:10-17
Song: "Standing on the Promises"

When Sir Walter Scott lay dying, he asked for his son-in-law to read to him. The son inquired as to what book he wanted to hear. "Need you ask? There is but one," said Scott. The son-in-law knew what he meant and began reading from the Bible. Everyone reading the Bible is blessed. Paul was a lover of the Old Testament Scripture. The early church would read the Scriptures in their assembly. To Paul, the Scripture was the method of passing on the truth from one generation to the next. It was the measuring rod for living a godly life. The Bible is of divine origin and it is able to change our lives in positive ways. It is the divine Word of God. This was something Paul wanted clearly understood by his son in the faith and personal envoy, Timothy.

A little girl was telling her friend about the Bible. She said, "It begins with Genesis and ends in revolutions." She was more right than she realized. If we read, study and apply the Bible to our personal lives, it will create a revolution in our personal lives, our church, and our society. The Bible changes us and those around us—all we need to do is apply it.

Almighty God and Father of all mankind, how blessed we are to have Your Word, the Bible. Help us to dedicate ourselves to seeing that others know and love this most important book, the Bible. Help us to live by the words we find in Your Word. Help us to show the wisdom found in Your Word by the way we live our lives. In the name of Jesus Christ, the Savior of the World, we pray. Amen.

A Credit to Your Account

However, to the man who does not work but trusts God who justifies the wicked, faith is credited as righteousness (Romans 4:5, *New International Version*).

Scripture: Romans 4:1-8
Song: "Jesus Paid It All"

When we have worked hard on a job, our employer pays us for the work. The amount of money that we have agreed upon is applied to our credit. It is an exchange for the work.

There are those who are trying to earn Heaven by their own power and works. It is a truth of the Gospel that one cannot get to Heaven on one's own merit. Isn't this a relief? If we wanted to get to Heaven on the basis of our deeds and hard work, how would we know when we would have done enough? Would it take one million good deeds or one million and one? We would never have any sense of peace.

God has created a system whereby we can obtain Heaven. This system is one recognized even by Abraham in the Old Testament, that God is willing to count our faith as if it was righteousness. The great irony is that the more faith we engage, the more we are enabled to live righteous lives. There is only one deed that can enable us to enjoy Heaven—that is our acceptance of Christ on the cross. Abraham looked forward with faith toward a perfect sacrifice. We live in the afterglow of it.

God of grace and power, we thank You that You have provided for our salvation. This is a gift that only You can give, and it is not earned by hard work. We receive it with joy. We know that the blessing of Heaven does not come to those who strain to achieve, but to those who trust in Your mercy and love. In the name of our Savior we pray. Amen.

What Is Your Inheritance?

Therefore, the promise comes by faith, so that it may be by grace and may be guaranteed to all Abraham's offspring—not only to those who are of the law but also to those who are of the faith of Abraham. He is the father of us all (Romans 4:16, *New International Version*).

Scripture: Romans 4:13-25
Song: "Faith Is the Victory!"

Have you ever received an inheritance? What was it? Did you receive land, money or stocks and bonds?

When I was a child, I would dream that I had a fabulously wealthy, long-lost relative. I dreamed that someday I might receive a visit from a stranger who would say, "I am the attorney for your long-lost cousin. He wants you to have his fortune." That never happened, but as I grew older I realized that I do have an inheritance. I received the heritage of faith from my relative in the faith, Abraham. In fact, Paul says Abraham is my father. Don't get Paul wrong; he knows that we have earthly fathers and that we have a heavenly Father. Paul sees that Abraham is the father of the faithful. Isn't it interesting that Abraham is honored in Judaism, Islam, and Christianity? He was a flawed man, but he had faith. What a great man! Every time we believe in the promises of God, we are enjoying our inheritance from Abraham. Every time we reflect on God's gracious covenants, we are enjoying our inheritance from Abraham. Come to think of it, that is a much better inheritance than land, money or stocks and bonds.

Dear Father, help us to realize how wealthy we are in Christ. This is not because we have earned it, but we have received it from You. We accept it in the name of Jesus, our Savior. Amen.

More Than a Cover-Up

Blessed is he whose transgression is forgiven, whose sin is covered
(Psalm 32:1).

Scripture: Psalm 32:1-5
Song: "Are You Washed in the Blood?"

The meaning of the word cover in Psalm 32:1 does not mean that a sin is hidden to avoid accountability. It means just the opposite. We acknowledge our sin to God. The term cover is only one of many used to describe forgiveness. Perhaps it finds its origin in the clothing God made for Adam and Eve in the Garden. At any rate, no one word is adequate to describe forgiveness. In the Bible it is described as cleansing or purifying (1 John 1:7) as healing (Psalm 103:3) as redemption (Ephesians 1:7) as reconciliation (Romans 5:10) as resurrection (Ephesians 2:4) as pardon (Isaiah 40:2) as washing, sanctification and justification (1 Corinthians 6:11).

The forgiveness of sins that comes to us through the Lord Jesus Christ is so grand no one word is adequate to describe it. The image of covering in Psalm 32 is found again in the book of Revelation. Those who follow Christ are described as being dressed in white robes; fine linen, white and clean (Revelation 7:13, 14). God covers our sin with His own clean white robes. In Him only do we find forgiveness.

O Lord and Creator of all, by Your grace we are covered and the deformities of our twisted lives are changed. Forgive us and make us pure. Teach us, O Lord, to live our lives in celebration of Your forgiveness. We pray in the name of the sinless Christ, our Savior. Amen.

March 18-24. **Robert Shannon** has been a minister, missionary and college professor. He and his wife are now enjoying retirement in Valle Crucis, North Carolina.

The Key to Our Faith

Christ died for our sins according to the Scriptures . . . and that he rose again the third day according to the Scriptures (I Corinthians 15: 3b, 4).

Scripture: 1 Corinthians 15:1-11
Song: "Christ the Lord Is Risen Today"

The Romans revolutionized architecture when they invented the arch. Stones could be held in place with nothing at all under them. They pressed against one another, and were held there by a key stone at the top of the arch. The keystone was shaped differently than the rest, and from its position at the top it held all the other stones in place. The resurrection of Jesus Christ is the key stone of the Christian religion. It holds all the other parts in place. Without the resurrection of Christ, all the various pieces of our faith would fall.

All Western music is based on the harmony produced by a keynote. The keynote is the central tone, and all the other tones in a piece of music revolve around that tone and gravitate to it. The resurrection is the keynote in our Christianity. Without the death, burial, and resurrection of Christ, there is nothing but discord. With the resurrection there is a harmonious relationship between all the parts of our faith. In today's Scripture we can see how Paul understood the resurrection to be central. The gospel which was preached to them, which they received, and which enabled them to stand could be summarized by the death, the burial and the subsequent resurrection of Christ.

O God, and Lord of all, we thank You for the resurrection of Christ; for the way it gives meaning to our faith, and for the way it gives hope to our lives. Help us to live our lives in such a way that the world will know of Your love to the world. In Jesus' holy name, we pray. Amen.

The Last Enemy

For he must reign until he has put all his enemies under his feet
(I Corinthians 15:25, *New International Version*).

Scripture: I Corinthians 15:20-28
Song: "Crown Him with Many Crowns"

In the Cairo Museum in Egypt one can see an actual footstool made for a Pharaoh. Carved on it are images of enemies of Egypt. When the Pharaoh used his footstool, his enemies were pictorially under his feet. Someday Christ will literally and actually put all enemies under His feet. The last enemy that will be destroyed is death.

The Bible is honest and realistic. It tells us that death is our enemy. There used to be a song "Death is Only a Dream" and a poem describing death as a friend holding open a door. Walt Whitman said "death is only a beautiful adventure" and George Eliot called death "a delightful journey." You will not find this idea in the Bible. Death is our enemy, but death will be destroyed. Someone once referred to Easter as "the day death died." Of course, death is still among us, but the death warrant for death was signed by the resurrection of Jesus and will eventually be carried out. It is thrilling to know that Christ our King will destroy all His enemies. It is most comforting to know that death is among them. For from our human perspective death is the ultimate enemy—the last enemy. It is good to know that in life and in death, in time and eternity, when we are followers of Christ, we are on the winning side.

Dear God and Lord of all, we thank You for the forgiveness we have in Christ Jesus our Lord. We thank You that He came to earth to be the Savior of the world. We celebrate the life everlasting that we have in Him. In His holy name, we pray. Amen.

Access to Grace

We have gained access by faith into this grace in which we now stand
(Romans 5:2a, *New International Version*).

Scripture: Romans 5:1-11
Song: "Amazing Grace"

Recently a popular magazine noted that it is now possible to own a handheld satellite receiver. Already installed on some new autos, the devices work with the global positioning satellite to tell you exactly where you are. They can now be carried and are designed for hikers and other walkers. The story's title was taken from John Newton's beloved hymn, "Amazing Grace." The title of the piece was "I Once Was Lost But Now Am Found." The original message of "Amazing Grace" must not be forgotten. To be lost in the spiritual sense is a very serious thing. To be the recipient of grace, through Jesus Christ, is a very sacred thing. Faith gives us access into this grace. Some of us have had the experience of standing before a door and seeing a sign: No Admittance. Before Christ died for us we did not have free access to grace. Remember that the veil of the temple, that curtain separating the Holy Place from The Most Holy Place, was torn in two when Christ died. It opened up a way that had been closed. It gave new access to the Most Holy Place. It illustrated the fact that faith in the crucified Christ would now give us all access to God and His grace in the most personal way. Today, we are able to approach the throne of God through Jesus Christ, the Savior of the world.

O Lord, forgive us. Cause us to fall before You. Increase our faith. Deepen our trust. Help us this day to live a life of celebration in Christ Jesus. Through our Lord and Savior's name, we pray. Amen.

Bad News and Good News

But not as the offense, so also is the free gift: for if through the offense of one many be dead, much more the grace of God, and the gift by grace, which is by one man, Christ Jesus, hath abounded unto many (Romans 5:15).

Scripture: Romans 5:12-17
Song: "Hallelujah, What a Savior!"

The water hyacinth plant is not native to Florida. It was brought from another area to grace a lily pond, but the plant spreads rapidly and has now clogged waterways throughout the state. Thousands of dollars are spent annually in an attempt to control the plant. It all began with the act of one person. The plant called Kudzu is not native to Georgia and its neighboring states. However, someone brought it in to that state to cover a bank of poor soil. But the plant spread until it now covers fences and trees and buildings. It all began with the act of one person.

The deeds mentioned here are eclipsed by the results from the act of the one man, Adam. By him the misery of sin entered our world. This is the bad news.

There is also good news. Christ destroyed sin in one single act. His death, burial, and resurrection bring life to all mankind who follow Him. This is amazing. One deed done by Christ in one day canceled all that had come upon us through Adam's sin and through our sins. Truly we can say with the songwriter P. P. Bliss, "Hallelujah, What a Savior!" We worship Jesus. This is the good news for all mankind.

O God, we confess to You that we have sinned. We confess that we have experienced the painful results of sin. Now we come to confess our faith in Your Son. Thank You for all the grace that has come to us through His death and resurrection. In His holy name, we pray. Amen.

The King is Coming

See, your king comes to you, righteous and having salvation, gentle and riding on a donkey (Zechariah 9:9, *New International Version*).

Scripture: Zechariah 9:9-13
Song: "Face to Face"

Before World War II the emperor of Japan was regarded as divine. Because of this, ordinary people were never allowed to see his face. When Emperor Hirohito rode through the streets of a Japanese city everyone looked down. It was considered irreverent—and dangerous—to look on his face.

When Jesus rode into Jerusalem people saw Him face to face. He was the King of kings, but He did not demand that people look down or look the other way when He passed. Jesus recognized that majesty should be accompanied by humility, that divinity should not be cut off from humanity. His entry into Jerusalem on the eve of His crucifixion we call His triumphal entry. The crowds impress us. We are impressed by their shouts of Hosanna. The palm branches they waved impress us. We are impressed that people covered the road before Him with their garments. But we are most impressed that He did not come into Jerusalem riding a prancing steed, as a warrior king might have done. He chose instead, deliberately, to ride on the lowliest beast of burden. What a stunning combination of kingship and servanthood! What a Sovereign! What a Savior!

Dear God and Father of all mankind, we bow before You in reverence, devotion, and love. Help us to show compassion, love, and wisdom as we walk in Your ways. Teach us to follow Your example in purity and holiness. Give us grace that we may follow Your example in humility and meekness. In the name of our Savior, we pray. Amen.

Praise Him! Praise Him!

And the disciples went, and did as Jesus commanded them, (Matthew 21:6).

Scripture: Matthew 21:1-11
Song: "All Hail the Power of Jesus' Name"

They were two Americans who spoke only English. They were attending a church service far from home. The service was in two languages because this church had many refugees from a neighboring land. So the service was in the national language and translated into the refugees' language. The two visitors knew neither language. So they understood nothing until the closing chorus. The closing chorus was that lovely little song, "Alleluia! Alleluia!" And this word is the same in every language. All three language groups represented in that worship service could understand it. Then they sang another song to the same tune. It was simply the praise and worship word, "Hosanna"—another word that needed no translation. The two most familiar words in praise and worship all over the world are words of praise: "Alleluia" and "Hosanna."

When we praise and worship God we often all say the same words! But the praise of today's text would not have been heard if the disciples had not been obedient. Our Lord deserves worship, praise and obedience. We cannot substitute one for the other.

Sometimes people want only to praise the Lord—literally! Let us remember to worship Him and to give Him both our obedience and our praise.

O God and Lord of all, forgive us, when we forget to praise and worship You. Help us to obey You. Give us grace that we will honor You with our lips, and with our lives. Show us, dear Father, how You want us to worship and serve You. Through Christ our Savior, we pray. Amen.

Are You Alive?

The wages of sin is death; but the gift of God is eternal life through Jesus Christ our Lord (Romans 6:23).

Scripture: Romans 6:1-11
Song: "Because He Lives"

There are many ways to divide all the adults of the world neatly into two categories: men or women, rich or poor, old or young, them or us. But the most important division from God's viewpoint is this one: dead or alive. All people everywhere can be classified as either dead in their sins or alive in Christ.

We see people everyday playing sports, going to work, mowing the lawn, raising a family and think of them as alive. Yet, without Christ, even though one is physically alive, one is spiritually dead. Anyone who lives without regard for God and His Son Jesus, has no hope of eternal life.

Believers live a celebrated life in Jesus Christ. In Him we are assured that we live today and for eternity. Just as Jesus died and was resurrected, we too have been raised to new life. As we continue to live for Jesus and put our trust in Him, we have the assurance "that whoever believes in him shall not perish but have eternal life" (John 3:16, *New International Version*). It is wonderful to know that we shall be forever with the Lord!

Heavenly Father, thank You for the life that we have because of the death and resurrection of our Lord and Savior, Jesus Christ. Give us a love for those who are still dead in their sins. May Your Holy Spirit work through us to draw others to life in Christ. Help us to follow You as we work, play, worship and serve You. Through the name of Jesus Christ, our Savior, we pray. Amen.

March 25-28. **Cheryl Frey** is a Christian writer living in Cincinnati, Ohio.

Free to Choose

A man is a slave to whatever has mastered him
(2 Peter 2:19, *New International Version*).

Scripture: Romans 6:15-23
Song: "Have Thine Own Way, Lord!"

Have you ever said, or heard someone say, "I'm my own man . . . . I do things my own way . . . and nobody tells me what to do."

Humans of all ages show a strong streak of independence. First comes the two-year-old, stamping her foot and saying, "Me do it!" Then there's the 16-year-old with his permit protesting, "Mom, quit telling me how to drive!" Next we see the young woman insisting on marrying a man who will make her life miserable. We also see the older man, hopelessly lost, but refusing to ask for directions. Even the elderly woman declines to take her medicine. It's in our nature to want to do things our own way.

Certainly God did give each person free will, and He expects us to use it to make life decisions. Our destiny is the result of our own choices. But according to today's passage, our only real choice is who will be our master. Paul says we are slaves to the one whom we obey.

When we listen to the seductive voice of pleasure, power, or possessions, then sin becomes our master. When we choose to die to ourselves and live for the Lord, we are slaves to righteousness. No matter how independent we think we are, we are all somebody's slave—either God's or Satan's.

Sovereign Lord, how gracious You are to give us the freedom to choose whom we will serve. Protect us from wrong choices. Give us wisdom to see the joys of life in Your service. In the Master's name, we pray. Amen.

Visions of Sugarplums

Is the law sin? Certainly not! Indeed I would not have known what sin was *except through the law* (Romans 7:7, *International Version*).

Scripture: Romans 7:7-13
Song: "I Need Thee Every Hour"

The only time I really obsess about food is when I'm on a diet. Most of the time I only give the most casual attention to my next meal. But when I'm on a diet, I start early in the morning thinking about all the food that I'll be allowed to eat that day.

Unfortunately, I also spend way too much time daydreaming about all the food I can't eat! When I'm on a low fat diet, all I want is a nice juicy steak. But when I'm on a high protein diet, I find myself longing for a big plate of spaghetti. And no matter what the diet, ice cream always sounds good! What I can't have is what I want.

Is it the diet that's bad? No, it helps me face up to the bad habits I've developed related to food. If it hadn't been for the diet, I wouldn't have known what a problem I have with self-discipline.

That's exactly what the law does for us. God's law is good because it helps us to see how much we want what we shouldn't have. It helps expose the sin in our lives and shows us what a strong hold it has over us. Then we can admit our weakness and look to the Lord Jesus to be our strength and our righteousness.

Father of mercy, Your law blesses our lives, for it reveals the sinful longings of our hearts. We confess our sins to You now, and ask for Your forgiveness. How wonderful to know that even though we are sinners, we are sinners saved by grace. In Jesus' name, we pray. Amen.

Delivered From Danger

What a miserable person I am. Who will rescue me from this body that is doomed to die? Thank God! Jesus Christ will rescue me (Romans 7:24, 25, *Contemporary English Version*).

Scripture: Romans 7:14-25
Song: "Jesus Is All the World to Me"

Newspaperwoman Lois Lane just couldn't seem to help herself. If there was a story somewhere in Metropolis, she would have to go after it. It didn't matter that she would cause grief to other people or put herself in all kinds of danger. The story was all she could see, and she had to go after it. She was fortunate to have Superman close by to help her when she got into all those messes.

Sometimes we have a lot in common with Lois. We know there are places that we should stay away from, but we go there anyway. Certain activities are sure to get us in trouble, but we can't seem to stop ourselves from getting involved. Even though our souls are in danger, we still allow our lives to become all messed up by sin.

How hopeless our lives would be—if it weren't for Jesus. Apart from Him, sin would overwhelm our lives and deliver us to death. Instead, we have a Savior who loves us so much that He came to Earth to rescue us. And unlike Superman, that fictional character who was never in any real danger, Jesus was a flesh and blood human being. He put His life on the line for us and died to save us from sin.

Loving heavenly Father, how can we ever thank You for saving us from sin and death? Your tender care for us caused You to send Your Son Jesus to deliver us from sin's trap and give us life everlasting. In the name of our Savior, Jesus Christ, we pray. Amen.

Rolling Stones

And his incomparably great power for us who believe. That power is like the working of his mighty strength, which he exerted in Christ when he raised him from the dead (Ephesians 1:19–20a, *New International Version*).

Scripture John 20:1–10
Song: "Great Is the Lord"

Christians believe the stone blocking Jesus' tomb was divinely removed and Jesus was, indeed, raised from the dead. We believe the power of God did something very unique as it made Christ alive again after He was beaten and crucified.

However Christians sometimes forget the same power that raised Jesus from the dead 2,000 years ago is at work within us today. God wants us to know of "his incomparably great power for us who believe. That power is like the working of his mighty strength, which he exerted in Christ when he raised him from the dead . . ." (See Ephesians 1:19–20a).

God can do anything. But do we live like we believe it? Are there "stones" in our lives we have not allowed Him to roll away? Are thoughts, habits or relationship troubles blocking our lives with God? The power that raised Jesus from the dead is the same power that is at work within us. God still rolls away every stone. But we must ask Him to take charge of our lives.

Powerful God, thank You for raising Jesus from the dead. Thank You for displaying Your awesome power to mankind and for offering salvation to all. Give us the strength and the wisdom to use the power You offer. Help us to eliminate impure thoughts, overcome bad habits, and restore troubled relationships. In the mighty name of Jesus, we pray. Amen.

March 29-31. **Erin Seta** is a student at Cincinnati Bible College and serving as an intern at Standard Publishing. She and her husband worship at Northern Hills Christian Church, Cincinnati, Ohio.

Comfort in Promises

My comfort in suffering is this: Your promise preserves my life
(Psalm 11 9:50, *New International Version*).

Scripture: John 20:11-18
Song: "Near to the Heart of God"

Why are you crying? Does there seem to be no comfort for the hurts of life? Has depression, disappointment, disease or death left you in grief? Do the tears flow without ceasing? These experiences are universal. Pain is part of life.

After Jesus' crucifixion and burial, Mary was left crying. Actually, Mary may more accurately be described as "wailing." She could be heard using a loud expression of grief. Before Jesus comforted anyone else, He appeared to console Mary.

In Psalm 119:50, we read, "My comfort in suffering is this: Your promise preserves my life." By someone's calculations there are more than 7,000 promises in the Bible. For example, God promises that He will never leave us or forsake us (see Joshua 1:5). God promises He will comfort those who mourn (read Matthew 5:4). God promises a new Heaven and a new earth (see 2 Peter 3:13). When we put our trust in Him, we will find true comfort.

When Mary was left crying, Jesus comforted her. The Holy Spirit too can comfort us, and when we read the Word of God, we can find comfort in the numerous promises offered to us in the Bible, God's Word.

Faithful God, thank You for being a God of promises. Help us to truly seek You in our times of pain. May we always look to Your Word for assurance that You give the comfort we need. Help us to honor You, no matter what our circumstances. In the name of Jesus, our Savior, we pray. Amen.

Waiting for Joy

Yet the Lord longs to be gracious to you; he rises to show you compassion.
For the Lord is a God of justice. Blessed are all who wait for him
(Isaiah 30:18, *New International Version*).

Scripture: John 20:19–23
Song: "Burdens Are Lifted at Calvary"

Imagine what it was like for the apostles after Jesus' death. Fear and uncertainty flooded their souls. The past few years of their lives had been a "mountaintop experience." They were with the Lord! Then suddenly, their leader was murdered. Almost immediately their mountain top experience sent them crashing into a valley.

Has this ever happened to you? Have you been on a mountaintop, and then suddenly, unexpectedly fallen into a valley? The apostles did not understand what was happening to them as they were walking through the valley. After God's plan was fulfilled, Jesus appeared to the disciples, and they were "overjoyed."

We walk through valleys sometimes, but God will always meet us, even though we may not see Him or understand what is happening at the time of our pain. God does reveal Himself, just like Jesus revealed Himself to the disciples. Isaiah 30:18 says, "Yet the Lord longs to be gracious to you; he rises to show you compassion. For the Lord is a God of justice. Blessed are all who wait for him!" Valley experiences may come, but God can, and will, turn our mourning into joy.

Gracious God, thank You for Your desire to bless us. Give us the courage and the strength to wait for You in times of despair. Help us to live a joyful life in Christ so that Your Word will reach all mankind. In the name of Jesus our Savior, we pray. Amen.

My Prayer Notes

_____

_____

_____

_____

_____

_____

_____

_____

_____

_____

_____

_____

_____

_____

_____

_____

_____

_____

_____

_____

_____

My Prayer Notes

_____

_____

_____

_____

_____

_____

_____

_____

_____

_____

_____

_____

_____

_____

_____

_____

_____

_____

_____

_____

_____

Devotions

April

photo by Chuck Perry

April 1

So Bright the Light Looks Dark!

If that which is done away was glorious, much more that which remaineth is glorious (2 Corinthians 3:11).

Scripture: 2 Corinthians 3:1-11
Song: "Living for Jesus"

If you want to guarantee that your front porch light comes on whenever it gets dark outside, all you need to do is purchase a socket with an electric eye. With the lightbulb in this socket and this socket in your fixture, you can leave the light switch on twenty-four hours a day. The electric eye will turn on the light in the dark and turn it off when the sun rises.

At least, that's how it's supposed to work. If the electric eye is broken, or if it is turned toward the wall so that it doesn't "see" the sun, the lightbulb will burn nonstop, day and night. Everyone knows this is a waste. That's why someone invented electric eyes in the first place. With daylight shining all around us, the glow of one bulb looks like nothing. A porch light isn't necessary in the brightness of the sun.

This underscores the message of today's passage. Although the Old Covenant, delivered by Moses, shone with glory, it was like a lightbulb burning in the blackness of midnight. That light is nothing like the brightness that came with the New Covenant of Christ. Today we have the privilege, and the responsibility, to walk in the light of Jesus our Lord.

God of glory, and God of light, shine on us today and show us Your will. Help us to reflect the newness that comes only from You. In the name of Jesus, our Savior, we pray. Amen.

April 1-7. **Mark A Taylor**, vice president and publisher with Standard Publishing and his wife, Evelyn, have two grown children, Jennifer and Geoffrey.

Just Like Jesus

We . . . are being transformed into his likeness with ever-increasing glory, which comes from the Lord, who is the Spirit
(2 Corinthians 3:18, New International Version).

Scripture: 2 Corinthians 3:12-18
Song: "O to Be Like Thee!"

Someone has said, "Whenever two people are together, one is influencing the other." When we think through our relationships, we can see that the saying is true. With some people the persuading is a one-sided proposition. One of the pair is always the leader; the other always follows. One dominates; the other submits. One talks; the other listens.

But often, we take turns taking the lead. She lets me choose the restaurant; I let her select the living room couch. I let her pick the place for our vacation; she lets me decide on the mutual fund for our retirement account. Sometimes the influencing bounces back and forth throughout a conversation. I see his point at first, but soon he sees my point of view.

There's one relationship where there's never a question about who should do the influencing. The Bible says that as we spend time in the presence of Christ, He transforms us into His likeness. As we grow close to Him, we become like Him.

It won't happen against our will. He won't make us change. But neither can we become more like Jesus just by trying hard to do so. It will happen slowly, over time, as we rest and revel in the glory of His presence.

Oh, to be like Thee, blessed Redeemer! This is the prayer and the plea of my heart. Help me to be transformed into Your likeness as I become more and more comfortable in the glory of Your presence. And help those around me today to know that I have been with You. In Thy holy name, I pray. Amen.

Jars of Clay

We have this treasure in jars of clay to show that this all-surpassing power is from God and not from us (2 Corinthians 4:7, *New International Version*).

Scripture: 2 Corinthians 4:1-15
Song: "All to Jesus I Surrender All"

If you have a beautiful plant, you don't worry about growing it in a fancy pot. In fact, if the pot is too ornate or colorful, it may distract from the loveliness of the plant itself. You choose a plain clay pot. The simple container will allow the plant's shiny leaves or striking flowers to stand out. Then, the plant and the pot will not compete with each other. The eye of every viewer will be drawn to what's most important.

In the same way, God's glory is best seen when it flourishes in the simple life of an unpretentious believer. Paul compared his life to a plain clay vessel, not worth much by itself. Its value came only with the remarkable product that it contained, the ministry of God's mercy and God's Word. Paul reminded those who had become Christians because of his teaching to look first and longest at the all-surpassing power of God, not at Paul himself.

Sometimes people serve God to draw attention to themselves. When this happens, the person's glory always competes with God's glory in the sight of those looking on.

If we want to serve God but don't believe we're anything special, that's OK. In fact, those who see themselves as humble "jars of clay" may accomplish the most for God.

Heavenly Father, thank You for the assurance that You want to work through Your servants for Your glory. Help us to recommit to You. May people around us today see You more clearly. In the name of Jesus, we pray. Amen.

His Control, and Ours

Those controlled by the sinful nature cannot please God
(Romans 8:8, *New International Version*).

Scripture: Romans 8:1-8
Song: "Under His Wings"

If you want to fly from New York to Los Angeles, you cannot force your body to do so. You need the power of an airplane to get you in the air and to take you to Los Angeles. But just as long as you are in control of your will, even a whole fleet of aircraft cannot *force* you to fly. You must choose to walk onto the plane and submit to its ability to transport you through the heavens. The power of the plane is much greater than yours but not greater than the strength of your will.

It's the same way with God and us. He demonstrated His unequaled power by overcoming all the forces of sin and all the limitations of the law to make possible life and peace for those who choose to follow Christ. But He will not use His power to violate our choice to choose. To experience the freedom of the Spirit, we must decide to submit to it. When we submit our will to His will, we receive the wonderful gift of eternal salvation.

If we board a plane to Hawaii, we won't reach Alaska. And, as Paul makes clear in today's passage, if we choose to submit to sin, we will not experience life in the Spirit. The Spirit rules only in the lives of those who give Him control.

We seek to give You control, O God. We know that life doesn't work when we try to keep total control of it. Help us to see You working through us as we yield more and more of self to Your command. In the name of Jesus, our Savior, we pray. Amen.

The Blessings of Being His Child

The Spirit himself testifies with our spirit that we are God's children
(Romans 8:16, *New International Version*).

Scripture: Romans 8:9-17
Song: "Children of the Heavenly Father"

A private beach club in Newport, Rhode Island, has such exclusive admission standards that not even New York multimillionaire Donald Trump could get in. To be considered for membership in this club, your wealth must have been in your family for three generations. In a community concerned about heritage, "new money" isn't enough. Not only must you qualify for consideration, but your family must qualify as well.

In many societies, through many periods of history, a person's forefathers were as important as his own accomplishments. Family breeding and family history were thought to tell as much about a person as anything he had done on his own.

In this light we should consider the importance of today's Scripture. As this passage states it, one of the greatest blessings of the Holy Spirit in our life is the fact that He confirms that God is our Father. "Those who are led by the Spirit of God are sons of God" (verse 14, *New International Version*). Because we are God's sons, we stand in line to inherit His riches. And this wealth is greater than any possession or perk that the world can offer. God promises His sons that they will "share in his glory" (see verse 17).

Dear God, thank You for qualifying us to experience the marvels of Your glory. We know that we have done nothing to earn such blessings but that they come simply because You have chosen to call us Your children. In the name of Your son, and our Savior, Jesus Christ, we pray. Amen.

Hope Amid Groaning

We know that the whole creation groaneth and travaileth in pain together until now (Romans 8:22).

Scripture: Romans 8:18-30
Song: "O That Will Be Glory"

Watch the news for 30 minutes any evening, and you'll hear many accounts of groaning. Hurricanes or tornadoes lash and batter; forest fires or volcanoes burn and destroy; man's inhumanity to man spawns murder and persecution and fear.

And away from the newscasts the groaning continues. Someone who appears to be in good health gets sick. Someone trusted betrays. We go to God again and again for comfort, but always we're left with questions. "When will this suffering cease?" "How can a person cope who does not know God?"

Today's Scripture gives answers to the first question. And it affirms that the second has no satisfying reply.

Paul promises that the groaning will one day end, "that the creation itself will be liberated from its bondage to decay" (see verse 21). We wait patiently for this grand day, confident in the meantime that God will work, even through life's pain, for the good of those who love Him (see verses 25, 28).

Sadly, those not living according to His purpose have no such expectation. Their only hope is in what they can see, and this "is no hope at all" (see verse 24). Today, let us lift our eyes above the suffering in the daily news and take comfort in our relationship with the eternal and everlasting God.

Dear God of the ages, we trust You to work through today's difficulties and to sustain us with the hope of eternity with You. Meanwhile, help us to see You at work even in the groaning of this life. In the name of Christ, we pray. Amen.

April 7

Nothing, Absolutely Nothing!

What shall we say in response to this? If God is for us, who can be against us?
(Romans 8:31, *New International Version*).

Scripture: Romans 8:31-39
Song: "O Love That Wilt Not Let Me Go"

The day my grandfather died, all of his children and most of theirs gathered in his home to be close to my grandmother. It was a sober afternoon in a house accustomed to loud talk and hearty laughter from a family that was large and close. Soon the minister came, and before he prayed, he read the beautiful prose in this passage, beginning with verse 35.

By the time he was finished, several were wiping away tears, expressions of the groaning described in yesterday's passage and reflections of hope inspired by today's. When faced with life's loss and confused by our inability to control it, we need hope that comes only from God. We find it in Paul's promise: nothing, absolutely nothing, can separate us from the love of God that is in Christ Jesus our Lord!

We can think of several crossroads that may seem to separate us. Grief. Loss. Failure. Sometimes success. But whatever we can imagine and no matter what we may experience, we can be confident in this reality: God's love is always waiting, always available, always around us. And if God is for us, who can be against us?

God of love, and God of hope, we take confidence in these verses, no matter what life may throw at us today. And we will put faith in You tomorrow, no matter what troubles may come. We believe that Your love is available now and will be with us forever. This is why we recommit our lives to You and will give all to live for You always. In the name of Your son, Jesus Christ, our Savior and Lord, we pray. Amen.

I Will Pour Out My Spirit

And everyone who calls on the name of the Lord will be saved
(Acts 2:21, *New International Version*).

Scripture: Acts 2:14-21
Song: "Spirit of the Living God"

God was doing something new. The prophet Joel had prophesied hundreds of years earlier that God's Spirit would be poured out on human beings. Until then, God had given His Spirit to a few select individuals, but from Pentecost on, he was doing something new.

Joel mentioned the end results: "And everyone who calls on the name of the Lord will be saved." The Holy Spirit cannot be divorced from evangelism. He was present at Pentecost, He was present in the home of Cornelius (Acts 10:44), and He is present at every cultural threshold over which the gospel travels today. God fills men, women, sons, and daughters with His Spirit. On Pentecost, there were signs and wonders. The result, however, was that three thousand responded to the message and called on the name of the Lord.

Each individual, Spirit-filled Christian, is unique. We have varied gifts, given for the common good (1 Corinthians 12:5-7). We must not lose sight of the fact that Spirit-filled lives call people to repentance and confession of the Lord Jesus Christ. Does our life call others to salvation that our Lord offers? If He has filled us, it must.

O Lord, we confess that we are prone to think of ourselves, desiring Your blessing. Help us to have Your perspective and to concentrate on sharing Your love. In Jesus' name, we pray. Amen.

April 8. **David Fish** is on staff at Ozark Christian College in Joplin, Missouri.

The Enabling Gospel

But Peter and John answered and said unto them, Whether it be right in the sight of God to hearken unto you more than unto God, judge ye. For we cannot but speak the things which we have seen and heard (Acts 4:19, 20).

Scripture: Acts 2:22-33
Song: "Tell Me the Old, Old Story"

Peter's courage was amazing. There he stood, before a crowd of thousands, of which many had been instrumental in putting to death the Son of God, stinging their ears with the charge of murder! Where did he get such boldness? Was it from anger or revenge? Was it blind daring, prompted by fear for his own safety? No, his boldness came from a confidence in the gospel and the power of God who raised Jesus from the dead. It was this truth Peter was confident would transform this multitude of Jews. So he spoke the simple truth of the gospel and trusted in the power of God to take a crisis and turn it into a celebration.

We may not stand before ten thousand people today, but God calls us to demonstrate the same confidence in the gospel that Peter displayed. Let us therefore stand up and speak the truth of God's plan of salvation wherever we are. The same power will not only strengthen us; it will transform a crowd of unbelievers who wait to hear His message through us.

O God of all creation and our personal God, we are often frightened by the world around us; but dear Lord, may we speak Your truth which alone is sufficient to change an unbelieving mob into faithful servants. Help us to have boldness in You, knowing full well that You will guide us into all truth. In Jesus' holy name, we pray. Amen.

April 9. **Gordon Clymer**. Reprint from DEVOTIONS™ 1977-78.

Who Made the Robins?

All things were made by him: and without him was not any thing made that was made (John 1:3).

Scripture: John 1:1-5
Song: "This Is My Father's World"

In Genesis, chapter one, the first verse says God created the heavens and the earth. Now John tells us that the Word was with God in the beginning. He created everything, and without Him nothing was made that was made. "Who is this Word?" we ask. John gives us clues in the following verses. John the Baptizer was sent from God to tell that the Word was coming (verse 6, 7). The Word became flesh and lived among men for a while (verse 14). Not every one accepted Him, but those who did could become God's children (verse 12). He is the one and only Son of the Father (verse 14). It is Jesus!

Jesus was there when this world was created! None of the wonderful beauty that surrounds us was created without Him. What an exciting thought that is! The tulips and daffodils that are staging a beautiful show in our yards were created by Jesus. The robin you may see building its nest knows how to build that nest because Jesus gave that robin the right instinct to build and reproduce. God's world was created from a perfect plan, and Jesus had a part in formulating that perfect plan. Jesus was there in the beginning! Jesus has always lived! He is eternal! (Colossians 1:17).

Loving **Creator**, we praise You for the glorified reliability of Your world. Give us wisdom to value its beauty, to protect its resources, to respond to its rhythms. In the name of the Savior of the world, we pray. Amen.

April 10. **Nancy Hunt Sams**. Reprint from DEVOTIONS™ 1996-97.

April 11

Avoiding Judgment Through Faith

He that believeth on him is not condemned: but he that believeth not is condemned already, because he hath not believed in the name of the only begotten Son of God (John 3:18).

Scripture: John 16:4-15
Song: "Tis So Sweet to Trust in Jesus"

Proof of an historical person's existence is based upon testimony from those who knew him and upon evidence which verifies his life and work. The Bible presents ample testimonies from men who saw and heard Jesus preach and teach, and those testimonies support each other in regard to truthfulness and accuracy. Evidence relating to His life and work forms the basis for spiritual truths which are revealed in the Bible. Those truths are valuable in knowing Christ, believing in Him, and understanding His work.

Christ's presence manifested God's power and revealed God's character in a way that could be believed by men. His presence exposed evil and established the basis for judgment. His resurrected presence supports a continuing belief in a Heavenly existence. We look forward to living eternally with our creator.

Although Jesus is presently with the Father and cannot be seen by us, He continues to bless us with His presence through the Holy Spirit. By this means Jesus is glorified, and we are provided an escape from judgment.

Thank You , God, for helping me to believe in things unseen and for giving me hope for eternal life. I praise You for Your grace and mercy. In the name of Jesus, we pray. Amen.

April 11. **Richard H. McVay**. Reprint from DEVOTIONS™ 1986-87.

The Christian's Armor

God is our refuge and strength, a very present help in trouble. Therefore will not we fear (Psalm 46:1, 2a).

Scripture: Ephesians 6:10-23
Song: "I Need Thee Every Hour"

Where could you find a suit of armor? And even if you could find one, what good would those old metal shields do against a machine gun or a rocket? Such things would be totally impractical. We don't fight that kind of war. Any modern military man would tell you that you have to prepare for the kind of battle your enemy is fighting. He is the one that determines your defenses.

Why is it, then, that today some still think the church can battle evil with money and political pressure? What good are swords against an atomic equipped enemy? Or what defense are the ways of man's thoughts against a spiritual foe? If you think the armor of God is strange, perhaps you do not understand the enemy. Note the equipment that our commander said we would need in our warfare against evil: truth, righteousness, the gospel of peace, faith, salvation, the Word of God, prayer, and boldness.

Are you prepared? Are you preparing? Only as we prepare in the Lord's way can we expect to stand strong and victorious. The world may call us foolish in not preparing to "live," but the enemy will overtake them, and they will not be prepared to die.

O Master, let me walk with Thee. I need Thee every hour, stay Thou near by. That will be glory for me. In Jesus' name, we pray. Amen.

April 12. **Gordon R. Clymer.** Reprint from DEVOTIONS™ 1975-76.

April 13

The Family of Faith

Behold, what manner of love the Father hath bestowed upon us, that we should be called the sons of God (I John 3:1).

Scripture: 1 John 1:1-10
Song: "Trusting Jesus"

Congratulations! It's an eight pound, nine ounce, twenty-one inch, bouncing boy! A baby in the home is a joy. A baby brings many delights and chores. The family is important to the baby. A baby needs the love, trust, and nourishment the family gives. The baby needs to learn to depend on the parent's love. She needs to learn that when Daddy playfully throws her gently upward he will catch her on the way down. The baby needs satisfying food when hungry. The family must make a baby feel secure and loved. As the baby needs a family for love, for security, and for the necessities of life, parents find their need to love satisfied in the little child.

So it is with the Christian. Without someone to love him, someone he can trust, and something to nourish him, he will surely die. He needs the personal prayer life. He needs to trust God to supply all of his needs. As a loving parent God showers His love upon us every day. It's great to be in the family of God.

Let us learn to trust God just as a little baby trusts the parents.

Most gracious heavenly Father, thank You for Your love and light, for Your security and comfort to care for me day by day. Help me to be an obedient child and bring honor to our family name. In Jesus' name, we pray. Amen.

April 13. **Journalism Student**. Reprint from DEVOTIONS™ 1977-78

Becoming

But as many as received him, to them gave he power to become the sons of God (John 1:12a).

Scripture: Romans 10:5-17
Song: "Only Trust Him"

Stationery, pins, and bumper stickers feature a small red heart to proclaim "love" for all sorts of things. The people to whom Paul was writing in today's Scripture, however, did not consider the heart the seat of sentimental emotion. Paul's readers considered the heart the seat of the will—the place of decision making.

Paul wrote, "For with the heart man believeth unto righteousness . . ." (Romans 10:10a). It is in the heart—the place of decision making—that man chooses to disobey God and to follow after sin. Here he will feel the weight of guilt and shame. But it is also in the heart that man may choose to forsake his sins and believe on Jesus Christ for his salvation. Here he will know forgiveness from sin and freedom from guilt.

Paul concluded his statement with, ". . . and with the mouth confession is made unto salvation" (Romans 10:10b). The heart filled with faith in the saving grace of Jesus will want to give witness of what Christ has done.

The joy of sins forgiven and the knowledge of sonship will inspire us to witness the thrill of becoming one with Him.

Our Father, thank You for forgiving our sins and helping us share the good news of salvation. May we tell to all the joy of Your saving faith. Through Christ our Lord, we pray. Amen.

April 14. **Yvonne Vollman Chalfant**. Reprint from DEVOTIONS™ 1986-87.

April 15

Sit and Soak Christians

Do not merely listen to the word, and so deceive yourselves
(James 1:22, *New International Version*).

Scripture: James 1:19-27
Song: "He Lifted Me"

William had never seen so much fresh, clean water. Having been born in a semi-desert part of Africa, he was a bit overwhelmed watching people dive into the swimming pool. He asked, "Do you mind if I jump in and swim with you?"

"If you can swim, come on in. The water is pretty deep at this end of the pool," the swimmers replied.

In an instant, William was in the pool and on his way to the bottom. Just as quickly, he found himself rescued and deposited on the edge of the pool again. After a moment of silence, William said, "I thought I could swim but I had never tried it before."

Self-deception is the couch-potato approach to athletics, the fool's approach to obedience before God. Jesus said, "Everyone who hears these words of mine and does not put them into practice is like a foolish man who built his house on sand. The rain came down, the streams rose, and the winds blew and beat against that house, and it fell with a great crash" (Matthew 7:26, 27, *New International Version*).

Let us not sit and soak less we drown in self-deception.

Lord, may we be wise today and build our lives on the solid rock of active obedience. Help us to include our hearts and our hands in service to You. In the name of Jesus, our Lord and Savior, we pray. Amen.

April 15-21. **Dr. David Grubbs** is the President of the Cincinnati Bible College and Seminary in Cincinnati, Ohio. For many years, he and his wife, Eva, served as medical missionaries in Zimbabwe.

Don't Show Favoritism

My brothers, as believers in our glorious Lord Jesus Christ, don't show favoritism (James 2:1, *New International Version*).

Scripture: James 2:1-13
Song: "More About Jesus"

If Jesus were on earth today, would He have a reserved parking space? Private entrances, executive restrooms, complimentary tickets, and other "perks" that have the flavor of favoritism. Discrimination is sometimes so subtle that one needs to understand the code words (Matthew 23:16).

During the days of severe racial discrimination in Rhodesia, black Africans were not permitted to use public restrooms that were reserved for white people. The sign on one door read "Gentlemen." The sign on the other door read "Public Restroom, Men." The meaning was clear.

Confronted with those signs, one of my black African friends decided to go through the door marked "Gentlemen." He was stopped by an attendant and instructed to use the other door. My friend replied, "I, too, am a gentleman." (And he is!)

Unfortunately, favoritism is sometimes practiced in the church. The person "wearing a gold ring and fine clothes" may still get the choice seats. Jesus said, "it is hard for a rich man to enter the kingdom of heaven" (Matthew 19:23). The up-and-coming person and the down-and-out person equally need Jesus. "Brothers, as believers in our glorious Lord Jesus Christ, let us not show favoritism."

Dear Lord, forgive us for showing favoritism. You have created all people, and provided salvation for all people. Help us to overcome our worldly values and to see people as You see them. In the name of Jesus Christ, our Savior, we pray. Amen.

April 17

Don't Trip Over Your Words

We all stumble in many ways. If anyone is never at fault in what he says, he is a perfect man, able to keep his whole body in check
(James 3:2, *New International Version*).

Scripture: James 3:1-12
Song: "Open My Eyes, That I May See"

Learning a new language is often a difficult task. One stumbles through a lot of conversation before fluency is ever noticed. Tripping over the obstacles of the new language is sometimes humorous, at other times humbling. I once told people that we should read the "monkeys" of God. I mispronounced "word." On another occasion, I told someone that a "little cow manure" was running down his pant leg. I had mispronounced "grasshopper."

When I was a young boy, the older people used to say, "I got my tongue over my eyetooth and I couldn't see what I was saying." James reminds us that we are often at fault in what we say. One must exercise great discipline in speech. It is all too easy to stumble.

Jesus informed us that our speech is a mirror of our inner person. If we listen to what comes out of a person's mouth, we will know what lives in his heart. Keeping our language under control reflects the discipline we exercise over our whole body. Let us keep a tight rein on the tongue. It will set the pattern for keeping a tight rein on the rest of life.

Dear Father and Almighty God, Creator of Heaven and Earth, may we devote ourselves to speaking the truth in love and compassion toward others. May our tongues be a healing balm and not a raging fire. And, may the words of our mouths glorify and praise Jesus, our Savior and Lord. In His holy name, we pray. Amen.

Reaping What You Sow

Peacemakers who sow in peace raise a harvest of righteousness
(James 3:18, *New International Version*).

Scripture: James 3:13-18
Song: "Bringing In the Sheaves"

When the first African preacher introduced the Gospel to the part of Zimbabwe where we later lived, he carried in his pocket the seed of a palm tree from his home area and planted it near his new home. Over the years the seed grew to be a lonely, but stately, palm tree. Since it was located about five miles from Mashoko Mission hospital, where we lived and worked, I frequently admired the tree as I drove past it at the now deserted home site.

One day in my travels I thought: It would be nice to plant a palm tree, the symbol of peace, to represent my efforts to bring the Prince of Peace and His righteousness to the continent of Africa. I planted the seed, and today that seed has grown to be a young palm tree.

James reminds us that if we sow in peace, we will bring about a harvest of righteousness. Attitude is very important. While the rule of nature is that you get more than you sow, the rule of the Kingdom of God is that gentleness and peace also bears fruit.

My palm tree is growing, but the growing church is a better memorial.

Heavenly Father, we want no other memorial than that we have been peacemakers. We thank You that we represent the Prince of Peace. May our lives today reflect the peace and righteousness that comes only through Him. In Jesus' name, we pray. Amen.

Don't Grumble

Don't grumble against each other, brothers, or you will be judged. The Judge is standing at the door! (James 5:9, *New International Version*).

Scripture: James 5:7-12
Song: "Jesus Is Coming Again"

In some parts of Africa, people believe that they can find God only through the help of departed ancestors. They explain it this way:

"Many years ago, God lived with people. He visited their villages, talked to them directly, helped them solve their problems and cured their illnesses. But God was often disturbed by the way people grumbled about everything and the way they scolded each other, even over small matters.

Because of this, God decided to distance himself from people, only visiting with their Elders. God chose a place on a high mountain for the proposed visits, but when the Elders were on their way, God heard them grumbling and scolding each other as they walked up the mountain. So, God went away, and no one knows where He lives."

Although this is an African myth, it reminds us that quiet patience is a wonderful virtue. James says, "Be patient, then, brothers, until the Lord's coming." Why do we grumble about things over which we have no control? God is in control, and He never makes a mistake. We are expected to enjoy each other as we gently wait for Christ's return.

Father, forgive our grumbling and complaining. You continue to shower us with blessings, but, like spoiled children, we keep asking for more. Thank You for everything. Thank You for the good friends we share in Your Kingdom. In the name of Jesus Christ, our Savior, we pray. Amen.

Come Down to Earth

For by the grace given me I say to every one of you: Do not think of yourself more highly than you ought, but rather think of yourself with sober judgment, in accordance with the measure of faith God has given you
(Romans 12:3, *New International Version*).

Scripture: Romans 12:1-8
Song: "Just As I Am"

During our second year of medical school, we began examining patients. The dress code included a white jacket, and we carried stethoscopes in our jacket pockets. We began to look like doctors, and often "thought too highly" of ourselves by wearing the coats and carrying the stethoscopes everywhere. One day just before leaving the hospital, I phoned my wife to ask her if there was anything that I could pick up from the supermarket on my way home. Stopping at the store, I wore my white coat and carried my stethoscope as I went in to pick up the items. As I neared the produce area, I was surprised to be stopped by a nice elderly lady, and was humbled by her question. "Young man," she asked, "how much is cabbage per pound?" She thought I was a produce clerk. I thought I was a doctor. We were both wrong. I was a student posing as a doctor.

Sober judgment also reminds us not to think to little of ourselves. God gives a variety of gifts and spreads them around to bless all people. Celebrate your own gift as you also celebrate the gift of your brother. There is no cause for pride or jealousy.

Dear God, thank You for all of our gifts and abilities. Help us to enjoy them and use them for You. Keep us from being jealous of the gifts You give to others. In the name of Jesus, we pray. Amen.

Share With God's People

Share with God's people who are in need. Practice hospitality
(Romans 12:13, *New International Version*).

Scripture: Romans 12:9-21
Song: "Count Your Blessings"

My wife and I flew into Sydney, Australia, and did not know a single person in the city. As we were unpacking our suitcases in the hotel, the phone rang in our room. A voice on the other end of the line said, "You don't know me but a friend of yours phoned long distance to let us know that you were arriving today. Would you join us for supper and then go to a home Bible study with us tonight?"

Over the next several days we met many wonderful Christian people who fed us, took us on tours of the city and its parks, and invited us to preach for them. Their hospitality and generosity is one of the fondest memories we have of our visit to their homeland.

Hospitality and generosity are identifying characteristics of Christ's church here on earth. More hours are given in volunteer service and more donations given for religious purposes than for any other purpose in America. Sharing with family and friends is one of life's joys. However, Paul reminds us to share with God's people "who are in need." Our hospitality and generosity must go beyond friendship. It must include God's people who are in need. While we were still sinners, Christ died for us.

Blessed Lord, thank You for being so generous, for opening up Heaven for us. Help us not to hoard but to share the blessings that You so generously give to us. In the name of Jesus Christ, our Savior, we pray. Amen.

Let God Do the Judging

Do not judge, or you too will be judged (Matthew 7:1, *New International Version*).

Scripture: Romans 14:1-6
Song: "0 Master, Let Me Walk with Thee"

For years I have eaten lunch in our college cafeteria. I usually choose milk—skimmed milk at that—because it is healthier than beverages with caffeine, sugar, or fat. A colleague usually chooses coffee, and teases me because I choose a drink best suited for babies. But in spite of bantering over this and several other issues about which we differ, we are the closest of friends.

Christians differ over many issues not much more important than these when viewed for the perspective of eternity. We argue about what hymnal to use or the color to paint classrooms. Some have split churches over worship styles. In today's Scripture, Paul mentions Christians who differed about whether they could eat meat. His advice was that they should not reject one another over such a matter.

There are some issues of basic doctrine which we cannot compromise. These are matters essential to the faith, but most of the issues that trouble us are not essentials. God is the master over all His servants, and we must leave the judging to Him.

Gracious God, give us the wisdom to distinguish the essentials from the incidentals in our walk with You. Teach us to love our brothers and sisters when we disagree with them about incidentals that are based on our culture or our personal idiosyncrasies. In Jesus' name, we pray. Amen.

April 22-28. **John Wade** is a professor at Atlanta Christian College and a former editor for Standard Publishing. He and his wife live in Atlanta, Georgia.

"No Man Is An Island"

For none of us liveth to himself, and no man dieth to himself (Romans 14:7).

Scripture: Romans 14:7-12
Song: "I'll Live for Him"

The title, coming from John Donne's famous line, paraphrases our verse for today. In a culture that is becoming increasingly self-centered, we need this reminder that "every man is a piece of the Continent, a part of the main." We need to be reminded that our very existence depends upon a host of others who contribute to our well being—parents, children, fellow Christians, doctors, lawyers, merchants, craftsmen.

The application of this verse for today's Scripture is that since we are a small part of the total human race, we should not set ourselves up as judges over others. For one thing, our own prejudices and experiences always condition our standards for judgment. Further, we don't know enough to pass eternal judgments upon those around us.

Only God has the infinite wisdom to know all. Understanding these things, we should be further humbled because all of us must someday stand before the Eternal Judge. In that day "every knee shall bow" and "every tongue shall confess" that we are sinful servants and that our only hope for salvation is through His wonderful grace purchased for us through the death and the resurrection of Christ, our Savior. It is in Him alone that we are saved.

Almighty and everliving God and Father of all, keep us ever mindful that You and You alone are the Judge of all creation. Forgive us when we are tempted to usurp Your authority and judge our fellow men. Teach us to walk humbly with You. In the name of Your Son, Jesus Christ, the Savior and Lord of all, we pray. Amen.

Our Brother's Keeper

If your brother is distressed because of what you eat, you are no longer acting in love (Romans 14:15a, *New International Version*).

Scripture: Romans 14:13-23
Song: "Purer in Heart, O God"

A large flock of sheep was once grazing on a hillside, when a big ram, the leader of the flock, decided that the grass on the other side of a stone wall was greener. Finding a low place in the wall, he jumped over it without looking. Unfortunately, on the other side of the wall was a dry well, and he plunged into it. The other sheep watched their leader and, in spite of everything that the shepherd could do to stop them, each sheep one after another followed their leader, the ram, over the wall to their destruction.

Of course, people are not like sheep—at least most of the time they are not. But every one of us, in one way or another, is, like that ram, a leader that others may follow. We may not even be aware that others are looking to us for guidance, which means that we must be sensitive to the needs of others at all times.

Actions and attitudes that may be appropriate for mature Christians can become stumbling blocks to those who are weaker. Let us so act that we will never "put a stumbling block or an occasion to fall" in the way of a brother. We are, after all, our brother's keeper.

Gracious heavenly Father, make us all sensitive to the spiritual needs of those about us, and help us always to act in such a way that we will be good examples of Your love and salvation to the world. May we never use our freedom in such a way that others may be led astray. In Jesus' holy name, we pray. Amen.

April 25

Bearing One Another's Burdens

We then that are strong ought to bear the infirmities of the weak, and not to please ourselves (Romans 15:1).

Scripture: Romans 15:1-6
Song: "Where He Leads I'll Follow"

In World War II, the men who made up our unit had all completed basic training and presumably were in good physical condition and ready for the more rigorous demands of advanced training. But one man in our unit, a man past forty, who had been a school teacher in civilian life, was really not prepared for the twenty-five mile hikes with full equipment nor the strenuous obstacle courses. On our first long hike, he struggled to keep up after we had gone only a few miles. A strong young man in his early twenties, who had somehow earned the nickname "Crow," saw his plight and took his pack and strapped it onto his own back, allowing the older man to finish the hike.

On future training operations, Crow stayed by the older man and helped him whenever he was needed. Crow's example inspired the rest of us also to help, and the older man was able to complete the training. But there was another side to this story. Crow had grown up in a rural area in the South, had dropped out of school, and had never learned to read. Quietly and without anybody knowing it, the old teacher had been teaching Crow to read. Certainly, the strong ought to help the weak, but sometimes the weak can help the strong.

Dear God, we thank You for the talents and gifts You have given us. Help us find ways that we can use these gifts to help those who are not so blessed. Teach us also to accept help from others when it is offered. In Christ's name, we pray. Amen.

No Respecter of Persons

Here there is no Greek or Jew, circumcised or uncircumcised, barbarian, Scythian, slave or free, but Christ is all, and is in all (Colossians 3:11, *New International Version*).

Scripture: Romans 15:7-13
Song: "In Christ There Is No East or West"

This paragraph is a logical conclusion to Paul's discussion about Christian freedom and the important truth that Christians must accept one another in love, even when they disagree about many matters. Already there had been controversy about whether a Gentile had first to submit to the Law of Moses before he or she could become a member of the church. Although the Jerusalem conference held a few years before Paul wrote the Roman epistle seemed to settle this issue, controversy still lingered.

For this reason, Paul shows that God began to reveal His plan for the salvation of the world through Abraham and his descendants. But His plan also included the Gentiles. In the Old Testament are frequent references showing that the Gentiles were included as a part of God's eternal plan. The Gentiles would "glorify God for his mercy" (verse 9). "In him shall the Gentiles hope" (verse 12). Because God is not a respecter of persons, we are urged to "receive one another, as Christ also received us to the glory of God" (see Romans 15:7). In a world that is torn by strife over race, language, and nationality, how important this message is!

Almighty God, we thank You for those who have been a part of Your plan for salvation, both Jew and Gentile. Keep us from fears and prejudices that separate us from all of Your children. In the name of Jesus Christ, our Savior, we pray. Amen.

The King Has Come

That I should be the minister of Jesus Christ to the Gentiles, ministering the gospel of God, that the offering up of the Gentiles might be acceptable, being sanctified by the Holy Ghost (Romans 15:16).

Scripture: Romans 15:14-21
Song: "Jesus Saves"

Above the Arctic Circle, the winter darkness lasts many months. As the spring approaches, the people living there look forward to its arrival with great anticipation. In one area, a messenger is sent up to the highest peak to watch for the first rays of the sun. When the sun is sighted, he sounds the cry. "Behold, the sun!" Then down the mountain and to the surrounding villages the cry is echoed, "Behold, the sun!" When the message has reached the most remote village, the celebration of the new season begins.

For centuries the world had been in darkness. Then God sent His messengers with the good news: "The King is coming!" After Jesus' resurrection, the good news that the King had indeed come was proclaimed at Jerusalem, beginning at Pentecost; then it was carried to Judea and Samaria. Finally, it reached the Gentiles.

God's special ambassador to the Gentiles was the Apostle Paul. Paul was uniquely equipped and uniquely called to be the messenger who brought the good news to the Gentiles. Now the gates of Heaven were open to them. Now the glorious celebration could begin.

Dear God, thank You that the message of salvation has reached us. We thank You for the apostle Paul and countless others who faced dangers that we might hear the message that the King has come! In the name of Jesus, we pray. Amen.

Man Proposes, But God Disposes

And I am sure that, when I come unto you, I shall come in the fulness of the blessing of the gospel of Christ (Romans 15:29).

Scripture: Romans 15:22-33
Song: "God Moves in a Mysterious Way"

Paul desired to preach in Rome, the capital of the mighty Roman Empire. But, as he indicates in verse 22 in today's Scripture, he had been "much hindered." His busy ministries in Asia Minor and Greece had commanded his time and his energies. Perhaps he had envisioned his entry into Rome as an act of triumph, walking to the city on the Appian Way, surrounded by friends and co-workers. Eventually Paul did walk the Appian Way and some friends were with him, but his entry into Rome could hardly be called triumphant. He came as a prisoner, bound in chains, to be tried in Caesar's court.

But if Paul felt any disappointment about this turn of events, he never showed it. Instead, he used this apparent disaster as an opportunity to witness for the Lord. God in His providence often deals with us in a similar way. We make great plans and even pray diligently that these plans will work out the way we want them to work. But God, in His infinite wisdom, chooses to answer our prayers in His own way. It has been said that "man proposes, but God disposes." The next time something doesn't work out the way we planned it or prayed for it, perhaps it is because God is dealing with us in His own way and His own time.

Loving Father, help us to plan and pray for great things for You and Your kingdom. Give us the strength for work for these plans, but also give us the patience to allow You to deal with them in Your way. In Jesus' name, we pray. Amen.

Not For Ours Only

And he is the propitiation for our sins: and not for ours only, but also for the sins of the whole world (I John 2:2).

Scripture: 1 John 2:1-6
Song: "So Send I You"

Our Bible college missions group searched for a theme for our annual missions program. One of the members, Phyllis Rine, suggested a phrase from 1 John " . . .not for ours only . . . " We all agreed to use it. Shortly after that, Phyllis went to Africa as a missionary. I was teaching school when I heard the news of the murders of missionaries in the area where Phyllis lived. No names had been announced by the end of the school day. I listened to the radio as I drove home. Suddenly an announcer interrupted and said, "A former Cincinnati resident, Phyllis Rine, has been identified as one of the massacre victims."

My hands shook, and tears streamed down my face as I maneuvered the car to a safe stopping place. In those few moments, I challenged God and His wisdom. How could He let Phyllis die while serving Him?

Then, just as quickly as the announcer had broadcast the news, I heard Phyllis speaking. "Let's use this verse from 1 John. After all, He died for everyone's sins, not for ours only." Phyllis gave her life because she believed that verse.

O Lord, help us to follow whatever path You have for our lives. When we fear the unknown, increase our trust. Thank You for those who have set an example of obedience, no matter what the cost. In the Master's name, we pray. Amen.

April 29-30. **Joyce Ann Munn**, teacher and writer, serves on the national board of Christian Educators Association.

Like the Father

My command is this: Love each other as I have loved you
(John 15:12, *New International Version*).

Scripture: 1 John 2:7-17
Song: "More Like the Master"

Years ago when churches held two or three-week revival meetings, many evenings were designated with special recognitions. My home congregation frequently held mother-daughter or father-son look-alike contests. Without fail, each year, Mother and I won the contest. One year the competition was changed to mother-son and father-daughter look-alike. Surprise! Daddy and I won that one too. Several years later a friend from college visited my home. We had been talking about families, and she turned to me and said, "You really look like your . . . " She then looked at both my parents and said in an amazed tone, "Your parents sure do look like each other." The three of us laughed hysterically.

Most of us resemble our parents in a variety of ways. Daddy and I also shared a lot of mannerisms, and several times I was mistaken for my mother on the phone.

God has so many attributes that we need to emulate. Perhaps His love is the one characteristic that needs to be shown most clearly. Loving our friends and family usually blesses us. What about that irritating neighbor, though, or the difficult boss? Do you look like your Father to them?

Father, forgive me when the world sees a marred image of You because of my attitude or actions. Help me to live in such a way that when the world looks at me they will see Your love. May they want to be part of Your family. In the name of Jesus Christ, Your Son and our Savior, we pray. Amen.

My Prayer Notes

Devotions

May

photo by Chuck Perry

Supporting the Weaker Brother

But take heed lest by any means this liberty of yours become a stumblingblock to them that are weak (I Corinthians 8:9).

Scripture: 1 Corinthians 8
Song: "Stepping in the Light"

Paul tells of the concern that we should have for the conscience of the weaker brother. Perhaps we do not have exactly the same conditions today that people did then, but we are under the obligation to use the same principles in dealing with problems now facing us.

The strong Christian of Paul's day understood that he could eat meat that had been sacrificed to an idol. The first temptation was to say, "It's my privilege. I can do as I please." But suppose a weaker brother believed that he was defying God and transgressing the law of God. What should he do then? Paul said this man will be offended and maybe lost to the truth, in which case the stronger brother would have destroyed the weaker one by doing something that was not wrong in itself. Here we are given the principle of sacrificing our liberty for the salvation of a brother.

Note that we are not required to leave off everything to which a brother simply objects, but we are encouraged to leave off anything that will cause him to sin by doing it himself when he believes it to be wrong.

Help us to build up our weaker brothers, O Lord, so that they may be strong enough to know when they are weak, and brave enough to face themselves when they are afraid, that we all may be honest in defeat and humble in victory. In His name, we pray. Amen.

May 1. **W. Edward Fine** and his wife Billye Joyce minister to the Central Christian Church in St. Petersburg, Florida.

Who's Watching?

Whether therefore ye eat, or drink, or whatsoever ye do, do all to the glory of God (I Corinthians 10:31).

Scripture: 1 Corinthians 10:23-31
Song: "To God Be the Glory"

As a young teen, I made the decision not to dance. Many friends and my parents took the news in stunned silence. I had personal reasons, but chose not to share them. Neither did I feel condemnation of those who chose to dance.

I served as freshman class president. That office included the duty of planning a dance, the first major dilemma of my Christian life. I had no one to talk to except God. I quickly learned to give Him my troubles. I believed it was important to fulfill my obligations, so I agreed to help with the planning only. This seemed to work well. Then one classmate asked what I would be wearing to the dance. Before I could answer, she stammered, "I'm sorry. I know you're a Christian and won't be going." Now came my turn for stunned silence. I finally managed to agree that I wouldn't be going. I tried, though, to explain that wasn't the best way to judge a Christian. Suddenly, I realized people were watching me.

What do people see in our lives? Are we a stumbling block or stepping stone? What do we encourage others to do as they follow us? Will they want to do all to the glory of God?

Lord, help us all to remember that when people look at Christians, they need to see You. Forgive us for the times that we have not been a good representative. Thank You for the work You are doing in the life of the church. Mold us according to Your will. Through Jesus, our Savior, we pray. Amen.

May 2-5. **Joyce Ann Munn**, teacher and writer, serves on the national board of the Christian Educators Association.

Called To Serve

Serve wholeheartedly, as if you were serving the Lord, not men
(Ephesians 6:7, *New International Version*).

Scripture: Galatians 1:1-5
Song: "Soldiers of Christ, Arise!"

Sitting in the hotel lobby in Colorado Springs, I observed several military families smiling broadly as they posed for pictures. Apparently, they had just been involved in a special ceremony. Most of the men held certificates, which they were showing their relatives, especially the children. Because of things happening in America at the time, I knew those men might soon be serving their nation in dangerous situations. The oath taken by members of our military service basically says they will be faithful, serve honestly, and obey orders. These men seemed ready to go.

The apostle Paul writes to the Galatians about his own commissioning from Jesus Christ. He then expresses astonishment at how some of them were deserting the faith, rejecting the commission they, too, had received from Christ.

In his greeting, Paul reminds them that Christ died to rescue them from evil. That's exactly what He has done for us, too. Just as the military personnel I observed were called to serve and protect our country, so Jesus Christ commissions us to stand firm in the faith once for all delivered unto the church of Jesus Christ. Today we seek to serve the one true and living God. Let us pledge to go forth obeying His orders, serving, and remaining faithful.

Lord and Master of our lives, help us always to be willing to serve in whatever place You need and want us. We know You go before us into battle, and we give thanks for Your protection. In Jesus' name, we pray. Amen.

Sharing the News

May he give you the desire of your heart and make all your plans succeed
(Psalm 20:4, *New International Version*).

Scripture: Galatians 1:11-24
Song: "I Love to Tell the Story"

In Eugene Peterson's New Testament translation, *The Message*, he conveys a feeling of excitement in today's passage. Paul tells of his return from Arabia. He spent fifteen days with Peter, and Peterson includes the words, " . . . but what days they were!"

Can you imagine the interchange between those two? Paul must have been trying to describe the three years that he had been away from Christians, while Peter brought him up-to-date on church happenings.

Often we return home from a convention bursting with enthusiasm. We share insights from workshops and speakers with friends. We plan to put ideas into practice. But what happens to that desire to do great things for God? Usually we get busy with our daily activities and routines and can't find time to carry out the grandiose plans we had anticipated.

How can you keep your enthusiasm and accomplish your goals? Try focusing on one simple way of sharing the Good News—perhaps by preparing new materials for a class or collecting supplies for a mission.

Let us spend time in our own Arabia (preferably not three years) and let God show us how He wants to use us.

O God, we know Your plan to spread the gospel is by using us. We humbly thank You for entrusting us with such an awesome responsibility. Today, help us to be willing to give all that we are to You that we may truly be Your servant. In the name of Jesus, our Savior, we pray. Amen.

God's Gift

For it is by grace you have been saved, through faith—and this not from yourselves, it is the gift of God (Ephesians 2:8, *New International Version*).

Scripture: Galatians 2:15-21
Song: "Faith Is the Victory!"

Most of us learn early in life: if you want something, you work for it.

Your son wants a special treat. You give him a few chores so he can earn the money. Perhaps it started even earlier when you held out a favorite plaything in front of your small daughter. To get the toy, the toddler had to take a few more steps.

By adulthood, that lesson is firmly embedded in our minds. We're willing to work a little harder for that raise or promotion. After all, that's the way life works, isn't it?

Perhaps that's one reason it's so difficult for us to accept salvation as a gift. We search for ways to earn it. We work more in church, but end up frustrated.

Think back, instead, to other aspects of childhood. Didn't you eagerly eat your food with no thought of paying for it? Did you readily climb into bed at night, knowing the heat would keep you warm?

Just as parents provide necessities for their children, God provides salvation for us. Yes, He expects us to work in His kingdom. That, however, is not to earn what He freely gives. Accept His salvation with simple, childlike faith.

Loving Father, we thank You for the privilege of working in Your kingdom. Forgive us when we fall into Satan's trap of making us think we can earn our salvation that way. What a wonderful gift You have provided. We praise You and accept it with grateful hearts. Through Christ, our Savior, we pray. Amen.

All or Nothing

You cannot drink the cup of the Lord and the cup of demons too; you cannot have a part in both the Lord's table and the table of demons (I Corinthians 10:21, *New International Version*).

Scripture: 1 Corinthians 10:14-22
Song: "Once to Every Man and Nation"

Consistency is one of the great challenges of the Christian life. Many times we are tempted to compromise our faith for the approval of those around us.

Bill Glass wrote of an experiment done in schools across America. Nine of ten students were told to lie about the length of two lines drawn on a chalkboard.

Two lines were drawn. The teacher then pointed to the obviously shorter line and said, "How many of you think this is the longer line?" Nine hands went up. The student who had not been informed, seeing all the other hands up generally followed suit. Then the teacher pointed to the obviously longer line and said, "How many think this is the shorter line?" Nine hands went up. In 85% of the cases, the tenth person went along with the other nine.

The apostle Paul warned Christians that they must stand firm in what they knew to be true. He pointed out that the Lord's Supper set them apart exclusively to Jesus. Let us remember this complete allegiance to Christ the next time we take communion.

Our Father God, help us to be unswerving in our devotion to You. Thank You for allowing us to be participants in the body and blood of Christ. Give courage and discernment for this present hour. In His holy name, we pray. Amen.

May 6-12. **Dr. Ward Patterson** is a retired educator living in Cincinnati, Ohio.

Faith That Blesses

The Scripture foresaw that God would justify the Gentiles by faith, and announced the gospel in advance to Abraham: "All nations will be blessed through you" (Galatians 3:8, *New International Version*).

Scripture: Galatians 3:1-9
Song: "Make Me a Blessing"

Robert Banks, in his book, *The Tyranny of Time*, wrote that there are both "extraordinary slowness and intermittent suddenness in God's way of working." He points to the slowness of God's working from the call of Abraham until the coming of Christ. Yet, within this slow development of God's people, there were "sudden explosions of saving activity," like the Exodus and the giving of the Law.

First century Jews had difficulty recognizing that Christ's death on the cross was a cataclysmic event. They saw the Christian gospel in terms of God's slowness. Faith in Christ represented to them something to be added to what they believed and did, not something that redefined their whole concept of their relationship with God.

Paul argued, however, that the way of Christ was not merely a continuation of what had gone before. It was the sudden culmination of what God had intended through all the ages. Paul contended that a "sudden explosion of saving activity" had taken place on the cross, that faith and trust in God are now the operative principles for us, as they were for Abraham.

Our heavenly Father, we thank You that our salvation does rest on Your love expressed in the shed blood of Christ. Help us to express our faith in ways that are a continual blessing to others. In His holy name, we pray. Amen.

Redeemed From the Curse of the Law

He redeemed us in order that the blessing given to Abraham might come to the Gentiles through Christ Jesus, so that by faith we might receive the promise of the Spirit (Galatians 3:14, *New International Version*).

Scripture: Galatians 3:10-14
Song: "I Know Whom I Have Believed"

Bruce Purcell put together what he calls "Toddler Property Laws." They are: 1. If I like it, it's mine. 2. If it's in my hand, it's mine. 3. If I can take it from you, it's mine. 4. If I had it a little while ago, it's mine. 5. If it's mine, it must never appear to be yours in any way. 6. If I'm doing or building something, all of the pieces are mine. 7. If it looks just like mine, it's mine. 8. If I think it's mine, it's mine.

While these "laws" catch the amusing ways of small children, they also reflect the self-centeredness that lies behind much of our legal system. Every year our local, state, and federal governments pass about 150,000 new laws and 2,000,000 new regulations. We view these sometimes as necessary parts of a regulated society and sometimes as unnecessary intrusions into our freedom.

The Jews saw the Torah, the Law, as what set them apart from all nations of the earth. The problem with the Law, however, was that no one could live it out perfectly.

In the Scripture for today, Paul explains, this is where Christ comes in. We are redeemed not by our ability to keep every rule of Old Testament Law but by our faith in Jesus Christ.

Gracious God, thank You for taking from us the curse of our wrongdoing. Please deepen our faith and help us to rejoice in the blessing of what You and Christ have done for us. In the name of Jesus, Your only Son, we pray. Amen.

Who Do You Think You Are?

So the law was put in charge to lead us to Christ that we might be justified by faith (Galatians 3:24, *New International Version*).

Scripture: Galatians 3:19-29
Song: "Now I Belong to Jesus"

Who do you think you are? We sometimes ask that question more out of derision than interest. It is our response to someone who oversteps our boundaries or imposes unwelcome influence on us.

According to psychologists Pauline Clance and John Harvey, 70% of successful people think that they are fakes. They are often people who have worked hard and accomplished much. Yet, they feel that if the truth were really known, they would be revealed as impostors.

In today's Scripture, Paul says some significant things about who Christians are. Read the passage again and see if you can list some of them? Christians are liberated from the prison house of sin, they are sons of God, they are clothed with Christ, they are united in Christ, they belong to Christ, they are Abraham's seed, and they are heirs to the promise of blessing.

Paul was at pains to impress his readers with the fact that this identity did not come from keeping the Mosaic Law. Rather it came through faith in Jesus Christ. The Law exposed sin but it did not cure it. The Law's purpose was to lead people to Christ. He alone brings the cure for human alienation and disharmony.

God of Grace and Promise, help us to live up to our high calling in Christ Jesus. Forgive us when we take pride in our good deeds, as if we merited Your good favor. In the name of Your Son, Jesus Christ, we pray. Amen.

Heirs in God's Household

So you are no longer a slave, but a son; and since you are a son, God has made you also an heir (Galatians 4:7, *New International Version*).

Scripture: Galatians 4:1-7
Song: "The Family of God"

Wills can be revealing. They not only expose the accumulations of a lifetime, but they also expose the relationships and values of the person making the will. In addition to disposing of his valuable properties, Benjamin Franklin's will left his gold-capped walking stick to George Washington and a Chinese gong and a Bible to grandsons. Further, he left a picture of the king of France to his daughter, with instructions that the four hundred and eight diamonds it was set with not be removed to make jewelry for her or her daughters, lest she "introduce or countenance the expensive, vain, and useless fashion of wearing jewels."

Most of us would gladly be an heir. Paul chose the household of his time, with its family members and slaves, for a metaphor of the special relationship of Christians to God because of their faith in Jesus. Children, though they would some day possess the whole estate, were treated little differently from slaves until the time came when they received their full rights. Paul asserted that Christians were now not merely slaves but sons. And even more than that, they were in the highest relationship with the Father that is possible. They were heirs

Abba Father, we thank You that You allow us to approach You with a child's unself-conscious love. We thank You that in the fullness of time You sent Your Son for us. We thank You for the wonders You have bestowed on Your children. We feel blessed. In Jesus' name, we pray. Amen.

To Tell the Truth

Have I now become your enemy by telling you the truth?
(*Galatians 4:16, New International Version*).

Scripture: Galatians 4:8-16
Song: "I Would Be True"

Mark Twain once said, "Most writers regard the truth as their most valuable possession, and are therefore most economical in its use."

It seems that we live in a time that is most economical in the use of truth. There are even those who insist that there is no such thing as truth. They ridicule the Christian belief that God's Word reveals truth and that Jesus is the way, the truth, and the life.

It is not always easy to be a bearer of truth. Paul knew that. He loved the Galatians greatly, and it broke his heart that they were turning away from what he had taught them. They had received him with great love and joy but now had been turned against him by those who wanted to enslave them in a yoke of bondage. He took no delight in confronting their errors, but love demanded he tell them the truth about what they were doing.

Do we ever have a conflict between love and truth? Are there people who we care a great deal about whom we are afraid to confront with the truth of salvation in Jesus Christ? Why should this be so? Is not love best expressed in truth?

God of truth and righteousness, we pray that we might have a heart for that which is true and right. Help us not to turn away from what Your Word has made known to us. Give our leaders boldness to speak the truth to us. Give us seeking and responsive hearts. In the name of Your Son, Jesus, we pray. Amen.

Slave or Free?

It is for freedom that Christ has set us free. Stand firm, then, and do not let yourselves be burdened again by a yoke of slavery (Galatians 5:1, *New International Version*).

Scripture: Galatians 4:17-5:1
Song: "Joyful, Joyful, We Adore Thee"

On August 1, 1838, slavery was to be abolished in Jamaica. On the evening before this date of emancipation, former slaves gathered around a large mahogany coffin on the beach. With great solemnity and ceremony they put into the coffin the symbols of their slavery—whips, padlocks, shackles, and chains.

A few minutes after midnight, the emancipated slaves lowered the coffin into a hole in the beach as they sang, "Praise God from whom all blessings flow. . . ."

As he wrote to the Galatians, Paul was sending an emancipation proclamation to them and to us. Using Sarah and Hagar as examples, he argued that Christians are "children of promise" (4:28), not children of slavery (4:31). He was rejoicing in the freedom to live abundantly that God gives to all mankind who follow His Son, Jesus.

Suppose you were standing beside a coffin and were to place in it the symbols of slavery in your life? What would you put in it? Or suppose you were standing beside a treasure chest and were to place in it the symbols of your freedom. What would you put in it?

Gracious God, freedom is sometimes a difficult gift for us to handle. We are so prone to choose lives of bondage rather than lives of freedom. Please give us discernment, wisdom, and joy as we seek to follow You in the exuberance of loving faith. Lovingly in Him, we pray. Amen.

Your Place in the World

Brothers, each man, as responsible to God, should remain in the situation God called him to (I Corinthians 7:24, *New International Version*).

Scripture: 1 Corinthians 7:17-24
Song: "I'd Rather Have Jesus"

Most of us are familiar with the old saying, "The grass is always greener on the other side of the fence." Most of us are also familiar with the "if-only" feeling. The feeling might be directed toward another person: "If only I had the talent she has! Or the feeling might be more general: "If only my circumstances were different!" Usually, our "if-only" statements are followed by the wonderful things we would do or be if we possessed what we don't.

It's easy to dream about what we would do if things were different. However, God is not really interested in our "if-only." He wants to know what we're going to do right now with the situation and resources that we have been given.

No two people are alike, and no two situations are alike. God doesn't expect us to do or be exactly the same that He expects others to do or be. If we are busy doing all the things we can for Him, we will have very little time to spend wishing that things were different.

What talents, personality traits, and resources has God given you? How are you using those things right where you are now for Him?

Dear God, You promised to give us all that we need for life and service. Help us to focus on fulfilling Your will for our lives. In Jesus' name, we pray. Amen.

May 13-19. **Paul Friskney** teaches communication arts at Cincinnati Bible College. He and his wife, Ann, have two children, Hannah and Ben.

Feeding an Ox

If we have sown spiritual seed among you, is it too much if we reap a material harvest from you? (I Corinthians 9:11, *New International Version*).

Scripture: 1 Corinthians 9:1-12
Song: "Help Somebody Today"

Two things from my childhood help me in understanding Paul's point in 1 Corinthians 9. First, I grew up in the country, and saw the way the farmers fed the animals that did the work. The ones they expected the most from received the most food. Second, I grew up as a preacher's son. My father's salary was never very large, but the members of the congregation to whom my father preached supplied our needs. We received milk, eggs, and an occasional chicken, as well as hand-me-down clothes, from the people of the church.

That relationship is exactly what God intends. Those who have committed their lives to feeding God's people spiritually should have their material needs met by God's people. While salaries for church workers have increased a great deal since my childhood, that is not the only application of this principle.

Those who labor in mission work, particularly where there are few or no Christians, also deserve to have their physical needs met by God's people.

Do you know of someone who has needs? If you do, find work to meet those needs. An ox can't tread out much grain when it's muzzled.

Dear Lord and Father of mankind, we often think about our own needs and how we can meet them. We may also be thankful for the ones who have helped to supply our spiritual needs. Help us to go the next step by taking the initiative to meet the needs of those working for You. In the name of Your Son, Jesus, we pray. Amen.

One For All

I have become all things to all men so that by all possible means I might save some (I Corinthians 9:22b, *New International Version*).

Scripture: 1 Corinthians 9:15-23
Song: "Seek the Lost"

Jesus was willing to become one of us and to experience life from our perspective. He lived in our world and dealt with the same situations, relationships, desires, and griefs that we must deal with in this world of sin. He understands us completely and can sympathize with us because He has been here on earth, living as we live. Taking on the experience and life of another is an example as to how we can learn to understand and relate to others so that we might reach them with the message of Christ. Of course, that doesn't mean that we violate other principles of Scripture to relate to those outside of Christ, but it does mean that we move outside of situations and circles of people where we are completely comfortable.

Our own society today is filled with people from many different backgrounds whose lives have many different focuses. What can we do to try to meet those people where they are so we might bring them to the Savior of the world? It may mean studying other cultures or occupations. It may mean taking the focus off of ourselves and placing it on others, observing and listening to others. But it will certainly still be less than the extent to which Christ emptied Himself to become one of us.

Our dear Savior, it is amazing to think of what You left and how You emptied Yourself to become one of us. Help us to be willing to make sacrifices so that we might increase our ability to reach others with the message of Your salvation. In His holy name, we pray. Amen.

The Spring of Hope

Praise be to the God and Father of our Lord Jesus Christ! In his great mercy he has given us new birth into a living hope through the resurrection of Jesus Christ from the dead (I Peter 1:3, *New International Version*).

Scripture: 1 Peter 1:3-12
Song: "My Hope Is in the Lord"

I can picture the day as if it were nine days ago instead of nine years ago. Nothing had prepared my wife and me for the incredible joy that we felt at the birth of our daughter, as we looked at the perfect life that God had placed in our care.

I can also see another day, when we learned that our second child had died before birth. The sense of loss and grief was tremendous.

When I stand those two days side by side, the contrast is stark: life versus death, hope versus grief. Still, the joy of the first day overwhelms the sadness of the second. Life continues, but death is temporary.

Jesus brought death and birth together at the cross. His death on the cross makes it possible for us to be born into eternal life. He made the sadness of death into the joy of life.

What does His transformation of death into life mean for us? It means that, no matter what obstacles we face or what temptations come our way, we can put everything into perspective by looking at the cross and the empty tomb.

Life is greater than death because we have a Savior who brought birth by dying.

Dear God, You worked an incredible miracle in bringing new life out of death. Help us always to be aware of Your power over death and to draw on that power to live victoriously each day. Through Jesus, our Lord, we pray. Amen.

Free to Do What?

Live as free men, but do not use your freedom as a cover-up for evil; live as servants of God (I Peter 2:16, *New International Version*).

Scripture: 1 Peter 2:11-17
Song: "Have Thine Own Way, Lord!"

A famous story is the story of the Prodigal Son. This young man could hardly wait to get away from the restrictions of his father and to be free to live life on his own terms, making his own choices. However, it didn't take him long to realize that his freedom wasn't all he expected it to be. He found himself living in a pigpen. He knew that being a servant in his father's house would be much better than the life he had made for himself. Yet, when he came as a servant, his father restored him as a son.

In a similar way, God has granted us freedom of choice. We decide how we will use that freedom. We can choose to live according to our own desires, but when we do, we end up paying the consequences for our choices. On the other hand, we can submit ourselves, as servants to God, following His will. The amazing thing is that when we surrender ourselves as servants to God, He adopts us as His children.

We must examine ourselves to see where we stand in our choice. Do we try to cling to all the rights that we think that we deserve? Do we make sure that our freedoms aren't limited by anyone? Or are we willing to be used as God chooses? We can't become His children without first becoming His servants.

Dear Father, we are so grateful for the freedom we have in You. Help us to use that freedom as You intend, as willing servants of Yours. Thank You for accepting us as Your children. In Jesus' holy name, we pray. Amen.

What Are You Afraid Of?

There is no fear in love. But perfect love drives out fear, because fear has to do with punishment. The one who fears is not made perfect in love (1 John 4:18, *New International Version*).

Scripture: 1 Peter 3:13-22
Song: "I Know Who Holds Tomorrow"

One of my favorite Christmas specials is *A Charlie Brown Christmas*. The primary conflict in the program is Charlie Brown's search for the real meaning of Christmas. As part of that search, he spends some time talking to Lucy. In her role as counselor, Lucy tries to determine just what it is that Charlie Brown is afraid of. After listing many different kinds of fear, they finally arrive at his problem: fear of everything.

People fear loneliness, failure, pain, death, and many other aspects of life. Even Christians have to deal with negative situations, people, and events that can lead to fear. However, we shouldn't fear what the people in the world fear because we have the hope that comes through our relationship to Christ. Knowing Him, we know that our lives are ultimately victorious. We need to be ready to point others to the only true source of hope and freedom from fear: Jesus.

What are you afraid of? What am I afraid of? Do you find yourself worried about situations or events beyond your control? Do I feel fear? Let us turn our fear over to Jesus. We know that He has both power to deal with the problem and the perfect love to save us.

Dear Lord, we know that we can trust You for everything. Help us not to lose sight of that truth when things come into our lives that could make us afraid. Help us always to be willing to share with others the One who gives us hope that overcomes fear. In Jesus' name, we pray. Amen.

Stumbling Runner?

You were running a good race. Who cut in on you and kept you from obeying the truth? (Galatians 5:7, *New International Version*).

Scripture: Galatians 5:4-15
Song: "Trust and Obey"

I love to watch track events, especially during the summer Olympics. The sight of a strong runner in top form and at top speed is a great illustration of freedom with a strong sense of purpose. But I remember one year when one runner cut in on the other, and both went down in failure. In one brief moment, all hope for victory and Olympic gold disappeared.

Many times, the Christian life is compared to a race. We move forward toward a goal and must throw off any hindrances that would slow us down in the race. Temptations of many kinds work to do just that. We might be distracted by other demands on our time. We might become confused in our true goal. Or we might become weary from the labors of life. Jesus wants us to trust fully in Him and to know that He will lead us to the successful completion of our lives. We can be certain that with Him we will win the race.

Are there aspects of life that wear us down in the Christian race? Do certain people influence us—try to get us to leave our commitment that we have to Christ? Have temptations tripped us up? Christ can lead us every day over any obstacles and run with us even beyond the finish line. In Him we can have victory!

Dear Father and God of all, please help us to stay completely committed to the way of life that You have set before us. Don't let anything pull us away from Your will or make us stumble in the race ahead of us. In Jesus' name, we pray. Amen.

Accessing God

So that through the church the wisdom of God in its rich variety might now be made known to the rulers and authorities in the heavenly places
(Ephesians 3:10, *New Revised Standard Version*).

Scripture: Ephesians 3:1-13
Song: "Rescue the Perishing"

The church has an important task as a community of people who have found new life in Christ Jesus. That task is to make known the wonderful riches that are made possible because of Christ's sacrifice on the cross. Our lives are made full and rich by the news that God's Spirit is alive and well in the world today. Our lives are enriched today by the knowledge that through Christ Jesus we have eternal life. We are the recipients of a secret, a mystery, that we have new life in Christ.

The followers of Christ can be confident that we can contact God through our faith in Him. To some, this is a strange approach. Our faith is in God. Our faith is not in our possessions. Our faith is not in our power. Our faith is not in prayer. Our faith is not in miracles. Our faith is not in our friends. Our faith is not in the government. Our faith is in God, the maker of Heaven and earth. Our faith is in the Lord of life, the One who has power over life as well as death. In Him we live and move and have our being.

Thank **Y**ou **H**oly **F**ather, for Your presence with us this day. We are indeed grateful that we can have access with You through Your Son, Jesus, and the Holy Spirit and that new life belongs to all who follow Your Son, in whose name we pray. Amen.

May 20-26. **Dan Lawson** is director of Development at Emmanuel School of Religion in Johnson City, Tennessee. He and his wife, Linda, have two children.

Living the Full Life

Now to him who by the power at work within us is able to accomplish abundantly far more than all that we can ask or imagine, to him be glory in the church and in Christ Jesus to all generations, forever and ever (Ephesians 3:20-21, *New Revised Standard Version*).

Scripture: Ephesians 3:14-21
Song: "Great Is Thy Faithfulness"

It is hard for some to imagine that people, even Christian people, might consider proceeding through daily trials and travails on their own. Why should we even begin to walk through life's challenges without the help that comes from Christ? To be filled with God's presence is to utilize the resources of His strength through His Spirit inside of us.

To be filled with God's fullness is to be filled with the hope and love that comes from Christ. A day filled with God's hope permits us to travel through this earthly life eagerly looking toward Heaven. There we will be free from pain and illness, free from stress and sorrow, free from the difficulties of earthly existence. When we see God's light at the end of the tunnel, we keep going on, knowing that He is forever faithful.

A day filled with God's love allows us to share in relationships wherein we rejoice when a brother rejoices, we hurt when a sister hurts, we experience a bit of illness when another is ill. Love causes that. We can rest our weary souls in God, knowing that life will be richer and fuller because of His love for us.

Heavenly Father, we know that in You there is not even a shadow of turning because of Your great faithfulness. You fill up our lives and give us a reason to live. We thank You for Your hope, compassion and love, for it makes our today worth living. Thank You, dear Lord. In Jesus' holy name, we pray. Amen.

In Faith, Unity!

*There is one body and one Spirit, just as you were called to the one hope of
your calling* (Ephesians 4:4, *New Revised Standard Version*).

Scripture: Ephesians 4:1-7
Song: "The Bond of Love"

Christians are eager to maintain unity. As we read in the
Scripture text for today, there is only one body, one Spirit and
one Lord. There is only one God who is the Father of us all.

So why today is the church so divided? Do we not worship
the same God? Did not Christ die for us all? Is not His cross
the source of all of our salvation?

It is true that many Christians today have different opinions
on many subjects concerning different ways in which to
worship You. We often do approach our churchly life and
worship differently. We do have different agendas. We do meet
in separate buildings. We do organize our work for Christ in
different orders. We even have different creeds or ways of
stating our faith. So how can we maintain the unity of the
church in a bond of peacefulness?

The answer is simple. Our faith is not in our opinions. It is
not in our worship styles. It is not in our list of common
doctrines. Our faith is in the same Lord. Jesus is the object of
our faith. We believe that Jesus is the Christ, the Son of the
Living God. We all have a common heavenly Father. In faith,
there is unity!

Father and God of all, please forgive us for making such divisive issues out
of our opinions. May You be the source of bringing us together for the
common work of continuing the ministry of Christ Jesus here on earth. Give us
wisdom that only comes from You and teach us to love Your church as You
love us. In the name of Jesus Christ, our Savior, we pray. Amen.

To Live Is Christ

So we are always confident; even though we know that while we are at home in the body we are away from the Lord
(2 Corinthians 5: 6, *New Revised Standard Version*).

Scripture: 2 Corinthians 5:1-10
Song: "When We All Get to Heaven"

I lost a good friend to cancer this week. He died, and that was his gain. He experienced the tremendous transformation of faith changing into knowledge. For years he has had to live as all Christians must do, believing in a God not made with hands, a God we cannot see nor touch but One that we can only know through faith. The apostle Paul wrote, "For now I see in a mirror, dimly, but then we will see face to face. Now I know only in part; then I will know fully" (1 Corinthians 13:12). We live by faith. We live by God's presence within us.

My friend was a man of deep and abiding faith in God. Not only did he believe that God existed, but he believed that the Lord was his strength and refuge, a very present help in his time of trouble. It was always a challenge for him to move when God said, "go." But he always moved, trusting God all the way, praying that God would lead him in the new and strange ventures of life. Now he has moved again to a land strange and different from anything he has known before. He has moved to a place that until now he has only known by faith, believing that God has prepared it especially for him.

Dear God and Creator of all the universe, we know You have our whole lives in Your hands. We rest at peace in Your holy presence. Thank You for preparing a place for us in Your heavenly realm. We look forward to the day that we will be at home with You and that we will see You face to face. In Jesus' holy name, we pray. Amen.

A Timely Faith

"At an acceptable time I have listened to you, and on a day of salvation I have helped you" (2 Corinthians 6:2b, *New Revised Standard Version*).

Scripture: 2 Corinthians 6:1-12
Song: "His Eye Is on the Sparrow"

In His own time, God uses all of life's experiences for a good purpose. He certainly uses our talents and abilities to minister to others in such a way as to bring about faith. That is the joy of our servanthood, knowing full well that our God will use us to fulfill His task here on earth.

He uses the good things in our life to accomplish a good in the lives of other people. He uses our love, our speech, our knowledge, our acts of kindness, our spiritual insights, and at just the right time they can help produce faith in others.

He can also use the bad things that happen as well. He uses our illness, our beating, our suffering, our pain, and even our weakness to show His strength and power.

The past several years have been a time of personal physical weakness for me. But the real joy of that horrific time in my life has been seen when in God's good time, He was able to use it to encourage others going through their valleys and times of darkness. Who would ever imagine that God could use the awful experiences in our lives for a good purpose? But the good comes in God's good time to strengthen faith when it is needed the most.

Heavenly Father and God of all, we thank You for every good and perfect gift that comes down from above. We thank You also for using the trials and travails of life for a good purpose. We put our time and talent in Your hands. Teach us always to trust in You. In Jesus' holy and blessed name, we pray. Amen.

They Look Just Like Their Father

If we live by the Spirit, let us also be guided by the Spirit
(Galatians 5:25, New Revised Standard Version).

Scripture: Galatians 5:16-26
Song: "Spirit of God, Descend upon My Heart"

Paul wrote that the whole law could be fulfilled in one word. Then he quotes Leviticus, "You shall love your neighbor as yourself." It is in the context of such a discussion that He lists the "fruit of the Spirit," love, joy, peace, patience, kindness, goodness, faithfulness, gentleness and self-control.

If the law of love is the foundation for God's law for His people, then the fruit of the Spirit is the produce grown in God's wonderful garden in our lives. It is these precious qualities that should be seen in the person whose life is made in the image of God. Living and walking by the Spirit of the Creator God should make a significant difference in the way we live our lives. God's Spirit should effect our inner being and our inner personality.

One of the most beautiful things about having children is that they are a delightful reflection of the parents who raised them. Their humor reflects that of their parents. Their disciplines are patterned after how they were raised. Their mannerisms, both good and bad, mirror the mother and father around whom they lived for some very formative years of their young lives.

The same is true of the children of the heavenly Father.

Thank You, heavenly Father, for making us in Your image. When others look at us today, may they see a reflection of Your love and compassion in us. In the name of Jesus Christ, our Savior and the Savior of the world, we pray. Amen.

The Good In Us All

So then, whenever we have an opportunity, let us work for the good of all,
and especially for those of the family of faith
(Galatians 6:10, *New Revised Standard Version*).

Scripture: Galatians 6:7-18
Song: "O Zion, Haste"

In the church we do experience tensions and conflicts. We have different opinions. We come from different backgrounds, we are aimed toward differing goals and possess different purposes. We have different strengths and weaknesses. We are on different committees and have different ministries. That diversity is our strength.

This tension can cause us to react and to do evil instead of good. We can gossip. We can say hateful things. We can give the silent treatment and ignore. We can openly oppose and try to destroy. We can keep others out of our group or clique. We can use others for self-gain. That's immorality. We can be angry. Paul writes, "I warn that those who do such things shall not inherit the kingdom of God."

Instead, let us do good as we have opportunity. In fact, let us make opportunities for doing good to our brothers and sisters. Where there is gossip, let us sow words of kindness. Where there is hate, let us sow love. Where there is a silent wall of exclusion, let us extend open arms. Where there is destruction, let us sow edification. Where there is evil silence, let us be aggressive to speak to a brother. Where there is self-gain, may God receive the glory.

Father, use us this day to sow seeds of goodness that Your will might be done here on earth as it is done in Heaven. May we reap a harvest of good. In Jesus name, we pray. Amen.

The Blessed Man

Ye shall know them by their fruits (Matthew 7:16).

Scripture: Psalm 1:1-6
Song: "Give of Your Best to the Master"

Jesus began the Sermon on the Mount with what we call the Beatitudes (Matthew 5:3-12). There are many beatitudes in the Old Testament. The Book of Psalms begins, in fact, with a beatitude. "Blessed is the man that walketh not in the counsel of the ungodly" (Psalm 1:1).

This fortunate individual is like a tree planted by a stream of water. His deep roots give him stability. He will not be blown down by the storms of adversity. From the roots come the shoots. His leaf does not wither. He is not shriveled when faced with hard times nor will he wilt away in the drought of depression. From the roots and shoots come the fruits, which Jesus told His followers we must bear.

Once a young man took a steamer from Baltimore to New York. The Captain was interested in him and asked him what he planned to do with his life. His reply, "Make soap." The Captain said, "Young man, if you will do that, and do it well, you will prosper; but you must make the Lord your partner. If your life is rooted in Him, you will succeed." When he set up his bookkeeping system, William Colgate headed one section, "Account with The Lord," and God prospered him.

Lord, may we find blessings in our lives in the same way that the blessed man in Psalm 1 found them. Let them be on our lips and in our lives. May we put You first in all of our lives. In Jesus' name, we pray. Amen.

May 27-31. **Ross Dampier** is a frequent writer for DEVOTIONS™. He is a minister emeritus of Central Christian Church in Bristol, Tennessee.

What God Loves

He loveth righteousness and Judgment: the earth is full of the goodness of the **Lord** (Psalm 33:5).

Scripture: Psalm 33:1-5
Song: "The Love of God"

The Taj Mahal in Agra, India is reputed to be one of the most beautiful buildings in the world. Shah Jahan promised to build a palace for his beloved wife, Princess Arjamond, but before it was built she died in childbirth. He built the palace which would be Arjamand's tomb. Engraved on it are these words, "To the memory of an undying love."

The evidence of God's love is seen everywhere in His creation. On each day of creation He looked at what He had made and called it good. He loved it all. When He created Adam and Eve, He loved them for they were most like Him.

The beauty of God's creation is not just the beauty of natural form. The psalmist says that we are to praise Him for His truth, justice and righteousness. Even when we fail Him, He still blesses us with unfailing love.

We can celebrate God's love for mankind in many ways; in our worship of Him, our service for Him, and our expressions of love toward Him including art, music, and even works of architecture.

We see His love expressed to us in the cross and the empty tomb where His son died, was buried and rose again. Its witness is found in redeemed lives that daily proclaim, "To the memory of an undying love."

Lord, may the things which You love be the first objects of our affection. Give us a love for truth and righteousness, but most of all give us a love for the souls of those who are lost. In Jesus' name, we pray. Amen.

The Ground of Our Hope

The Lord taketh pleasure in them that fear him, in those that hope in his mercy (Psalm 147:11).

Scripture: Psalm 33:10-22
Song: "The Solid Rock"

Theocritus said it first. "For the living there is hope, but for the dead there is none." Several hundred years before Theocritus, the Hebrew Psalmist called attention to the fact that having hope is not enough. What is really important is the ground of our hope. People who depend on military preparedness are likely to end up hopeless. Still, today, we depend on military strength for our physical salvation. We still place our trust in politicians to solve our social problems. We still hope that someone else's economic genius will drive up the value of our stocks. Then when the trust we put in the schemes of men fail we are bewildered, frustrated and hopeless. When we put our trust in the Lord we can be assured of His unfailing love, which has given us an eternal hope.

A tragic earthquake and tidal wave struck the little fishing village of Hope, Alaska. The town was almost completely wiped out. It was decided not to rebuild on the old site but to seek a new location. On the old town site someone erected a sign, "The Town of Hope will move to higher ground." There is no higher ground for our hope than this. "According to his abundant mercy hath begotten us again unto a lively hope by the resurrection of Jesus Christ from the dead" (1 Peter 1:3).

Heavenly Father and Lord of all, forgive us for trusting in our own wisdom and in our own accomplishments. Give us a spirit of humility, for our hope is in You. Help us to follow You day by day. In Jesus' holy name, we pray. Amen.

The God of Great Deeds

If God be for us, who can be against us? (Romans 8:31).

Scripture: Psalm 11:1-7
Song: "Who Is on the Lord's Side?"

When we face problems, we are often tempted to take the safe course even if we know that it is not right. The friends of David urged him to flee from his enemies. He did not take their advice. His decision was to trust God, and God did not fail him; nor will He fail us if we do what is right in His sight.

In May of 1776 Patrick Henry delivered a speech before the House of Burgesses in Williamsburg, Virginia. In it he said, "I repeat, Sir, we must fight! An appeal to arms and to the God of Hosts is all that is left to us! Sir, we are not weak, if we make proper use of the means which the God of Nature has placed in our power. Besides, Sir, we shall not fight our battles alone. There is a just God who presides over the destinies of nations and who will raise up friends to fight our battles for us. The battle, Sir, is not to the strong alone; it is to the vigilant, and the active, and the brave. Should I keep back my opinions at such a time as this through fear of giving offense, I should consider myself guilty of treason toward my country, and an act of disloyalty toward the Majesty of Heaven, which I revere above all earthly kings."

May God help us today to face our responsibilities and with His support, do what is right.

We come to You, Lord, God of the universe knowing that when we depend on ourselves that we often fail. Knowing, too, that when we trust in You we can but succeed. Give us the courage to attempt great things for You. Help us to be Your servants here on earth. Let others see Your love through us. In Jesus' holy name, we pray. Amen.

How God Judges Us

Justice and judgment are the habitation of thy throne: mercy and truth shall go before thy face (Psalm 89:14).

Scripture: Psalm 7:9-17
Song: "One Day!"

When we understand how God judges, we understand how He will judge us, and we will also understand how we can make right judgments ourselves.

The decade of the sixties should be known as the "Age of Immorality." It was a time of drug culture and sexual revolution and rebellion against authority. Even more significant was the God-Is-Dead theology and situation ethics. The idea that absolute values no longer exist swept away the moral foundation of our culture. There was no more right and wrong. God's Word was no longer counted as the true authority.

The triumph of the sixties was putting a man on the moon. Wernher Von Braun headed the program of the Army Ballistic Missile Agency that sent rockets into outer space.

We would have been well advised to listen to Wernher Von Braun's spiritual advice as well. He said that two stimuli are necessary to make people conform to ethical standards. One is the belief in ultimate judgment and the other is the belief in the immortality of the soul. He believed that our faith in a living God, and the fact that we will stand in judgment before Him should be the basis of our actions in our daily lives.

Almighty and everliving Lord and Master of all, forgive us our sins, for they are many. Lead us back to Your word as the only safe guide to the doing of Your will. Help us to follow Your wisdom for living. In Jesus' holy name, we pray. Amen.

Devotions

June

photo by Chuck Perry

How Big Is God?

The heavens declare his righteousness, and all the people see his glory
(Psalm 97:6).

Scripture: Psalm 19:1-6
Song: "The Spacious Firmament on High"

When I was in high school they told us that the known universe was so many million light years across. I had no idea how far that was, and I still don't know. It doesn't matter! By the time I got to college they had discovered that the known universe was at least twice as far across. When my son went to college it had doubled again. Then they sent out the Hubbell telescope, and guess what! It had doubled again!

The question now becomes "Is there any limit to the size of the universe?" There is a theory that the universe is expanding so rapidly that man will never see the end of it. I guess we can safely say that it is a whole lot bigger than we ever thought.

The next question is what effect does the concept of an expanding universe have on our understanding of the God who made it? Like the universe, we can safely say of God that He must be bigger than we can ever imagine Him to be.

We must add to all our knowledge of the world of infinitely small things molecules and atoms, for He is the God of the miniscule, as well. Our increasing comprehension of the natural world can only add to our wonder and awe of Him.

When we consider Your eternal nature, O God and Lord of all, we are reminded of our own mortality. So when we think of Your righteousness, let it emphasize our own sinfulness. When we think of Your love, let us be reminded to be Your servants. In Jesus' holy name, we pray. Amen.

June 1-2. **Ross Dampier** is a frequent writer for DEVOTIONS™. He is a minister of Central Christian Church in Bristol, Tennessee.

The Law of the Lord

I will put my law in their inward parts, and write it in their hearts; and will be their God, and they shall be my people (Jeremiah 31:33).

Scripture: Psalm 19:7-14
Song: "Immortal, Invisible, God Only Wise"

One of the great mistakes we make is to talk about the Laws of Nature and the Laws of God as though they were two separate things. The Creator who made the one is the Judge who enforces the other. In Psalm 19 we have both functions of God proclaimed. The first verse talks about the heavens, which declare His glory. The seventh verse introduces His law, which directs our lives.

When God created the heavens and the earth, He made them in such a way that they conform to natural laws. I remember a cartoon, which showed a startled Isaac Newton sitting under an apple tree. The caption read, "The law of gravity was there all the time. He just wasn't smart enough to see it until it hit him in the head with an apple." God is the author of natural law.

God is also the author of moral law. Recently we have heard a great deal about whether it is appropriate to display the Ten Commandments in public places. The question is not really whether they should be displayed so much as whether, in a civilized society, they can be ignored. It makes about as much sense to repeal the moral law of God as it does to try to ignore the natural law of God.

Lord of the world and of all our daily lives, forgive us for thinking that there is any part of our existence that is not controlled by You. We were created in Your image. Make us more like You in all we do through Jesus Christ our Lord, in Whose name, we pray. Amen.

God Is Our Hope in Distress

My tears have been my meat day and night, while they continually say unto me, Where is thy God? (Psalm 42:3).

Scripture: Psalm 42:1-11
Song: "Never Alone!"

How can a good God allow the innocent to suffer? Job wrestled with this question in the Old Testament, and many of us wrestle with it today. Suffering, unfortunately, is something we will all experience living in a fallen world. Many blame God for every "ill-fated" event in their lives. Actor Woody Allen, for example, once factiously accused God of letting him get his "tongue caught in the roller of an electric typewriter." Many Holocaust survivors emerged from their suffering very skeptical of God's existence. Nobel Peace Prize recipient Elie Wiesel wrote, "faced with unprecedented suffering and agony, [God] should have intervened . . . . Which side was He on?"

The existence of suffering is a riddle many of us won't adequately solve in this lifetime. But we can be encouraged by the fact that God has promised to remain by us as we suffer and that we, as Christians, can look forward to the day when we are finally delivered from our suffering on earth. "Why are you downcast, O my soul? Put your hope in God" (Psalm 42:11, *New International Version*).

Our souls pant, dear Lord, for You! Please be our comfort in time of distress, and please continue to remind us that we are not alone in our suffering. Give us the confidence to live a victorious life in You today so that others might see Your power in our lives. In the holy and righteous name of Jesus Christ, our Savior, we pray. Amen.

June 3-9. **Steve Simpson** is a journalist living in Cincinnati, Ohio. He is currently pursuing a master of arts in English literature.

Those Who Are Persecuted

In God I will praise his word, in God I have put my trust; I will not fear what flesh can do unto me (Psalm 56:4).

Scripture: Psalm 56:1-7
Song: "O God, Our Help in Ages Past"

Christians are not strangers to religious persecution. The Christian church has suffered unjust persecution at the hands of worldly powers since its inception. Many are familiar with the plight of the early church fathers at the hands of the Romans starting with the rule of Emperor Domitian in A.D. 95. Likewise, many are aware of how Christians devoted to translating the Bible into the language of the common people were excommunicated and executed for their efforts. Many, however, fail to realize that this persecution continues. A recent report stated that over 160,000 Christians were martyred in 1996 alone and that more Christians have died for their faith in the twentieth century than in the first nineteen combined.

Naturally, one need not be martyred to be persecuted. Most Christians have been persecuted to some extent. Some have been teased at school or ridiculed at work. Some have been ostracized from long-time friends or berated by family members. And all of us have been marginalized by a culture that insists public life should be godless. Thanks be to God. Our God is powerful! We should not fear worldly powers, for, though they can harm our flesh, they can not touch our spirit!

God, **You are powerful and mighty**, and we praise You for Your willingness to protect us. Often we fear the world, but help us to know that You have conquered the world and are all-powerful. In Jesus' holy name, we pray. Amen.

I Am Not Afraid

In God have I put my trust: I will not be afraid what man can do unto me
(Psalm 56:11).

Scripture: Psalm 56: 8-13
Song: "The Lord Is My Shepherd"

It was in FDR's first inaugural address that he coined the familiar phrase, "The only thing we have to fear is fear itself— nameless, unreasoning, unjustified terror which paralyzes needed efforts to convert retreat into advance." Fear, as FDR said, is rarely reasonable. Many of us, for instance, can remember being afraid of the dark as children. Even though our parents assured us countless times that our bedrooms were perfectly safe at night, the thought of waking in the dark and not knowing if there was a monster in the closet or a goblin under the bed was terrifying. Surely, uncertainty bolsters many of our most irrational fears.

Many parents have found that the remedy for lygophobia is a nightlight. True, a nightlight can't protect a child from monsters, but it can allow him to see that there's nothing harmful in his bedroom and thus nothing to fear.

The thought of being alone in a dark world is a scary thought for Christians. This is not, however, something we need to fear as God's Word assures us that we are not alone. God has promised to protect us—we need only remember this to vanquish all fear from our minds.

Dear Father, the world can often be a dark and frightening place. We have all been afraid and have all doubted Your presence in our lives. Help us to trust in You, and let our minds be comforted by the fact that You have delivered us from death and will protect us from harm. In Jesus' name, we pray. Amen.

God, Our Faithful Fortress

He only is my rock and my salvation; he is my defense; I shall not be greatly moved (Psalm 62:2).

Scripture: Psalm 62:1-2
Song: "A Mighty Fortress is our God"

The U.S.S. Constitution is the oldest commissioned ship in the United States Navy. It has survived forty-two naval battles and numerous ambassadorial missions. It was first constructed in Boston in 1794 from nearly 1,500 trees harvested from Maine to Georgia.

The Constitution was built to protect American merchant ships from pirates and to defend the young country from the British fleet. By all accounts, it performed these tasks brilliantly. In fact, during the War of 1812, several crewmembers reported that they saw the British cannonballs bouncing off the ship's flanks. This claim earned the Constitution its more familiar appellation, "Old Ironsides."

In times of adversity, people seek refuge. When confronted by the prospect of a very formidable British navy, Americans trusted "Old Ironsides." Similarly, when those in the world assail us, Christians do not trust in nor depend on money, political power, or any other worldly contrivance. They are sure to buckle and crumble when attacked. God is our rock and our fortress—He is the one edifice that does not quaver in a relentless torrent of worldly philosophy. He is the unmovable Prime Mover in whom we can seek refuge.

Our most loving heavenly Father, we exalt You for Your everlasting mercy, Your power, and Your might. You alone give salvation and our protection—nothing in this world is as secure as You! Help us always to depend on You and Your power. In Jesus name, we pray. Amen.

A Hope That Will Last

For thou art my hope, O Lord God. Thou art my trust from my youth . . . Let my mouth be filled with thy praise and with thy honor all the day (Psalm 71:5, 8).

Scripture: Psalm 71:1-8
Song: "Take the Name of Jesus with You"

Many have heard the old English proverb, "Hope for the best, but prepare for the worst." Somehow we have come to equate the word "hope" with the uncertainties of life. Perhaps it is our experience with false hope that encourages this attitude in life. Indeed, all of us have experienced false hope at one time or another.

It is said that nothing in this world arouses more false hope than the first four hours of a diet. Most diets begin with the best of intentions but often end as a terrible disappointment. We buy that expensive exercise bike hoping to use it every morning, but we do not. We try countless lose-weight-quick schemes, hoping maybe one of them will work, but few do.

This should not surprise us, however. According to the *Dieting for Dummies* manual, the reason why most diets fail is because they are based on fads rather than on proven and lasting weight loss programs. This can be said of all our hopes. Hope is only uncertain when it is rooted in unstable soil. Hope is certain when it is founded on God—our rock and our fortress. He alone is the only constant in the world of uncertainty in which we live.

We praise You, O God, for Your constancy and Your certainty. Help us to always base our hope of salvation on You alone and not on the things of this world—things that will perish and fail. We know that we can place our hope in You. In the name of Jesus, we pray. Amen.

Justice Will Be Served in the End

Let them be confounded and consumed that are adversaries to my soul; let them be covered with reproach and dishonor that seek my hurt (Psalm 71:13).

Scripture: Psalm 71:12-24
Song: "Come, Ye Disconsolate"

One of the more fulfilling aspects of a Charles Dickens novel is that the "bad guy" always gets what's coming to him at the end of the story. In his final novel, *Our Mutual Friend*, a large sum of money is left to a rich man's servant, Mr. Boffin, when it is believed that the rich man's only son and heir has died. Mr. Boffin is a simple man and comes close to being bilked of his newfound wealth by Mr. Wegg, a conniving con man. Fortunately, everything is resolved at the novel's end. The rich man's son, it turns out, is not dead, and he returns, exposes Mr. Wegg as a villain, and expels him from the father's estate.

Naturally, we all like to see justice served to all. Though God has promised to judge the wicked, we need to remember that judgment is served in His time, not ours. It may seem at times as if the wicked prosper in assailing the righteous. We should not be discouraged, however. Rather we should continue living a life of compassion, love and forgiveness. Living in righteousness, we know that at the end of time the righteous will be rewarded for their obedience, and the wicked will be punished for their negligence.

Dear heavenly Father, we pray to hasten the day of Your coming, though we understand that all things happen in Your time and not our own. We pray for the strength to remain faithful, just as You have remained faithful to us in the past. Thank You for Your everlasting faithfulness. In the name of our Savior, Jesus Christ, we pray. Amen.

Maintaining Christian Character

Judge me, O God, and plead my cause against an ungodly nation: O deliver me from the deceitful and unjust man (Psalm 43:1).

Scripture: Psalm 43:1-5
Song: "The Rock That Is Higher Than I"

The life of Japanese novelist Shusaku Endo is an object lesson in maintaining strong Christian character. He was not intimidated living in a Buddhist country that had historically opposed Christianity and had encouraged cultural conformity. Rather, he stuck to his Christian beliefs and lifestyle. Likewise, his secular literary contemporaries did not sway him—he discussed overtly Christian themes and values in his literature. His masterpiece, *Silence*, portrays the suffering of Japanese Christians during the Shogun Era of Japanese history.

Maintaining Christian character in such an adverse environment was not easy for Endo. Like many in similar situations, he suffered from frequent bouts of discouragement and doubt. He battled the urge to just give up and conform. What he came to realize, however, is that the strength to overcome adversity comes not from oneself but from God. It is our belief in the person of Christ and the legitimacy of His Gospel that fuels our commitment to Him.

Strength comes from God; this is what provides Christians with the will to persevere. When we allow God to show us the way, we will be able to live a life of victory.

O God You are all powerful, and we are in awe of Your holiness. Teach us to persevere. Guide us through the pitfalls of our daily worldly living and direct us toward a more perfect understanding of You and Your ways. In Jesus' name, we pray. Amen.

O Shepherd of Israel

Turn us again, O God of hosts, and cause thy face to shine; and we shall be saved (Psalm 80:7).

Scripture: Psalm 80:1-7
Song: "Dear Lord and Father of Mankind"

One problem common to shepherds is that of "cast" sheep. A cast sheep pathetically lies flat on its back in an utterly helpless position. It may kick its legs furiously in an effort to stand, but to no avail. Unless it is found within a short time it will certainly die.

A sheep may get into such a silly state by lying down in a comfortable depression in the earth. When it paws at the ground in order to raise itself, it tends to upset its equilibrium causing it to roll completely over on its back. In such a vulnerable position the sheep is completely at the mercy of the elements or its predators.

Sometimes Christians, the sheep of the Lord's flock become "cast." When, through carelessness or neglect, we become too comfortable with sin, we may find ourselves in a totally helpless condition. Eternal damnation would be imminent were it not for a loving Shepherd who hears our bleating cry for help and saves us from our folly. Only in Him can we find true comfort.

Heavenly Father and Lord of all, we praise You for Your patience with Your people—we are often wayward sheep. It seems as though we are always becoming "cast," yet You are always there to help us when we ask, and You help us to get back on our feet. It is so good of You never to have a weary ear to our pleas of helplessness. In Jesus' holy and righteous name, we pray. Amen.

June 10. **John Chesnut** ministers to the Pickerington Christian Church in Pickerington, Ohio.

God's Covenant People

He hath remembered his covenant for ever, the word which he commanded to a thousand generations (Psalm 105:8).

Scripture: Psalm 80:8-19
Song: "We Gather Together"

There is a story about the famous Presbyterian missionary, John G. Paton, who served for many years in the island of Tanna in the New Hebrides. For a long time he served among savage cannibals without making a single convert. When his wife and infant son died, it almost broke his heart, but he continued to preach the gospel. More than once he was forced to leave all his earthly possessions behind and escape only with his life.

The missionary group that sponsored him wrote to him, "What are your prospects?" Patons reply was 'My prospects are as bright as the promises of God which cannot fail!"

For a time it seemed as though his faith had been misplaced. He was forced to leave the island of Tanna without making a convert. Years passed, and he remarried. He had another son who grew to manhood and joined him in the mission work. Years later, his son returned to the island of Tanna and preached the gospel. This time many were converted to the Lord. God is not slack concerning His promises, and His covenant is unto His children's children.

Eternal heavenly Father, we are thankful that Thou art eternal. Men forget. Their promises are often broken. We praise Thee that Thou wilt remember Thy covenants even unto a thousand generations. In the name of Your Son, Jesus, we pray. Amen.

June 11. **Ross Dampier** is a frequent writer for DEVOTIONS™. He is a minister emeritus of Central Christian Church in Bristol, Tennessee.

Push Into the Water

There is a river, the streams whereof shall make glad the city of God, the holy place of the tabernacles of the Most High (Psalm 46:4).

Scripture: Psalm 46:1-11
Song: "It Is Well with My Soul"

Whether racing down river at top speed or bobbing gently at anchor in a shady cove, my family loves to go boating. As we break away from the dock and listen to the soft slap of the waves against the side of the boat, all the problems and cares of our "landlubber life" are left behind. There is something about being on the water that invigorates, calms, and refreshes us like nothing else can.

The world we live in is a dry place. The demands on time, emotions, and physical resources often leave us feeling stressed or drained. We long for a place where we can find refreshment and peace. Scripture tells us that there is a river which flows from the very throne of God. Jesus has invited us to be a part of that river, to let its life-giving waters flow through us. As we push farther and farther into its waters, the problems on the shore seem less urgent and less troublesome. Whether we are racing or resting, when we are on God's river there we will find all that we need. We know that in Him there is peace.

Gracious heavenly Father, how pleasant it is to rest in Your unchanging love. Thank You for sustaining me day by day, moment by moment. Praise You for Your goodness and Your everlasting love. Help me to live this day in Your calm, peaceful and restful love. May others see Your spirit of gladness within me. Let me show Your goodness to the world. In the name of Jesus Christ, we pray. Amen.

June 12. **Susan Petropulos** is a writer and former church finance assistant. She and her husband, Peter, have two grown children.

Praise the Lord

He hath put a new song in my mouth, even praise unto our God (Psalm 40:3).

Scripture: Psalm 40:1-10
Song: "O for a Thousand Tongues"

An angry king and his army tramped the wilderness to find young David and kill him, but God saved the fugitive's life (1 Samuel 23:14). As an older man, David sank deep in the mire of sin, but God rescued him with forgiveness (2 Samuel 12:13). What rescue was in David's mind when he sang, 'he brought me up also out of a horrible pit, out of the miry clay"?

Perhaps David was remembering both the pit of danger (Psalm 40:14) and the mire of sin (Psalm 40:12). Certainly we can trust the Lord to save us.

Saved from the pit and the mud, David responded in three ways. We see them in our Scripture for today. First he praised God, singing of His wonderful works and pronouncing a blessing on those who trust in the Lord (verse 3-5). Second, with opened ears he heard God's will and with delight obeyed it, knowing that obedience is better than sacrifice (verse 6-8). Third, he told others how God had saved him, announcing the Lord's righteousness, faithfulness, loving-kindness, and truth (verses 9, 10).

Saved from sin and kept safe in the dangers of life, are we responding in these same ways?

Father, You know and we know how muddy our feet have been. Thank You for a new way on the solid rock of truth and righteousness. In Jesus' name, we pray. Amen.

June 13. **Orrin Root** is a former editor at Standard Publishing. He resides in Cincinnati, Ohio, where he enjoys gardening and writing.

A Refuge In Troubled Times

God is our refuge and strength, a very present help in trouble (Psalm 46:1).

Scripture: Psalm 40:11-17
Song: "Beneath the Cross of Jesus"

Most of us are eager to possess the strength of character to meet even the most alarming situations with quiet calm and courage. Recall Stephen, the first Christian to give up his life for faith in his Lord. He faced persecution because he was "full of grace and power." As he was stoned to death, his face shone with radiance. This made a terrific impression on Saul, who, after his conversion, became the great missionary and apostle.

The ancient Israelites, as revealed in this psalm, learned that the one true and living God is a shield and a rock, a refuge and a sure defender. Many of the psalms are cries of the human heart under stress and strain, trial and sorrow. Grief, pain, and hurt find vivid expression in these prayers for healing, cleansing, and forgiveness.

When the storms of life close in around us, and we cannot see our way clear, we can be sure that our God—the true and living God—is near. He knows our predicament. He comes to our aid, saying "Have no fear." In Him we know that we have protection and are able to walk in the light of His word with confidence that He walks before us.

Calm our fears, almighty God and Lord of all, and grant us the faith to trust in Your presence in stormy times as well as in the good times. Encourage and comfort those who find themselves in difficult places. May we support them with our prayers, our gifts, and our love. In the name of Jesus Christ, our Savior, we pray. Amen.

June 14. **Raymond Veh**. Reprint from DEVOTIONS™ 1977-78.

"The Lord Is My Shepherd"

The Lord is my shepherd; I shall not want (Psalm 23:1).

Scripture: Psalm 23:1-6
Song: "Savior, Like a Shepherd Lead Us"

The Lord is my shepherd; I shall not want—a confession of absolute trust with no reservations, no limitations.

As the sheep found their shepherd adequate for guidance, affection, protection, food, and bodily care, so we find our all in all in Christ our shepherd. We can help each other, but sometimes this help is insecure and uncertain. Christ is always adequate.

As a patient is wheeled to the operating room, he has spiritual needs, and so do his loved ones in the waiting room. What can we say? Yes, we can give assurances and words of confident hope. But in those moments the surest thing is, "The Lord is my shepherd." Success or failure by the skilled surgeon, the Lord is adequate to the need.

The Shepherd of our souls sustains us not only in times of crisis and sadness, but also in times of joy and celebration as well as in our everyday walk of life. At all times we can rest safe and secure in His arms, for we know that it is He who holds the universe in His hands! Since He has taken charge of our keeping, how can we ever want?

Dear heavenly Father and Lord of all, Thy Son's faithfulness as our Shepherd humbles us because it shows us that we are often unfaithful as His sheep. We ask O Father, that You guide us to walk daily in the way of the Lord. Cleanse us. Help us to be faithful to Him forever. In Jesus' holy name, we pray. Amen.

June 15. **John Mills**. Reprint from DEVOTIONS™ 1977-78.

The Lord Is Our Keeper

I will say of the Lord, He is my refuge and my fortress: my God; in him will I trust (Psalm 91:2).

Scripture: Psalm 121:1-8
Song: "He Hideth My Soul"

The story is told of a servant girl in London who, as she was hurrying home in the dark, was accosted by a pair of ruffians. The frightened girl began repeating in a low voice the fourth verse of Psalm 91: "He shall cover thee with his feathers, and under his wings shalt thou trust." Hearing only something about "fathers" and "wings," the men decided the girl was mentally unbalanced and turned away, leaving her unharmed.

How wonderful are the ways of our omniscient and omnipresent God! He is the God of the unexpected, using ways and means to protect His trusting child, that to the unbeliever may seem simple or coincidental. But the Christian knows that God had directly intervened in his behalf.

A woman was facing surgery for the third time in less than three years. She felt she could not face the ordeal again and spent the day before surgery in a state of agitation. Finally, that night she committed all to the Lord, and immediately such peace flooded her soul that she wondered at her former state. When God is concerned with the fall of a sparrow, will He not keep His own blood-bought child?

Heavenly Father, we cannot thank and praise You enough for Your loving care over us. Help us to trust You in all things and be thankful. In Your precious name, we pray. Amen.

June 16. **Clara Brandon**. Reprint from DEVOTIONS™ 1977-78.

Light Comes With God's Word

The entrance of thy words giveth light (Psalm 119:130).

Scripture: Psalm 119:130-144
Song: "The Light of the World Is Jesus"

Many of us enjoy the long days of late June, when sunset and darkness are delayed their longest and light is available for reading and strolling and playing games. That extended daylight is so highly valued, in fact, that in some of the world we changed our clocks and watches a few months ago in order to delay the evening darkness to a later hour.

Consider especially, though, the relief that comes with dawning light of a new day after a long and difficult night. Perhaps you have made an overnight drive to meet an emergency. You've never been over that road before and the route is not well marked. Your eyes burn with the strain of searching out road signs and directions. At last comes the dawn, and you can see the road and the signboards and the other traffic. Now you can continue safely on to your destination.

The words of God, spoken by His prophets, written in His Book, and ultimately seen in His Son Jesus, provide the way of seeing and understanding and following our way home to Him. The wise will do their traveling on life's road in the Son light of God's living Word.

Thank You, O God of love and light, for the light of Your words that shows us the way home. We ask of You, O God to give us wisdom as we schedule all our activities so they may be seen clearly in the light of Your Word. We praise Your holy name. We pray in the name of Jesus, our Savior. Amen.

June 17-23. **Edwin V. Hayden,** minister and retired editor of the Christian Standard, continues to write and edit from his home in Cincinnati, Ohio.

God's Tender Mercies

Great are thy tender mercies, O LORD: quicken me according to thy judgments
(Psalms 119:156).

Scripture: Psalms 119:149-160
Song: "Turn Your Eyes Upon Jesus"

My school teachers way back in the dim distant past included one who considered it her duty to open our innocent eyes to the real world out there. One of her more memorable seventh-grade assignments directed us to do a layout for the front page of a daily newspaper, complete with headlines—the more sensational the better. We were to stretch our imaginations for stories of crimes, especially if committed by prominent citizens. The more horror, the bigger the headlines, the better they pleased the teacher. We came up with some dandies. Not many stories were required to fill a front page.

Some very different teachers and assignments blessed our classrooms in the following years. One made a habit of flavoring each class period with at least one practical and memorable saying, frequently from the Proverbs of Solomon. Another excellent teacher persuaded us to memorize John 14:6 as a guide for life purposes: "I am the way, the truth, and the life: no man cometh unto the Father, but by me."

In the face of godless violence such as so deeply disturbed the psalmist, the tender mercies of God persist and bless. With the apostle Paul in Philippians 4:8, they invite us to fix our minds on the lasting true and life-giving love of God.

We thank and praise You, dear God our Father, for the patient love that sees through front-page wickedness to find and save what is eternally valuable in each of us, for Jesus' sake. We pray in the name of Jesus, our Savior. Amen.

God's Righteous Reign

The Lord reigneth; let the earth rejoice; let the multitude of isles be glad thereof (Psalm 97:1).

Scripture: Psalm 97:1-12
Song: "Joy to the World"

Perhaps the phone is answered and you hear, "Thank you for calling our company office. If you wish to open an account with us, press 1. If you wish to inquire about your current billing, press 2." And so goes the roster of eight successive numbers while you wait to ask some listening and talking person when you can expect fulfillment of the service that was promised for last week. Instead you are ultimately assured repeatedly and mechanically that you will receive the undivided attention of the first available one of their busy personnel. When that does happen you'll probably find that you are talking to a specialist in a department entirely different from the one with which you did business.

It is not so with God. He reigns! He reigns in Antarctica and America and in outer space alike, for He made them all. He reigns in the Chinese nursery and in the Hawaiian retirement home alike, for He loves every patient and serves through every nurse in both. The channels of His mercy are directed through His servants, but it is God who reigns. As the psalmist rejoiced to see and say: God reigns! And access to Him in prayer is instantaneous and direct.

Help us, dear God, to build our understanding and confidence in the marvelous communication that we have with You in prayer. May it be more and more clear to us that You listen, and hear, and understand, and care, and respond because You do reign. In that, may we increasingly rejoice. In Christ our Lord, we pray. Amen.

God's Justice

Defend the poor and fatherless: do justice to the afflicted and needy
(Psalm 82:3).

Scripture: Psalm 82:1-8
Song: "Jesus Loves the Little Children"

David, the psalm-writing king was once guilty of sin against God and great injustice to persons around him. He took another man's wife and caused that man's death in a clumsy effort to cover his own guilt (see 2 Samuel 11 and 12). But when God's prophet Nathan went to face David with his sin, he did not charge him directly with adultery and murder. Instead he told a story of a rich man's injustice in taking and using a poor neighbor's pet lamb. David called that a villainy worthy of death and was condemned with his own words.

Both the psalm and the teaching of Jesus, however, call for a justice higher than a rich man's respect for his poor neighbor's meager possessions. The poor or the afflicted—the widow or the orphan—has a need that constitutes a legitimate claim on the believer who has the ability to relieve that need. "If anyone has material possessions and sees his brother in need but has no pity on him, how can the love of God be in him?" (1 John 3:17, *New International Version*).

Jesus did not speak of it as justice, but He did make it a part of judgment—"Inasmuch as ye have done it unto one of these my brethren, ye have done it unto me" (Matthew 25:40). Shall we withhold fair treatment of our Lord?

We praise You, O God, because You care for us, Your children, more than for the rest of Your creation. Teach us to share Your sense of values, and to show it by the way we use what You put into our hands so may we show justice to others for Jesus' sake. Amen.

Compassionate God

He raiseth up the poor out of the dust, . . . that he may set him with princes, even with the princes of his people (Psalm 113:7a, 8).

Scripture: Psalm 113:1-9.
Song: "All for Jesus"

During the years following Ruthie's accident, with her extensive skin grafts and other surgeries, clothes shopping for her became an exercise in exhausting futility. It was impossible to find anything that she could put on and tolerate wearing; anything presentable in appearance. Then she remembered her old sewing machine, and brought it out to create her own wearables. The result was so satisfying, both in activity and in result, that she invested in a fine new sewing machine and extended her activity to cover family members and neighbors, especially those with unusual needs not otherwise met. None gave quite as much pleasure as the fashioning of first baby clothes, complete with stitched-in names, in readiness for twins to be born to folk unable otherwise to meet the special need.

Called to mind is Dorcas (Acts 9:36-42), whose death was mourned by "all the widows" who showed coats and garments Dorcas had made for them. Dorcas was restored to life after prayer by the apostle Peter, who then presented her alive to the assembled believers and widows! May we assume that the nonbelieving widows became believers soon afterward. May Ruthie's sewing machine be implemental in similar results.

Thank You, our glorious God, for the love that reaches from the highest Heaven to the lowest depths of human shame, to touch, save, and lift sinners to Your presence in Christ Jesus our Lord. May we take a glad part in the lifting process for His sake. In Jesus' name, we pray. Amen.

God's Guidance

Give the king thy judgments, O God, and thy righteousness unto the king's son. He shall judge thy people with righteousness, and thy poor with judgment (Psalm 72:1, 2).

Scripture: Psalm 72:1-7
Song: "Cleanse Me"

God will guide a person who prays that his life be as God wills it to be. It is especially hard for a ruler so to humble himself. Observe the prayer of General George Washington after his inauguration as the first President of the United States: "Almighty God, we make our earnest prayer that Thou wilt keep the United States in Thy holy protection; that Thou wilt incline the hearts of the citizens to cultivate a spirit of subordination and obedience to government to entertain a brotherly affection and love for one another and for their fellow citizens of the United States at large."

Better known is the prayerful conclusion of Abraham Lincoln's dedicatory address at the Gettysburg battlefield during of the Civil War: "It is rather for us to be here dedicated to the great task remaining before us: that from these honored dead we take increased devotion to that cause for which they gave the last full measure of devotion; that this nation, under God, shall have a new birth of freedom, and that government of the people, by the people, and for the people, shall not perish from the earth."

All powerful God, we are not all heads of state, but we recognize how much such men need Your wisdom, and how much they need the prayers and the support of citizens such as we. May they have it, for their sake, and for ours as a nation, and especially for the sake of Your kingdom. In Jesus' name, we pray. Amen.

God's Continuing Concern

Blessed be the L{ORD} God, the God of Israel, who only doeth wondrous things. And blessed be his glorious name for ever: and let the whole earth be filled with his glory (Psalm 72:18, 19).

Scripture: Psalm 72:11-19
Song: "Guide Me, 0 Thou Great Jehovah"

In Mark 14:7, 8, Jesus says, "The poor you will always have with you, and you can help them any time you want. But you will not always have me. She did what she could" (*New International Version*). Jesus spoke up for Mary of Bethany.

The poor—those who have needs they can not meet without help—are always present on God's mind. He expects His people to be aware of them, too. He expects compassion and love to be expressed most by those who are most able to help—rulers and leaders of men.

Need and responsibility are not limited to material things. Jesus himself needed the kind of selfless devotion that came with the anointing at Bethany. He needed supportive friendship even more desperately in Gethsemane and in the courts of the Jewish council and of the Roman governor. Who was ever more neglected in His need?

Many of the "poor" folk around us need encouragement and understanding as well as food and clothing. God's people are the kind of kings who have the wealth most needed by those poverty-stricken ones—even those called "rich and famous." We have what the world needs—the love of God.

Thank You, God our heavenly Father, for making us kings and priests in Christ Jesus our Lord. Help us to accept our responsibility to deal generously with the wealth, spiritual and material, entrusted to us, and so to relieve affliction around us in Jesus' name, we pray. Amen.

The Faithfulness of the Father

For I have said, Mercy shall be built up for ever: thy faithfulness shalt thou establish in the very heavens (Psalm 89:2).

Scripture: Psalm 89:1-7
Song: "Jesus is all the World to Me"

A few years ago, I stood amidst a pep rally as the school's football team was welcomed to a new season. Over the loudspeaker, each player's name was read as he jogged across the gym floor with arms waving to the cheers. As the line of player's continued forward, I noticed one player with his head down. When his name was called, the few claps were muffled with an entourage of "boos" from the stands. The hurtful jeers poured from the crowd. As the boy was finishing his trot, my eyes were drawn to the shouting and clapping man. Though the negative crowd surrounded him, he continued his cheering. He did not relent in his show of support regardless of what others did. You see, this man was the boy's father.

Since that day, I've forgotten much about the team and even who was quarterback, but I'll never forget what that father did for his son. A father's faithfulness, support and love echoed louder than a myriad of fruitless noises.

We have a heavenly Father who cheers for us and loves us. Despite our failures, fallings and fumbles, He is ever faithful. Let us proclaim His name to all generations.

Almighty and everliving heavenly Father, We praise You and we proclaim Your majesty before all generations. We stand in awe of You and worship Your holy name. In the name of Jesus Christ, Your son, and our Savior and Lord, we pray. Amen.

June 24-30. **Andrew S. Caldwell** is pursuing an advanced degree in Fire and Emergency Management Administration at Oklahoma State University.

No Matter What

The heavens are thine, the earth also is thine: as for the world and the fulness thereof, thou hast founded them (Psalm 89:11).

Scripture: Psalm 89:8-18
Song: "I Sing the Mighty Power of God"

When we look around us, we see so much pain in our world today. When we look at our families, we can see family members who are hurting. When we look at the church family, we can see those who are hurting there. Our neighborhoods, towns, and cities need Your love. Everywhere we look we can see the pain and hurt among all nations of the world. This world is cold—so cold that stories laced with tragedy become commonplace. Our compassion is smothered with indifference and busywork. And often we see the hurt and pain so much that we forget to thank God for the good in life.

Nearly two thousand years ago, God came down and walked amongst the thorns of life. He touched those whom society had shunned, He loved the unlovely, and He knew the very ones He called "friends" would soon betray Him to a world of hate. He was innocent, yet this world handed Him a death of suffering and loneliness. He endured a death that presented Him a cup and a choice—a cup we could not drink and a choice we could never make. He chose to die so that the whole world could live. Because of Christ, our present world of turmoil and suffering will end—for He is in control—no matter what!

Dear Lord, maker of Heaven and earth let us turn to You and give You thanks and praise. Help us to see the good in others and to display Your love to all we see and touch this day. We know that You rule everything in the name of Jesus, Your son and our Savior, we pray. Amen.

Think of Eternity

For a thousand years in thy sight are but as yesterday when it is past, and as a watch in the night (Psalm 90:4).

Scripture: Psalm 90:1-6
Song: "I Belong to the King"

Have you ever pondered the concept of eternity? Take one single drop of water and let it fall in your hand. Let it roll across your palm and fall into a river. That single drop of water represents one year of life. The endless flowing river represents eternity. The water of the river keeps coming, never stopping. No one knows where the water of the river has come or where it's going. The river just keeps flowing right on by.

God is the Creator of Heaven and earth. He is the one who sets time into motion. He is the God from everlasting to everlasting. He is forever and forever. Sometimes we tend to put God into our time frame. We think that He sees only our point of view. We expect Him to answer our prayers as we think they should be answered. Our minimal understanding of God doesn't allow us to understand why our prayers are not always answered right away. We focus on our plight whilst ignoring the fact that God alone is in control. He knows the proper time to send His answer. For He sees beyond our days and knows exactly what to do and what is best for us—His children. Sometimes it is tough to wait, but we must hang onto the hope and provision of Christ as we travel through our day—for our eternity is just around the corner!

Heavenly Father, You are the Creator of time and eternity. Give us patience when we are restless—give us wisdom when we are confused, and remind us in this very hour that, no matter what happens today, in Christ we'll always have a tomorrow. In Jesus name, we pray. Amen.

He Will Be There

He will regard the prayer of the destitute, and not despise their prayer
(Psalm 102:17).

Scripture: Psalm 102:12-22
Song: "Hear Our Prayer, Oh Lord"

Change is rampant in our society. In the recent past, we called our loved ones on rotary dial phones. Now with the invention of the computer and the Internet, we can not only speak to them but also see their faces across the miles. The field of medicine continually changes with the advent of new procedures and new practices and new treatments altogether working to provide better patient care. In nearly every facet of society, change is continuous—continuous at a blistering pace.

Coupled with rapid change comes indifference. People tend to care more for their own needs while not having the time to lend a helping hand to those who need it most. In societal crises—like homelessness and child abuse—we blame the government and then move on with our own lives. The cries of suffering and loneliness continue to fall on deaf ears.

However, within our society is something that will never change—that is the love of God for His children. His hand protects our every movement. He hears our pleas and prayers of desperation. For He shall deliver the destitute, the despised and the unlovely. He will always be there for us and for every passing generation. His Name shall endure forever!

Heavenly Father, You love and care for Your children despite our senseless actions and failures. You are Master of every broken heart and You are willing and able to heal our broken lives. O God let us learn to turn to You for our needs. In the name of Christ, our Savior, we pray. Amen.

The God of Countless Wonders

Thou art the God that doest wonders: thou hast declared thy strength among the people (Psalm 77:14).

Scripture: Psalm 77:11-20
Song: "All Hail the Power"

Let us take a walk through biblical history for a moment. Can you imagine sitting on the bank of the Red Sea as it had just closed upon the powerful Egyptian army after the people of Israel are safely delivered through the Sea? Can you imagine watching Elijah being ushered into eternal bliss on a chariot of fire? Can you imagine standing over the Philistine giant, Goliath, after you defeated him in a battle that only the Lord could have won.

God worked wonders in the past. Better still, He is working wonders today. There are doors being opened now that have never been opened before. People seem to be questioning more and more . . . "What is life really about?" What will be the response to these opportunities from God's children? We must convey the hope that is in Christ Jesus our Lord. For God is the God of all comfort. He is the God of the oppressed and the mercy giver to the downtrodden. He is King and Lord over all creation, and He is the God of countless and unending wonders.

And today, right now, He rests in your heart loving you—ready to deliver another wonder to your weary soul. He is there for us all.

Dear Heavenly Father, You are truly the God of all wonders. For with You in our lives, all things are possible. Let us not fall into the trap of thinking we are self-sufficient, but rather let us remember Your awesome power and Your unconditional love. In the name of Jesus, we pray. Amen.

Up and Down the Road Again

We will not hide them from their children, showing to the generation to come the praises of the LORD, and his strength, and his wonderful works that he hath done (Psalm 78:4).

Scripture: Psalm 78:1-8
Song: "I Will Sing the Wondrous Story"

While on duty at the fire station, I noticed a man pushing his wheelchair up Main Street. As he came near, I could see his smile and hear his pleasant words. I noticed his strong arms and scarred face as he introduced himself. John was a new resident at the local assisted living facility. And already he was out in the neighborhoods, wheeling up and down the roads witnessing to whoever crossed his path. His witness consisted of a smile and a word about how good God had been to him. John stated that he loved the Lord and had taught Sunday school for years. He loved to visit people and with every visit left a gift—either a pamphlet from the church he attended or a small gift. And always he said a prayer for them.

Whenever I saw John, it made me think of my faith. John was out pounding the pavement with his wheelchair for Christ every single day. Even though he couldn't walk, it did not stop him from proclaiming Christ to the next generation and encouraging another brother like me. I know God truly smiles when He sees John loving a dying world in the Name of His Son—Jesus Christ.

Heavenly Father, I thank You for sending faithful saints out into the world to spread Your Word. I pray that we will always reach out to future generations and let them know true life rests in Jesus Christ. In His precious name, we pray. Amen.

The World From God's Viewpoint

For I know that the LORD is great, and that our Lord is above all gods
(Psalm135:5).

Scripture: Psalm 135:1-7
Song: "How Great Thou Art!"

I stood atop the mountain, which had a small forest fire raging below. Before me lay a few acres of flames and charred underbrush. The teams of firefighters from our department and from other governmental agencies scoured up and down the mountain all through the night attempting to extinguish the blaze. Though there was much action going on all around, my eye caught a glimpse of the countless mountaintops which rested in peace in the far distance. The bright moonlight reflected across the tops of the endless mountains and foothills on this midnight horizon. The moment was brief, yet it was serenity amidst the chaos.

And then a thought crossed my mind. At the present moment this fire seemed like a huge problem. It seemed to occupy the minds and actions of numerous agencies and their personnel. Yet, from God's point of view, this fire was very small. The mountains surrounding the fireground dwarfed its existence. And then I thought of our heavenly Father. He dwarfs all of the distant mountains combined and beyond. He is God Supreme. He is the Almighty. He, alone, is the true and living God and He is above all gods for there is none like Him!

Heavenly Father, we thank You for loving mankind. You alone are God and worthy of praise! Help us to surrender the hustle and bustle and think upon You and Your power. God, we praise You! In the name of Jesus Christ, our Savior, we pray. Amen.

My Prayer Notes

_____

_____

_____

_____

_____

_____

_____

_____

_____

_____

_____

_____

_____

_____

_____

_____

_____

_____

_____

_____

Devotions

July

photo by Chuck Perry

Deeds to Prove His Mercy

*O give thanks unto the L*ORD*; for he is good: for his mercy endureth for ever*
(Psalm 136:1).

Scripture: Psalm 136:1-9
Song: "Great Is Thy Faithfulness"

It's nice, it's probably even necessary to *hear* that someone loves you. But, as important as the words are, even more important are actions to support them.

A child may tell his parent, "I love you." But if the child never calls home, forgets birthdays, and mocks the parent's values, the parent wonders what kind of love this is.

A young man may tell his sweetheart, "I love you," but if he won't listen to her, help her, or consider her, she may doubt that his love is real. A lover's actions prove his love.

A wife fixes her husband's favorite food. A mom refuses to say, "I told you so," when her son gets into trouble. A dad works extra hours to pay for his daughter's college. A daughter sacrifices to buy her dad a special Christmas gift.

Each of these actions might be accompanied by the words; "I love you." But in each case, are the words really necessary?

Today's psalm reminds us that God loves us; His mercy for us endures forever. To underscore his claims about God, the psalmist shows us what God has done: He has created our universe. He has defeated our enemies. He has provided our needs. Can anyone doubt that God's mercy is real?

Thank You, God, for proclaiming Your mercy to us, and for demonstrating that mercy so marvelously. In Jesus' holy name, we pray. Amen.

July 1-7. **Mark A. Taylor,** vice-president and publisher at Standard Publishing, first came to the company as editor of The Lookout in 1976.

Me Do It

The Lord taketh pleasure in them that fear him, in those that hope in his mercy (Psalm 147:11).

Scripture: Psalm 147:1-11
Song: "Immortal, Invisible"

With set jaw and a determined tone, the toddler refuses her parent's help and says, "Me do it!" She's sure that she is able, that she possesses in her hands and in her great experience every resource she needs to reach her goal. And so she struggles with the puzzle until her parent shows which piece fits where. Or she tugs at her shoes, unable to tie the bows herself. Or she spills her juice, falls down the stairs, or stomps away from an unsorted pile of toys with tears of frustration.

This stubborn determination to do it herself may anger or befuddle or amuse her parents, but shortly it will be over. Soon enough the child learns what her parent is trying to teach her. But it will probably take many years for her to learn that her parents have more to teach and that she desperately needs to accept what they have to offer.

"Me do it" is an attitude that can characterize anyone at any age. With our education, our jobs and our abilities, we think we're in charge of our lives. But we can't control something even as simple as the weather. We can't make the grass grow. We can't count the stars. Our efforts to run things on our own must make God smile. He knows how much we need Him. And He waits each day for us to realize this too.

O God, great God, controller of the universe and Lord of life, we need You today to make life meaningful, to smooth the rough paths, and to show the way. We trust You more than we trust ourselves. We rely on Your strength alone. In Jesus' name, we pray. Amen.

Prepared for the Surprise

As for man, his days are as grass . . . but the mercy of the Lord is from everlasting to everlasting (Psalm 103:15, 17).

Scripture: Psalm 103:15-22
Song: "Bless His Holy Name"

I love my garden, but I must admit that it constantly surprises me. It is difficult in April for me to imagine the bounty that spring's new seedlings will create by end of summer. But in the summer I enjoy the health of my sprawling vines and bushes as if they will last forever. In July I give little thought to the frost that will come in October. And I cannot even picture the clean up of dead stalks that will be my gardener's task in November.

Sometimes we are so caught up in any given moment of our lives that we don't think about how our lives will change. Enjoying our health, surrounded by our vibrant children, we don't acknowledge that beauty fades and that all earthly life pursues a cycle that must end in death.

He who worships God is prepared for this surprise. For God warns us to trust Him and not to count too much on ourselves. Like the bright flowers in my summer garden, my smile and my strong voice will one day fade. "But the mercy of the Lord is from everlasting to everlasting upon them that fear him."

Heavenly Father, giver of life, help us to enjoy life without taking it for granted or insisting that it never change. Help us to learn to trust You today so that we will be prepared to trust You through the changes of tomorrow. In the name of Jesus, our Savior, we pray. Amen.

Mightier Than the Sea

Mightier than the thunder of the great waters, mightier than the breakers of the sea—the LORD on high is mighty (Psalm 93:4, *New International Version*).

Scripture: Psalm 93:1-5
Song: "Make a Joyful Noise"

There's just something about the seashore that can't be resisted.

The beaches of the world are crowded at this time of the year. Sun worshipers, shell collectors, and children who want to cool off in the waves—they flock to the ocean side to enjoy the pleasures that come only there.

Even when the weather is cool, even when a walk on the beach must be in long pants and a sweatshirt, the chance to be close to the ocean is an opportunity that can't be missed.

Sometimes, however, the ocean turns ugly. A tropical storm blowing ashore sends fearful waves ahead of it. We remember television pictures of hurricanes when we read verses 3 and 4 of today's psalm. Pounding waves thundering against piers, docks, and beach houses damage with a power that surprises and frightens us.

Perhaps this is why the ocean fascinates us. It is so much bigger than we are, larger than we can see or control. But, as the Scripture reminds us, even the raging expanse of the ocean is not mightier than our God. He created it all. He is above all. And He will prevail, from the beginning of eternity until it ends, and it will never end.

Mighty God, how wonderful it is to realize that You are our God, and You are large enough to rule the world, and strong enough to solve all our problems. Help us to yield to Your power and to experience Your rule—this is our prayer today. In Jesus' name, we pray. Amen.

The Ultimate Creator

He set the earth on its foundations; it can never be moved
(Psalm 104:5, *New International Version*).

Scripture: Psalm 104:1-9
Song: "This Is My Father's World"

What does it take to create a classic painting? Time—hour after hour, then days, and maybe month after month of painstaking work with the oil and the canvas. This is talent, to be sure. But talent alone did not create the Mona Lisa. Years of experience preceded it, and hard work produced it.

What does it take to create a beautiful piece of furniture? Patient measuring and sawing, planing and gluing, sanding and staining and varnishing. A home carpenter may give a whole summer of Saturdays to such a project.

What have you created? A patio? A flower garden? A team? A casserole? All of us are creative in one way or another. It's evidence that we are made in the image of God, the first and the ultimate Creator. But there's a great difference between our creations and His. We labor to create. God created the whole world with just a few words. "Let there be light," He said, and the world saw its first morning and evening. "Let there be a sky and land and seas." "Let there be trees and plants." "Let there be stars and sun and moon." "Let there be living creatures—in the water and on the land." "Let us make man in our image." As He spoke, the earth took its form. And by His Word we have our hope of salvation after this world is no more.

Heavenly Father, we worship You because You created our world with a few words. We live for You because Your Word shows us how to live. In the name of Jesus, we pray. Amen.

Quenching Our Thirst

As the deer pants for streams of water, so my soul pants for you, O God
(Psalm 42:1, *New International Version*).

Scripture: Psalm 104:10-23
Song: "As the Deer"

Do you remember the last time you were really thirsty? Maybe it was just this week, as you mowed the lawn or coached a Little League game, or took your daily walk in the afternoon sun. You were thirsty, but you probably weren't desperate for something to drink.

Few of us have ever been that thirsty. We've seen men stumble and fall for desert mirages in the movies. We've read books about people bobbing on tiny lifeboats, thirsty castaways with parched lips, swollen tongues, and sunburned brows. But most of us have never experienced such thirst.

We probably take our water for granted. Even though some communities negotiate, spend, and sue to guarantee that they have water, we usually just expect clean water to be there when we turn on the tap to fill our water bottles.

Today's Scripture reminds us that God has provided the life-giving water—and everything else—that we need. As we thank Him for His physical provision, we can remember that He satisfies our spirit as well. He wants us to seek Him the same way we long for a tall glass of ice water on a summer afternoon.

We thank You, Lord, for giving us every good gift. As we enjoy the abundance of Your provision for our physical needs, help us to remember that You alone can satisfy the spirit and quench our thirst for satisfaction, fulfillment, and peace. Help us to find each of these in You today. In Jesus' name, we pray. Amen.

Struck by Wonder

Praise awaits you, O God, in Zion; to you our vows will be fulfilled
(Psalm 65:1, *New International Version*).

Scripture: Psalm 65:1-13
Song: "I Am His, and He Is Mine"

To different people, at different times, different gifts from God mean the most.

The person burdened with guilt thanks God for lifting his chin, wiping his tears, and forgiving him for his wrongdoing. "When we were overwhelmed by sins, you forgave our transgressions" (verse 3, *New International Version).*

The person who realizes that God assembled the whole universe is awestruck at His power and creativity. He bows in fear before God (verse 8) because no one can do what God does.

The person who has run to God to meet his need may actually be amazed when he sees God provide. Have you ever been surprised to see God clearly and specifically answer your prayer? It is a feeling of wonder and worship to taste the abundance of what He gives (see verse 9).

Each of us has experienced many of these reasons to worship Him. When we see all He has created, when we feel His hand at work in our own lives, and when we realize that He invites us to come close to Him in spite of our sin (verse 4), we are driven to our knees before Him.

We realize, our Father, how many reasons we have to worship You! Help us to see signs of Your power, evidence of Your provision, and memories of Your grace as we walk through the details of our day. Help us to see all the ways You are at work in our world, even as we recommit ourselves to bringing that world under Your control. In Jesus' name, we pray. Amen.

Great Is the Lord

Great is the Lord and most worthy of praise; his greatness no one can fathom
(Psalm 145:3, *New International Version*).

Scripture: Psalm 145:1-7
Song: "O Worship the King"

Worship of God is central to the believer's life. The Old and New Testaments both end with a book of worship as a testimony to the place of worship in God's scheme of things.

In worship there is activity in two directions: God comes to man, and man goes to God. This provides for a spiritual relationship. The psalmist says that he will praise the Lord. It was early January and in the doctor's waiting room every seat was occupied. There was the usual atmosphere of tension, each person concerned with his/her own problems. The waiting patients looked down at their feet, flipped through old magazines, and gazed at the pictures on the walls. Suddenly a woman spoke up. "Why don't we sing? Are you tired of Christmas carols?" Every head turned in her direction. Startled at such an idea, the others in the room couldn't help returning the smile on her happy face. Without waiting for an answer, her strong soprano voice began, "O Come, All Ye Faithful." Another joined in with his tenor voice. Then another added an alto and soon others joined in. In a moment the waiting room was filled with joyous music and worship as we sang.

Every day Christians praise and worship God everywhere.

Almighty God and Lord of all, create in us a desire to praise You everyday in worship. Help us to see the importance of kneeling before You. Humble us before Your Throne of grace and love. In Jesus' name, we pray. Amen.

July 8-14. **Dr. Willard Walls** serves as the Europe Coordinator with Christian Missionary Fellowship. He and his wife, Ruth, live in England.

Our Kind God

Your kingdom is an everlasting kingdom, and your dominion endures through all generations. The LORD is faithful to all his promises and loving towards all he has made (Psalm 145:13, *New International Version*).

Scripture: Psalm 145:8-13
Song: "Holy God, We Praise Thy Name"

We have a kind and loving God. The psalmist David knew this. "The Lord is gracious, and full of compassion; slow to anger, and of great mercy." What a quartet of attributes! The Lord makes the sun to rise on the evil as well as the good, and He sends rain upon the just as well as the unjust (Matthew 5:45). "All thy works shall praise thee, O Lord, and thy saints shall bless thee." Truly, He is a great God. His creation worships Him. The saints cannot contain themselves. They must speak of His Kingdom and of God's eternal dominion.

When Jesus entered Jerusalem for the final time, the disciples could not restrain themselves and worship the Lord openly with great enthusiasm. Some of the religious leaders told Jesus to tell these unruly followers to quiet themselves. Jesus replied, "I tell you, if they keep quiet, the stones would cry out!" (Luke 19:40).

There are some lines from an ancient prayer from the church, "Lord, I want to thank You that you've allowed my golden moments to roll on. You could have stopped my life at any point, but you allowed my golden moments to roll on."

God is good. Let us praise and worship Him.

Almighty God and Lord of all, thank You for allowing our golden moments to roll on. You are the God of grace and mercy. Your love extends to all. We return Your love in worship and praise of Your name and mighty works. In the name of Christ, our Savior, we pray. Amen.

Our God Who Is Near

The LORD is near to all who call on him, to all who call on him in truth
(Psalm 145:18, *New International Version*).

Scripture: Psalm 145:14-21
Song: "Lord of All Being"

Whoever you are and wherever you are, if you want to meet the God of the universe, you can come into His presence through Christ. "The Lord is near unto all them that call upon him." What obstacle is keeping you from coming near to the Lord? Are there other overwhelming calls on Your time and attention? The psalmist reminds us that the Lord God is ready to hear our cry and to fulfill our desires. He is ready for our worship. The author, Erwin Lutzer says, "If we haven't learned to be worshipers, it doesn't really matter how well we do anything else."

One of the great doctrines that the Reformation brought back to us was the doctrine of the "priesthood of believers." The apostle Peter wrote, "But you are a chosen people, a royal priesthood, a holy nation, a people belonging to God, that you may declare the praises of him who called you out of darkness into his wonderful light" (1 Peter 2:9 *New International Version*).

When we trust Jesus Christ as Lord we have direct access to God. He will come near to us. To the unsaved, God invites them to come to Him for salvation. God is available to all mankind. Our Redeemer is worthy of our praise and worship.

Lord God, our Redeemer in time of need, praise Your mighty hand that can save us for eternity. Praise Your name for the love that sent Your Son Jesus in human form to be near us and experience our humanity. Praise Your holy name for all the goodness we find in You. Through obedience to Him our salvation is assured. In His holy name, we pray. Amen.

Worthy of Worship

Let everything that has breath praise the LORD. Praise the LORD
(Psalm 150:6, *New International Version*).

Scripture: Psalm 150
Song: "All Hail the Power"

God is the object of worship. The Psalms accentuate two things: God is Creator and Redeemer. He is worthy of our worship because He is the Creator. He is also worthy of our worship because He is the Redeemer. Furthermore, God is the only Creator and only Redeemer. God said to Moses, "You shall have no other gods before me" (Exodus 20:3).

John, on the island of Patmos, attempted to worship the angel who brought the visions to him, he was told: "Do not do it! I am a fellow servant with you and with your brothers the prophets and of all who keep the words of this book. Worship God!" (Revelation 22:9). He alone is to have our worship and adoration. Let everything that has breath praise the LORD."

Gregory of Nazianzus, fourth century church father who defended the doctrine of the trinity against the Arians, said, "I love God because I know Him; I adore Him because I cannot understand Him; I bow before Him in awe and in worship and adoration." Let everything that has breath praise the LORD." Praise Him alone as Creator and Redeemer.

A three-year-old was dancing and singing. Her song of praise was, "I love you, Lord, and I lift my noise! " While the psalmist desires the trumpet, harp, lyre, tambourine, strings and flute be used in worship—God wants us just as we are.

Lord, with every breath we praise and worship You, Creator and Redeemer. We offer service and honor to You. In Jesus' name, we pray. Amen.

Heavenly Worship

Praise the Lord. Praise the Lord from the heavens, praise him in the heights above (Psalm 148: 1, *New International Version*).

Scripture: Psalm 148:1-6
Song: "O Jesus, King Most Wonderful"

In Psalm 148 we learn that praise begins in the heavens. The Puritan John Trap notes that in framing the world, God began in the heavens and moved downward; so in this exhortation to all creatures, the psalmist proceeds to praise the Lord from the heavens downward. Psalm 103:20-22 demonstrates this order: "Praise the LORD, you his angels, you mighty ones who do his bidding, who obey his word. Praise the LORD, all his heavenly hosts you his servants who do his will. Praise the LORD, all his works everywhere in his dominion." Praise to God begins in the most exalted regions of His creation.

Do you have in your heart a song that leads you to worship God? As a young man in the church youth group I was quite concerned that I did not have the singing gifts or abilities of my peers. I longed to be able to sing as well as they did. I have learned to make the "Joyful noise" before the Lord. But more importantly I have learned that the real question is not, "Do you have a voice?" The question to ask is, "Do you have a song?" What has God done in your life today that you can sing and praise Him for His wonderful works? Stop for a moment, reflect, listen, and discover. Praise Him!

Thank You, almighty God and Lord of all, for giving us a new song today. A song that praises Your work in our lives. We can all join the heavenly host in worship because we are servants who desire Your will to be done in our lives. We pray this prayer in the name of Jesus, our Savior and Lord. Amen.

Praise His Name

We give thanks to you, O God, we give thanks, for your Name is near; men tell of your wonderful deeds (Psalm 75:1, *New International Version*).

Scripture: Psalm 75
Song: "All People That on Earth Do Dwell"

The following verse can be translated, "For I will take hold of the set time, I will judge in uprightness." When the Lord comes it will be at a set time. Jesus in human form said, "But of that day and hour knoweth no man, no, not the angels of heaven, but my Father only" (Matthew 24:36). The Lord is coming at that appointed time. No man knows the hour. The psalmist declares that it is God who is in control of the cosmos and all of His dominion. His judgment will come in His time.

The parents of a three-year-old decided to let him record the message for their home answering machine. The rehearsals went smoothly: "Mommy and Daddy can't come to the phone right now. If you'll leave your name, phone number, and a brief message, they'll get back to you as soon as possible."

Then the Mom pressed the record button and the three-year-old said sweetly, "Mommy and Daddy can't come to the phone right now. If you'll leave your name, phone number, and a brief message, they'll get back to you as soon as Jesus comes." Jesus is coming at the appointed time. William Barclay said "The best way to prepare for the coming of Christ is never to forget the presence of Christ." Worship keeps us in His presence.

Father, we thank You for Your many promises. Keep us alert Lord to the signs of the times that keep us sensitive to Your imminent return. Thank You Lord for Your memorial supper that keeps our attention to Your promise of return. Our prayer is in the name of Jesus. Amen.

Worship in Gladness

*Shout for joy to the L*ORD*, all the earth, serve the L*ORD *with gladness;*
come before him with joyful songs (Psalm 100: 1, *New International Version*).

Scripture: Psalm 100
Song: "Crown Him with Many Crowns"

This psalm is the grand finale of a cluster of psalms that
began with Psalm 94. These psalms speak of God's judgment,
salvation, authority, dominion and greatness. A doxology is an
expression of praise and Psalm 100 is a great doxology, a
hallelujah chorus. There are many doxologies in the Scriptures.
Ephesians 1:3: is one we can sing, "Blessed be the God and
Father of our Lord Jesus Christ, who hath blessed us with all
spiritual blessings in heavenly places in Christ."

Young Teddy Roosevelt was afraid of the Madison Square
Church. He refused to set foot inside it alone. He was terrified,
his mother discovered, of something called the zeal. It
crouched in the corners of the church ready to jump at him.

She asked, "What is the zeal?" He said, "I am not sure, but
it is probably a large animal like an alligator or a dragon." He
had heard the minister read about it from the Bible. Mrs.
Roosevelt read him a few passages containing the word 'zeal'
Suddenly, very excited, he said, "Stop." The line she read, John
2:17: "And his disciples remembered that it was written, "The
zeal of thine house hath eaten me up." The psalmist had no
fear of zeal for the Lord!

Shout for joy to the LORD all the earth."

Lord God of Heaven and earth, create in me a heart that is zealous for Your
holiness in my life. Create in me radiate joy and enthusiasm for the truth of
Your Word. May my life pass on the joy of Your salvation. Let me, O Lord,
show Your love to all around me. In Jesus' holy name, I pray. Amen.

Learning From the Sins of Others

Salvation is found in no one else, for there is no other name under heaven given to men by which we must be saved (Acts 4:12, *New International Version*).

Scripture: Psalm 106:1-12
Song: "Jesus Saves"

Often a child hears a parent say, "Don't do that." And then, the child forgets and repeats the wrong once again. Then, the parent asks the question, "How many times do I have to tell you not to do that?" As a child of God, we can identify with that problem, can't we?

All through history, people have sinned and forgotten about God. The psalmist, talking to God, reminds us that the children of Israel sinned because they did not remember God's kindness. The one question for us to answer is whether or not we want to sin. We must never lose the desire to not sin. We should never easily accept any sin in our lives without turning that sin over to the Lord for forgiveness. We're in trouble with God when we begin to make excuses for our sins or to blame others for them.

Psalm 106 reminds us that God saved the children of Israel and we know it is His desire for us also to have our sins forgiven. We are His creation, and it is His desire that we find forgiveness for our sins. Sin separates us from God, and God desires His creation to spend eternity with Him.

Heavenly Father, thank You for giving us life in Christ who died for us. Forgive our sins and help us to not sin. It is the desire to do what is pleasing in Your sight. We pray this prayer in the name of Jesus, our Savior. Amen.

July 15-21. **Kenneth Meade** has ministered to the Church of Christ at Manor Woods in Rockville, Maryland, for more than 44 years. He and his wife, Jan, have two children and four grandchildren.

God Loves to Forgive Us

The Lord is not slow in keeping his promise, as some understand slowness. He is patient with you, not wanting anyone to perish, but everyone to come to repentance (2 Peter 3:9, *New International Version*).

Scripture: Psalm 103:1-14
Song: "Love Lifted Me"

Do you realize that bad habits are like comfortable beds—easy to get into but hard to get out of? Bad habits lead to sin. Sin disturbed the heart of God. He gave His Son to die for and to pay the price for our sins that we might live.

A teacher took his students for a walk through a forest. He stopped and pointed to four plants. The first was just beginning to rise above the ground, the second had rooted itself well into the earth, and the third had already become a small shrub, while the fourth was a full-size tree. The teacher asked for a student volunteer to pull up the first plant. The student did it easily. The teacher then instructed him to pull up the second one. The task was more difficult but he did it. The student had to use all his strength to pull up the third and the tree didn't even budge. We need to remove bad habits quickly before they take over our lives and are more difficult to uproot.

The holding power of sinful habits cannot be overemphasized. The power of God's love through Jesus can take away our sins and free us to spend eternity with Him in Heaven.

O God, thank You for loving us. When bad habits come into our lives, give us the strength to turn them over to You quickly. Take away even the desire to sin. Teach us to never want to intentionally do anything to bring shame to You. We pray this prayer in the name of Jesus, our Savior. Amen.

We Need God's Unfailing Love

Show us thy mercy, O Lord, and grant us thy salvation (Psalm 85:7).

Scripture: Psalm 85
Song: "Love Divine, All Loves Excelling"

Several years ago on a lonely three-mile stretch of a Florida beach, 100 pilot whales hurled themselves onto dry ground. These huge creatures had beached themselves in a kind of follow-the-leader fashion. People came from miles around to try to turn them back. At one point, a human fence was formed between the whales and the shoreline. But even when those sea mammals were pushed, pulled, and forced back into deeper water, many of them repeated their death surge and threw themselves onto dry ground again.

Is it possible that we humans look like that to the angels? God has provided so much for us as Christians. We can live in His will and His Word and also have a good life. Yet some people seek to throw themselves into what is sinful and destructive. We might well ask the question, "Why?" Why would we do something that we know is not pleasing to God?

We must realize how much God loves us and wants to help us live each day! He gives a purpose to our life and promises peace and eternal life as a beautiful reward. "This is love: not that we loved God, but that he loved us and sent His Son as an atoning sacrifice for our sins" (1 John 4:10, *New International Version*).

Today, let us strive to live an obedient life in Christ Jesus!

Almighty and everliving God and Creator of all, we thank You for Your unfailing love. Teach us to have wisdom to follow Your teachings. Keep us safe from the power of Satan. Fill our hearts with Your Word and Your love. We pray this prayer in the name of Jesus, our Savior. Amen.

God's Forgiveness Is a Precious Gift

Be kind and compassionate to one another, forgiving each other, just as in Christ God forgave you (Ephesians 4:32, *New International Version*).

Scripture: Psalm 130
Song: "Precious Lord, Take My Hand"

Have you ever said these words to someone, "Oh, please forgive me. I'm so sorry. I didn't mean to do it." Probably most of us have had to say this. Forgiveness is important because we don't always do the right things. We need people who are kind enough to us or love us enough to forgive us. Where would we be in life if people weren't willing to forgive us? Our most important forgiveness comes from God. All sin pains the heart of God and separates us from Him, so it was God's plan to provide salvation and forgiveness of our sins.

Every once in a while, you'll hear someone describe someone else as being just like his or her father. All Christians should strive to live in a manner that will cause people to see God living in us. God, our heavenly Father, loves us and forgives us through His grace. We ought also to forgive one another because we have been forgiven. No one has to forgive you for anything you do wrong. It is their choice. God chooses to forgive us, and we must also give forgiveness to others as a precious gift. Notice the first part of verse 7 in our Scripture, "O Israel, put your hope in the LORD, for with the LORD is unfailing love . . .."

God, thank You for forgiving our sins. We can't imagine what life would be like without Your forgiveness. We appreciate what Jesus has done for us. May we be Your vessels to tell the world about Your forgiveness and the sacrificial death of Jesus to forgive our sins. You are truly an awesome God. Through the name of Jesus Christ, our Savior, we pray. Amen.

Jesus, I Need Your Forgiveness

Bear with each other and forgive whatever grievances you may have against one another. Forgive as the Lord forgave you (Colossians 3:13, *New International Version*).

Scripture: Psalm 51:1-9
Song: "Just as I Am"

It's a wonderful gift when someone helps someone else who has a special need. This is what God wants us to do.

Many years ago, I heard about a man who worked in a railroad yard through which several freight trains passed every day. The owner of the yard was a Christian. The owner threw chunks of coal over the fence at various places along the track. One day the man asked the owner why he did that. With some embarrassment he replied, "A poor elderly woman lives across the street, and I know that her old-age pension is inadequate to buy enough coal. After the trains go by, she walks along and picks up the pieces she thinks have fallen from the coal car behind the engine. Her eyesight is failing, and she doesn't realize that diesels have replaced steam locomotives. I don't want to disappoint her, so I just throw some pieces over the fence to help her."

The greatest need we have is for our sins to be forgiven. God knows that need and He freely saves us through the precious blood of Jesus, His Only Son! We must let God know that we appreciate and need His forgiveness. He is truly a God of love.

Father, we need Your forgiveness, and we thank You for wanting to forgive us. Take away any desire we may have to sin. Help us to be honest with You in confessing our sins. Fill us with Your power to overcome sin. We honor You! In Jesus' holy name, we pray. Amen.

Create In Me a Pure Heart

Thy word have I hid in mine heart, that I might not sin against thee
(Psalm 119:11).

Scripture: Psalm 51:10-19
Song: "Cleanse Me"

What would happen to you if your heart stopped beating? That's right, you would die. Aren't you happy that your heart keeps beating? You should be.

Ask yourself how important it is for your heart to be kept pure and clean as a Christian. If your heart stops beating for the Lord, you will be spiritually dead. We must have a desire to do things that are right in the sight of God regardless of what anyone else does.

A friend told about a companion of his in the armed services who was living immorally. His companion responded to his word of warning by saying, "Jim, you live your way and let me live mine. I'm having fun. Nothing terrible has happened to me so far, and I don't expect it will."

There isn't always an immediate result for sinning, but in due time there will be a consequence. Christians should not have to wait for something awful to happen before they quit sinning. They should ask God immediately not only to forgive them for sinning but also to remove the very desire to sin and to create in them a pure heart. The psalmist writes, "I have hidden your word in my heart that I might not sin against you" (Psalm 119:11, New *International Version*).

Dear God, thank You for life. Fill our hearts with Your love. We want to be spiritually alive for You! Thank You for the many blessings in life. May we always live in such a way as to honor and glorify You. We pray this prayer in the name of Jesus, our Savior. Amen.

Filled With Joy—We're Forgiven

I have no greater joy than to hear that my children are walking in the truth
(3 John 4, *New International Version*).

Scripture: Psalm 32
Song: "He Keeps Me Singing"

Think of a time when someone did something really nice for you. Remember the good feelings you had when you learned that somebody really cared about you.

One early spring, my mower was in the repair shop and the rain and sunshine were causing the grass to grow taller and taller. I called the shop and found out my mower wouldn't be ready for a long time. My son told me he had a mower he wasn't using now and said I could borrow it until mine was repaired. It was even self-propelled. He called on a Saturday morning to say he was loading the mower in his truck and his wife would be coming our way and would bring it to us. Then he said, "Oh, I'll send Greg along with the mower to mow your lawn. Is that okay?" You can imagine how quickly I said yes that it would be fine for our grandson to cut the grass.

Now, that may seem like a small kindness to do for someone, but it reminded me of the heavenly Father who did something far more wonderful for all of us. He sent His Son to die for us. We are filled with joy because Jesus has taken away our sins and we can now spend eternity with God.

We love You, Lord! We love You, Jesus!

Heavenly Father, thank You for loving us enough to give Your very best for us. Thank You for Jesus who took away our sins. May our hearts always be filled with the desire to do good for others, even as You have done so much for us. Thank You for hearing my prayer. In Jesus' name, we pray. Amen.

His Majesty Is Beyond Knowing

Through him all things were made; without him nothing was made that has been made (John 1:3, *New International Version*).

Scripture: Psalm 47
Song: "How Great Thou Art"

Pagan peoples of bygone years commonly worshipped a multitude of gods. One of their gods ruled the waters, another the forest and yet another was found in fire. Almost every part of nature had its own god. Polytheism was inevitable. Such a plethora of gods would have made for chaos in the world.

The One, true and living God created all things and made Himself known to man. The psalmist knew this, and he addressed his praise to God, but the psalmist couldn't even dream of the vast magnitude of the universe God had created.

With our powerful telescopes we can look at planets millions of miles away, and we can't even imagine the limits of space in God's vast universe. Along with the psalmist we have reason to bow in awe at God's great power. It is beyond our ability to imagine or comprehend. We must worship Him.

It might seem that a God who is so vast would not be concerned about human beings on one of His smaller planets. Amazingly, this is not so. We are created in His likeness. We are His people. He loves every one of us. He even sent His Son to redeem us from sin and to offer us life in Heaven.

O God of majesty and power, You are greater than we can even think. We bow in awe of Your glory, which is revealed in Your vast creation. You gave us life, and You give us salvation. We praise and worship You. In the name of Your precious Son and our Savior, Jesus Christ, we pray. Amen.

July 22-28. **Dr. Henry E. Webb** is a minister and retired college professor. He and his wife, Emerald, reside in Johnson City, Tennessee, where they continue in service to Christ and His church.

Praise God, Judge of All Earth

Righteous art thou, O LORD, and upright are thy judgments (Psalm 119:137).

Scripture: Psalm 98
Song: "Blessed Assurance"

Psalm 98 is a song of joy. The joy is based in confidence that God, who rules this universe, is a God of righteousness and justice. This means that though it might appear that evil is triumphant in the world such is only an illusion. God is in charge. The seeming triumph of evil is, at best, only short-lived. The Hitlers of the world cannot win. Ultimately evil will be overcome because the universe God made is subject to God's justice, and evil cannot prevail in God's universe.

All of us have periods of discouragement and times when we can't see far enough ahead to realize this. Many psalms in the Bible reflect the frustration of the faithful who struggle with evil! Their frustrations are too often mirrored in our own experiences in life. But we live with the assurance that God is still in control and that He will not permit evil to triumph. This basic conviction gave courage to the martyrs in the early history of Christianity. It sustained the Allies in the dark days of World War 2. It enervated the free world in the long struggle with communism. Evil is always with us, but never ultimately wins.

God is still sovereign, and He is the God of righteousness and justice. He will never leave us or forsake us. He loves and cares for His people.

Almighty **heavenly Father and Lord of all**, strengthen in us the faith that assures us of Your continuous presence and care. Help us to triumph over our failures and discouragement. Fill us with Your Spirit. We pray in Jesus' holy name. Amen.

The Privilege of Praise

Praise ye the LORD: for it is good to sing praises unto our God; for it is pleasant; and praise is comely (Psalm 147:1).

Scripture: Psalm 68:1-6
Song: "Praise God, from Whom All Blessings Flow"

God's people are encouraged by the psalmist to sing and to praise Him. To praise God is appropriate for several good reasons. We praise God because He is our Creator. He has asked us to worship Him. We owe our very existence to Him. He provides that the gift of life is transmitted from generation to generation. He continues to bless mankind.

We praise God because He provides everything for us. He supplies both our daily bread and the Bread of Life.

We praise God because He has promised to save us. Our hope for eternity is the gift of God's grace. It is right and good that we praise and worship the Creator God.

The psalms ring out with thanksgiving and praise to God. It is most natural to break forth in song when one is thankful. We sing when we are happy.

Songs of praise are an essential part of our worship. Many of the great and best-loved hymns of the church are directed to the praise and worship of God. They bless us when we lift our voices to express the thoughts they contain. Many compositions of praise are choruses, and these are widely used in some worship services today. We are blessed when we join our voices with others in praise and worship of our God!

When we consider Your awesome majesty, O God, our words cannot express the joy and thanksgiving we feel. We rejoice in Your goodness and love which comes to us in daily blessings. We praise Your name and exalt Your majesty and power. In the name of Jesus, our Savior, we pray. Amen.

One God, For All Mankind

After this I looked and there before me was great multitude that no one could count, from every nation, tribe, people, and language, standing before the throne and in front of the Lamb. They were wearing white robes and were holding palm branches in their hands (Revelation 7:9, *New International Version*).

Scripture: Psalm 148:7-14
Song: "Praise Ye the Lord, the Almighty"

Initially all humans came from the same source. In the far recesses of antiquity, God created man and woman. Every detail of God's creative actions has not been recorded for us. Much speculation has attempted to provide us with details. Yet the fact remains that all human beings are God's creatures and He is the Father of all mankind. God chose to reveal Himself and His ways to Israel so that Israel could mediate His truth and His will to all peoples. God has never ceased to love all of His people—every human being bears His image.

The Old Testament states clearly that God is concerned about all mankind. When the temple was dedicated it was called "A house of prayer for all people." Jesus commissioned His disciples to preach the gospel to every creature. God is not willing that any should perish.

In a day of racial and ethnic animosities it is easy to blend in with prevailing attitudes toward people who are different from us. Beneath all the differences are human beings whom God loves and who He wants us to love. There is already too much hate in this world. Jesus taught us to love. Let's do it.

Loving heavenly Father, who looks down on Your unlovely creatures and still loves us, help us to show a world that is filled with hate that there is a better way, as Your Son, Jesus, showed us when He died on the cross to redeem all people. In His holy name, we pray. Amen.

Doing God's Will in a Bigger Way

Therefore go and make disciples of all nations, baptizing them in the name of the Father and of the Son and of the Holy Spirit (Matthew 28:19, *New International Version*).

Scripture: Psalm 96:1-6
Song: "We've a Story to Tell to the Nations"

It is God's will that all peoples should know Him and accept His ways and the salvation He offers. That is why the followers of Jesus are commissioned to "preach the gospel to every creature"—no territorial, racial, or national bounds. The modern missionary movement, which began late in the seventeenth century, seeks to do exactly that. Today thousands of men and women are engaged in spreading the good news of Christ to every nation on earth.

Today more people in the world look to Jesus as Lord than to any other religious leader. He is the only way of salvation. He alone gives us eternal life.

But there are still people isolated by language and geography that have never heard of Jesus. Efforts are being made now to identify and evangelize them.

The missionary effort needs the support of Christians. It operates by voluntary contributions. We all can be missionaries to our acquaintances, but we can't "go into all the world." Do you know any missionaries? Does your church have a vigorous mission program? Do you support it? Are you involved? Be a missionary today to someone.

Heavenly Father, we thank You for Christians who share their faith, for those who are willing to go far away to do so. Father, bless them, give them courage, and fruit for their labors. Help us all to be a part of the effort to reach this world for Christ. In His holy name, we pray. Amen.

God Is So Good!

Rejoice in the Lord always. I will say it again: Rejoice!
(Philippians 4:4, *New International Version*).

Scripture: Psalm 96:7-13
Song: "Sunshine in My Soul"

The psalm for today urges all mankind to join with all creation in praising God. Even nature praises God in many ways. One way is seen in nature's beauty, which surrounds us every day. Another way that nature glorifies God is seen in the stability we find in nature (v. 10). What we call "The Laws of nature" do not change. We rely on their constancy when we build, when we take medicine, when we travel on land, sea, or in the air. (Wouldn't we be in a terrible plight if this were not so?) The God who created us placed us in an orderly world.

The God of creation and redemption is stable and dependable. We can count on Him to keep His promises, both to save us or to judge us.

The psalmist rejoiced over this. So should we. Rejoicing is an expression of joy. Rejoicing is part of our Christian experience. It is always thrilling to share the joy of a new Christian. What a pity that for many, this joy doesn't last very long. It is a stratagem of the devil to transform the joy of new life in Christ into a burden. It happens when we forget the reasons we have for rejoicing—God's great love for us is seen in the many provisions He has made for our needs and happiness both here and in a life to come. Let us all REJOICE!

Father in Heaven, You have not rewarded us according to our failure and sins. Rather, You have blessed us more than we deserve or can know. We praise You for Your goodness and love. May we never forget the magnitude of Your blessings and grace. In the name of Christ, we pray. Amen.

The Hope of All Mankind

At the name of Jesus every knee should bow, in heaven and on earth and under the earth, and every tongue confess that Jesus Christ is Lord, to the glory of God the Father (Philippians 2:10-12, *New International Version*).

Scripture: Psalm 67:1-7
Song: "All People That on Earth Do Dwell"

The prayer in today's psalm is for the realization of an ideal. It envisions the day when all peoples will praise the one true and living God.

Ideals are critically important to us. Ideals lift our eyes to better things and better times. Ideals motivate us to achieve what we would otherwise never accomplish. One theologian called ideals: "The Impossible Possible."

One might think that it is too much to hope that the time will come when mankind will "beat their swords into plowshares and their spears into pruning hooks" (Isaiah 2:4). Even though this ideal has not been realized in centuries past, does that prove that it will not happen?

Is it too much to hope that in some future time no little child will go to bed hungry, or a mother does not have to watch her baby die from starvation? If we abandon our ideals and do nothing, no suffering will ever be relieved.

Human beings working with God, according to His will and purpose, can surely bring His Kingdom on the earth. Every Christian has a contribution to make.

Almighty Creator God and Father of all, teach us to follow Your leading. We want to be a part of bringing Your kingdom and salvation to all peoples of the earth. We know that there is only hope and salvation for all mankind through Your son, Jesus Christ, our Savior and Lord. Help us to live each day in such a way that others will see You living in us. Today we want to walk with You. In the name of the Savior of the world, we pray. Amen.

July 29

Learn For Eternity

The fear of the LORD is the beginning of knowledge, but fools despise wisdom and discipline (Proverbs 1:7, *New International Version*).

Scripture: Proverbs 1:1-7
Song: "Be Thou My Vision"

I looked down with amusement at the big brown eyes staring up at me. He said, "Mrs. Coffey, how long does it take before you know everything."

"Travis, you never know everything. When you stop learning, you stop living. Even I don't know everything."

It's one thing to learn how to tell time. It's quite another to understand God's time. It's one thing to know the ins and outs of the latest technology. It's another thing to understand the Creator of technology. It is one thing to be able to graduate with honors. It is quite another thing to be able to face the future with the One who has already been there.

Until I begin to understand who God is, how I fit into His plan for mankind, and develop a reverence and awe of His very presence, all the wisdom I have obtained in life will be like beautiful siding on a shaky house. It looks good on the outside, but when storms come, little remains. Earthly wisdom may give you a diploma, but godly wisdom gives you eternity.

Your Word, O Lord, is eternal; it stands firm in the heavens. Your faithfulness continues through all generations. Your Word is a lamp to my feet and a light for my path. May my lips overflow with praise, for You teach me Your decrees (see Psalm 119:89, 90, 105; 17:1, *New International Version*). May we all, heavenly Father, follow Your ways. Teach us to be like Jesus. Let us show love to all those around us. In the name of Jesus Christ, our Savior, we pray. Amen.

July 29-31. **Pam Coffey** is a minister's wife and mother to twin sons. She lives in Arcadia, Indiana.

Whose Wisdom Is Leading?

For the foolishness of God is wiser than man's wisdom, and the weakness of God is stronger than man's strength (1 Corinthians 1:25, *New International Version*).

Scripture: Proverbs 1:20-33
Song: "Open Our Eyes, Lord"

Seeing the ruins of Pompeii was a sobering experience. As our family walked down its streets with chariot ruts still evident and market places in prominent locations, we pictured the crowd hustling and bustling about, oblivious to its impending doom. A regular day in the city, Mt. Vesuvius probably smoked out its warnings, but everyone was too busy seizing the day. Then the business deals stopped and food went untouched.

As we walked in quiet reflection, we saw the rest of the story. The wisdom of that world became melted in lava and solidified into stone. The artifacts remain, but the life is gone.

In direct contrast to Pompeii was the visit to the catacombs where the early Christians hid to worship, in fear for their lives. They were considered foolish according to the world's wisdom as they willingly gave up their lives for the cause of Christ. Yet, their legacy lives on.

One group lived in "security" and lost everything. The other group lived in peril and gained eternity. The world's wisdom gives security that lasts for a moment. God's wisdom lasts forever. We ask, "Whose wisdom is the driving force in us?"

Open our eyes, Lord. Teach us to follow Your decrees; then we will keep them to the end. Turn our eyes away from worthless things; renew our life according to Your Word (see Psalm 119:18, 33, 37, *New International Version*). In Jesus' holy name, we pray. Amen.

Wisdom That Leads to Salvation

For the Lord gives wisdom, and from his mouth come knowledge and understanding. He holds victory in store for the upright, he is a shield to those whose walk is blameless (Proverbs 2:6-7, *New International Version*).

Scripture: Proverbs 2:1-15
Song: "I Will Sing of the Mercies of the Lord"

The ultimate gift a father can give to his child is God's wisdom. The writer of Proverbs had this in mind as he laid out instructions. He wanted his son to experience the complete joy in life that comes from being a child of God.

Paul, as a spiritual father to Timothy, also had that as a goal as he addressed him in 2 Timothy 3:15 by saying, "Since you were a child, you have known the Holy Scriptures which are able to make you wise. And that wisdom leads to salvation through faith in Christ Jesus" (*New Century Version*).

What kind of wisdom was Paul talking about? Is it the wisdom that leads to salvation and gives purpose and direction to life? This wisdom is the wisdom we all need.

Are you facing difficult choices? Search out God's wisdom. Do you feel you are being attacked? Let God's wisdom guide you. Is the task of parenting searing you? Let God be your model. Is your future uncertain or shaky at best? Allow God to go before you and direct your every step with His wise and loving hand. But most of all, have you allowed God's wisdom to lead you to salvation in Him? Who's hand are you clasping right now? Let it be God's.

Your hands made us and formed us; give us understanding to learn Your commands. May they who fear You rejoice when they see us, for we put our hope in You (see Psalm 119:73-74, *New International Version*). In Jesus' precious and holy name, we pray. Amen.

Devotions

August

photo by Chuck Perry

Are We Listening?

*Trust in the LORD with all your heart and lean not on your own understanding;
in all your ways acknowledge him, and he will make your
paths straight* (Proverbs 3:5-6, *New International Version*).

Scripture: Proverbs 3:1-12
Song: "Seek Ye First"

August came too soon. The inevitable moment had arrived.
The van, just a few hours earlier loaded to the ceiling, was
empty and the college dorm room was full. Final hugs. (No
tears, please.) Then Mark and I hopped in the van and headed
down the hill wondering (with a funny little lump in our
stomachs), did we teach our twin sons all they need to know?
Will they apply what we did teach them?

One can almost hear the same concern in the father's words
in Proverbs 3, as he seems to be filling his son with final words
of wisdom. "Don't forget my teaching . . . Let love and
faithfulness never leave you . . . Trust in the Lord with all your
heart . . . Don't be wise in your own eyes . . . Fear God . . .
Turn away from evil . . . And allow Him to lead you."

God is saying to each one of us. "Don't forget my teaching
. . . Trust Me . . . Let love and faithfulness fill your life . . .
Don't try to go it on your own . . . Let Me lead you straight
through life . . . Honor Me with your earnings first and I will
bless you. Let Me teach you and discipline you, for I love and
delight in you . . . . Let Me fill you with My wisdom and you
will have a treasure beyond compare." Are we listening?

We seek You, dear Father, with all that we are, we want to follow Your
commands. In the name of Christ, our Savior, we pray. Amen.

August 1-4. **Pam Coffey** is a minister's wife and mother. She lives in Arcadia, Indiana.

Hold On And Look Up

For the LORD will be your confidence and will keep your foot from being snared (Proverbs 3:26, *New International Version*).

Scripture: Proverbs 3:21-26
Song: "Higher Ground"

The novice rock climber nervously put on his helmet and gave a final check to his gear. "Ready to climb!" he shouted.

"Climb on!" echoed the reply.

He began his ascent. The first few steps were somewhat easy. "This isn't too bad," he thought. But as he climbed past his comfort zone, his foot started to shake a little. He stopped, breathed deeply, then went for another step. Feeling for a good handhold, he lifted himself up, but as he stepped up, rocks gave way and his whitened knuckles dug in with the weight of his dangling feet. "I can't do this!" he shouted.

"Yes, you can! You are doing great! Come on! You can do this. Hang on!"

As we are climbing in life, the wisdom God gives us is like footholds that carry us upwards. Some steps may be sure. At other times, we may feel like the very foundation beneath us is giving way. We may cry out in desperation, "I can't do this!" But the One who has gone before us is reaching down with open arms saying, "Come on! You're doing great!" He will lift us up to His powerful presence so that we, too, might taste the thrill of victory, and rest in His presence. Is your foot shaky today? Hold on! Look up! Trust God.

Mighty and everlasting Father, we have chosen Your precepts. We long for Your salvation, O Lord, let us live that we may praise You, and may Your laws sustain us. Help us to be like Jesus, in whose name we pray. Amen.

Direction for Life's Maze

I guide you in the way of wisdom and lead you along straight paths. When you walk, your steps will not be hampered; when you run, you will not stumble (Proverbs 4:11-12, *New International Version*).

Scripture: Proverbs 4:10-17
Song: "O Master, Let Me Walk with Thee"

In past years, our youth group has enjoyed going through a life-size human maze. We all started with confidence thinking, "It won't be hard to make it to the end. No problem!" But then choices appeared and they all looked good. We chose the one we thought was the best and found ourselves at a dead end. Then we had to backtrack and try the less obvious choice.

Sometimes we would run into a small crowd of people who had found themselves off track, but because "misery loves company" they would talk others into going with them. (At least they wouldn't look foolish alone.) Peer pressure suddenly became an issue and the group became larger.

Once there was a tower in the middle of our maze climb and we stopped to take a peek. We saw a little clearer where we had been. "Go that way!" we shouted to those who were behind us. We could also see where others were running into roadblocks up ahead.

By the time we finished, we had laughed, been frustrated, had to retrace several times and had learned more about life.

There are choices in life that appear right but lead to dead ends. Until we look for wisdom from God we will wander aimlessly. Let us seek His direction through life's maze.

Your compassion is great, O Lord; we know that all Your words are true; all Your righteous laws are eternal. Great peace have they who love Your laws. Thank You for life, O God. In the name of Jesus, we pray. Amen.

More Precious Than Gold

Choose my instruction instead of silver, knowledge rather than choice gold, for wisdom is more precious than rubies, and nothing you desire can compare with her (Proverbs 8:10-11, *New International Version*).

Scripture: Proverbs 8:1-12
Song: "Lord, You Are More Precious Than Sliver"

Proverbs encourages us to choose wisdom over silver and gold. That's quite a paradox to the cries of the world that entice us to gain more and more possessions.

The truth is that God's wisdom is a treasure. When we tap into God's wisdom, we have access to something that the rest of the world does not have.

Take time to read 1 Corinthians 2 as Paul describes to Christians the wisdom that can be obtained from the Spirit—wisdom straight from Heaven and beyond the thoughts of mortal men. Through the blood of Jesus Christ, we can now go boldly before the Father. The Holy Spirit interprets our cries and teaches us more personally about His ways. Through God's Word, the salvation we have in Christ Jesus, and the help of the Holy Spirit, we have understanding beyond what the world's wisest men appear to have. God has given us a gift and we need to gratefully accept it and use it for His glory!

Are you wiser now than you were a week ago? Then thank God. He is teaching you His ways. May His wisdom and glory be reflected in our lives as we prepare to meet Him in eternity!

Lord, Your statues are wonderful; therefore I obey them. The entrance of Your Word gives light; it gives understanding to the simple. You are my refuge and my shield; and I have put my hope in Your Word. Make Your face shine upon Your servant and teach me Your decrees (see Psalm 119:129, 130, 114, 135, *New International Version*). Amen.

Just Say No

My son, if sinners entice thee, consent thou not (Proverbs 1:10).

Scripture: Proverbs 1:8-19
Song: "I Have Decided to Follow Jesus"

We have all seen the ads with the admonition to "just say no." I'm pretty good at saying no—at first. But as the enticement grows, I often weaken.

I feel bad about myself when I do that (obviously, not bad enough!) but imagine how Peter felt when the cock crowed. He had assured Jesus that he would never deny him. Peter felt that he would always be able to "just say no" to the temptation of denying his Lord. But he was enticed, and found he wasn't strong enough to say "no" to temptation.

"Just say no" is simple, straightforward advice on one hand, but difficult, and sometimes complicated, to follow.

Do you remember what Scripture tells us happened after Jesus said "no" to Satan's three temptations? Apparently, that was not the end of the lure to yield to temptation placed in Jesus' path. Luke's account in Chapter 4 of his Gospel concludes the temptation story with a chilling comment that the devil then left Jesus for a season.

When we have said "no" to Satan, he only leaves us for a season, waiting for a better opportunity to snare us. We have to "just say no" and keep on saying it.

Dear **Lord,** help us to "keep on keeping on" saying "no" to Satan's temptations. Help us to learn not to place ourselves in positions that will make it easy for unbelievers and other's to entice us to disobey You. In Jesus' holy name, we pray. Amen.

August 5-11. **Wanda Trawick** is a Christian writer living in Audubon, Pennsylvania.

Close My Mouth; Open My Ears

The wise in heart accept commands, but a chattering fool comes to ruin
(Proverbs 10:8, *New International Version*).

Scripture: Proverbs 10:1-12
Song: "Open My Eyes, That I May See"

My grandson came home from the ice rink with a frown on his face. He had been assigned to help a young girl in the "Learn to Skate" class.

"She says she really wants to be good at it," he complained, "but all she does is talk during the whole lesson. She never stops to listen to what I'm trying to tell her."

We thought perhaps his inexperience with coaching might be the problem, but he claimed she did the same thing with the head coach.

Maybe the child just talked too much because she was nervous and unsure of herself. Or maybe she didn't really want to hear the instructions because, if she heard them, she would be expected to follow them and risk failure and embarrassment. Maybe she had watched skaters and thought she already knew all about it. Whatever the reason, her ears were closed to instruction, and she never learned to skate.

There are many reasons that some of us talk too much, but the bottom line is—we can't talk and listen at the same time. We can learn from others if we listen long enough. We can learn from God if we take time and effort to listen to Him as well as talk to Him in prayer.

Lord, those of us who read Your Word and pray regularly sometimes think we know it all. Help us to open our ears to what You have to say to us—through Your Word, through prayer, and through others. In Jesus' holy name, we pray. Amen.

Feeding The Hungry

The lips of the righteous feed many: but fools die for want of wisdom
(Proverbs 10:21).

Scripture: Proverbs 10:13- 25
Song: "Lord, I Want to Be a Christian"

When she talked about the poor and hungry, Mother Teresa of India used to say that people were hungry for more than food and shelter. She insisted that everyone wants to feel that they matter to somebody.

Look at today's verse again. The hunger the writer speaks of is received by "the lips of the righteous." We can nourish others by our words and actions.

Have you met those who seem to hunger for significance and yearn for knowledge? Have your lips nourished them? Do you encounter daily those who desperately need encouragement? Do they receive it from your lips?

How do we go about "feeding the hungry" in this sense. First, by introducing them to Jesus, who found us all significant enough to die for us and who offers encouragement and the attainment of wisdom through the Holy Spirit and the Scriptures.

We who have attained righteousness bear a responsibility to provide for those who hunger for righteousness, significance, and wisdom. The very qualities are demonstrated by the words we say and the actions we do.

Dear Lord, help us overcome our reluctance to openly share You with others. Give us discernment to recognize those who hunger to be loved, to feel significant to someone. Give us courage to be Your spokespersons. In Jesus' holy name, we pray. Amen.

Am I Guaranteed Long Life?

The fear of the LORD adds length to life, but the years of the wicked are cut short (Proverbs 10:27, *New International Version*).

Scripture: Proverbs 10:27-32
Song: "He Hideth My Soul"

My sister and I had a Paul-Timothy relationship. She played Paul to my Timothy. She was a committed Christian who strove to do God's will. She died of breast cancer at the age of forty-six. Later, I contracted the same disease. I am now twenty years older than my sister was when she died. Why she died and I didn't has always been a mystery to me. So it troubles me when I read a verse like the one for today. Many wicked people live and prosper to a ripe old age. Many good people die young.

Victor Frank, a Jewish psychiatrist who lived through the holocaust in a concentration camp, claimed that those who survived were not necessarily good people—that the good were "the first to go." Think of examples of people in Scripture who died young because they were good—Abel, Uriah, Naboth, John the Baptist, and, of course, Jesus.

Should we regard this verse as a guarantee to a long life, or should we regard it as a "rule of thumb" statement regarding those who "fear the Lord" and thus avoid destructive habits and cultivate healthy ones, which, in turn, lead to a long life? This is the kind of verse that drives me to pray earnestly for trust and discernment.

Lord, we don't always understand what goes on in this world, and we don't always understand the meaning of Your written Word. But we trust You, and we say with the psalmist, "My times are in Your hand" (see Psalms 31:15). In the name of Jesus Christ, the Savior of the world, we pray. Amen.

Deceiving Myself

The integrity of the upright guides them, but the unfaithful are destroyed by their duplicity (Proverbs 11:3, *New International Version*).

Scripture: Proverbs 11:1-8
Song: "Jesus, I Come"

I was only eight years old, but I remember it well. I stomped around my bedroom, crying and saying that I was innocent and I was being mistreated. In the midst of my histrionics, the truth hit me like a punch from my little brother. I had done something I was told not to do and then lied about it. I was neither innocent nor mistreated—just foolish and lacking in integrity.

Many years later I had an agnostic roommate who told me in no uncertain terms that she did not believe in Heaven, but just in case there is one, she fully expected to be there. I lost track of her a few years later but have often wondered if she ever realized the foolishness of that statement. She was deceiving herself as much as I was at the tender age of eight.

We always fool ourselves when we try to justify ourselves rather than face the truth. We may fool others and ourselves, but we can never fool God. Maybe it was good for an eight-year-old to discover she couldn't fool her mother. It helped prepare me for the sometimes-daunting task of being truthful to God, even though I am often tempted to try to justify my words and actions.

Dear Lord and Father of all mankind, develop in us the integrity the writer of Proverbs talks about. When we try to deceive ourselves, place the truth squarely in front of us, no matter how painful it might seem at the time. Teach us Your ways, O Lord, God. We pray this prayer in the name of Jesus, our Lord and Savior. Amen.

Looking Beneath the Cherry

All a man's ways seem innocent to him, but motives are weighed by the LORD
(Proverbs 16:2, *New International Version*).

Scripture: Proverbs 16:1-9
Song: "Breathe on Me, Breath of God"

Exhausted, hungry, and thirsty, my grandson came off the ice rink and headed for the snack bar. Out of the array of salads, puddings and sandwiches, he chose a pudding with a cherry on top. Back at the table, he flourished the cherry in front of us and ate it with relish. But when he tasted the first bite of pudding, his expression changed from delight to disgust. "It's horrible!" he croaked

His Dad grinned. "And what have you learned from this?" The boy hung his head and muttered, "Don't judge a pudding by the cherry on top!"

But that is how we all tend to evaluate things, isn't it? If it is attractive, we think it must be okay—which explains why beautiful people get away with things a homely person could not. God, on the other hand, is never misled by the "cherry on top." He goes by my grandmother's admonition: "the proof is *in* the pudding!"

What we think, do, and say may look and sound good, but God looks beneath those surface things. In so doing, He reveals the frequent impurities in my motives that I keep myself unaware of. Maybe that is why we are told not to judge others. We cannot see beneath the cherry as God does.

Dear Lord, help us to understand and appreciate the fact that we can't fool You by "sugar coating" our words and actions. Give us the wisdom not to be fooled by the words and actions of those whose unseen motives are to fool and manipulate us. In the name of Christ, we pray. Amen.

Avoiding "Greener Pastures"

Be not thou envious against evil men, neither desire to be with them
(Proverbs 24:1).

Scripture: Proverbs 24:1-9
Song: "Near to the Heart of God"

We used to have horses. Once they had devoured the grass in our limited pasture, they would begin to eye the neighbor's lush pasture. Only a barbed wire fence separated the two fields. You can imagine how often we had to repair both the fence and the barbed wire injuries on our wayward horses!

In the spring, when there was plenty of grass in our own field, they preferred the familiar. But when summer came, and they had eaten down the good grass, they grew dissatisfied with their own pasture and looked for another.

Isn't that the secret to saying "no" to those who tempt us to enter what looks to be a "greener pasture"—having something we would rather say "yes" to? Something we love so much that we do not feel envious of others? The love of Christ "constrains" us, as Scripture says. When we say "yes" to Him, we automatically say "no" to things that would displease Him. The secret is having our heart's desire keyed on Jesus.

Let us begin this week by "just saying no." To keep on saying "no," I have to want to say "yes" to something more important to me—something more valuable. Following Christ is our priority, and to keep that as our priority, we have to love Him more than the "greener pastures" that might lure us.

Father, Your Son has shown us the way to go. Your love expressed through Him nourishes us in ways that nothing else can match. Thank You for green pastures, and keep us sensible enough and faithful enough to stay near You and enjoy what You give us. In Jesus' holy name, we pray. Amen.

The Troublemaker

A man who lacks judgment derides his neighbor, but a man of understanding holds his tongue (Proverbs 11: 12, *New International Version*).

Scripture: Proverbs 11:9-14
Song: "Take My Life and Let It Be"

The headlines on the front page of the morning paper in Phoenix read, "Four Minutes of Terror." It seems that a sixty-one-year-old angry man entered the club house of Vantano Lakes Resort where there was a home owners meeting in progress and did the unthinkable—leaving every man's life changed and many families grieving the terrible deed.

It seems that he had been an angry man for a long time. His wife had left him and moved to California because she could no longer take his angry tirades. He had managed to offend all his neighbors with abusive language. He 'had it in for' the Home Owners Association and would not abide by any of the rules and restrictions that were imposed by them. The anger that this man had kept in his heart all this time turned to rage and exploded in the clubhouse that day.

Jesus warned us all that it was what comes out of a person's mouth that makes him/her unclean, not the food he eats. James said: "If anyone is never at fault in what he says, he is a perfect man, able to keep his whole body in check . . ." (see James 3:2*)*.

Almighty God, help us to have the courage to look within and see whatever needs to be cleansed so that our thoughts and our words will bring only honor to You, our Lord. Give us courage to stand for what is right in Your sight. In the name of Jesus Christ, our Savior and Lord, we pray. Amen.

August 12-18. **Don Cox** is Pastor/Counselor at Central Christian Church in Mesa, Arizona, where he has served since his retirement from the Christian Church in Beaverton, Oregon.

Watch Your Words

Reckless words pierce like a sword, but the tongue of the wise brings healing
(Proverbs 12:18, *New International Version*).

Scripture: Proverbs 12:13-22
Song: "Search Me, O God"

The Vatican, in the pope's first Easter message of the new millennium, "offered wishes of peace in 61 different languages. He called on the world to end racism and xenophobia." If you are like me you may need to look up that last word. It means "hatred of foreigners." This probably related to the rather long journey that the Pope made through several countries offering apologies for the past behavior of the organized church in history and seeking forgiveness of those who had been offended.

How many languages does God speak? I don't know. But I am certain that in every language God says, "I love you." There are certain times and places that God may use your voice to speak those life changing words . . . "God loves you."

I spend much of my time in personal counseling. Some of it is with husbands and wives who are having difficulty communicating with each other. I recall one couple who was obviously very angry with one another. I encouraged them to listen to the words they were saying to each other.

Often family members say mean and hurtful words to one another. It is then that I suggest that they treat each other as they treat their friends. Kindness and love must be expressed to family members as well as to friends.

Dear Lord and Father of mankind, help us to guard our words and actions. Help us all to express Your love and kindness to family and friends alike. In Jesus' holy name, we pray. Amen.

Words That Make You Smile

A cheerful look brings joy to the heart, and good news gives health to the bones (Proverbs 15:30, *New International Version*).

Scripture: Proverbs 15:12-14, 23-30
Song: "Joy to the World!"

It was years ago, but it is still a vivid memory. It had to do with Vacation Bible School in my home church. It may have been the opening event of the two weeks of Vacation Bible School or the closing program. But I do remember that we all stood and sang—

"Smile, Smile, Everyone Smile"

"Show you are happy by wearing a smile,
Smiles are from Heaven and worketh like leaven.
So . . . help win the world with a smile."

Once I saw an artist portrayal of Jesus in a video. It was the text from the book of Matthew . . . word for word. But what really caught my attention was the smiling face of Jesus. It was as if He knew something wonderful and was about to let us in on it. The genuine smile touched me. In the midst of a storm, Jesus comes to His disciples walking on the water. He tells Peter to come to Him on the water. Peter takes a few steps before he begins to sink. As Jesus lifts him up He says to Peter, "You of little faith, why did you doubt?" Jesus and Peter, both wringing wet from the storm, embrace, and Jesus smiles as He embraces him. That's the real Jesus, smiling the smile of God even in the midst of a storm.

Dear heavenly Father, help us to express the happiness that we know comes only from You. Let us be examples of Your kindness and compassion to the world. In the name of Jesus, our Savior, we pray. Amen.

On Being a Wise Man

A wise man's heart guides his mouth, and his lips promote instruction
(Proverbs 16:23, *New International Version*),

Scripture: Proverbs 16:21-29
Song: "Wonderful Words of Life"

There are some words that we enjoy hearing again and again. They are helpful words, words that lift us up and give encouragement. There are words that bring a smile. There are words that bring tears and words that stir up anger within us.

Jesus spoke a few words, and a storm was stilled . . . eyes that were blind could see . . . lame began to walk . . . lepers were made clean . . . a dead child was given back to a grieving parent . . . sin was forgiven . . . hope was given . . . and peace was realized . . . just because Jesus spoke a word.

The words that we speak have more power than we realize. Just one word spoken by a parent may always be remembered forever by a child. Kind words will teach a child to love and hateful words will teach a child to hate. May we always remember that encouraging words spoken at the right moment can change a life in the right way. It has been said that Winston Churchill turned the tide of World War II and saved England by his words.

The Centurion's servant was paralyzed in much pain. The Centurion came to Jesus and asked for help. Jesus offered to go with him to see the servant, but the centurion said he didn't need to go. "Just say the word, and my servant will be healed" (see Matthew 8:8).

Dear Father, teach us all to say, "May the words of my mouth, and the meditations of my heart be acceptable unto You, my Lord and my God." In the name of Jesus, the Savior of the world, we pray. Amen.

When You Need A Friend

A friend loves at all times, and a brother is born for adversity
(Proverbs 17:17, *New International Version*).

Scripture: Proverbs 17:14-20
Song: "What a Friend We Have in Jesus"

It has been rightly said that to have a friend you must be a friend. Over the years I have been especially blessed to have some wonderful friends, and I thank God for them.

We may ask, "What is a friend?" I believe that a friend is one who is available. He is there night or day, whether it is convenient or not. He is believable . . . you can trust him. You can trust him with your life and your reputation. He is caring. He will listen with a discerning ear. He shares your pain, he is dependable. You can count on him . . . He'll be there if at all possible. He is effective, he will do something . . . whatever is needed he will do it. He is faithful. He will hang around and be there as long as needed.

That describes the kind of friend you need. Does that also define the kind of friend you are to Jesus? The ultimate Friend, said: I have called you friends, for everything that I have learned from my Father, I have made known to you" (John 15:15, *New International Version*).

Friendship is initiated and perpetuated by effective communication on the part of both. Friends talk. Friends listen. Friends know each other. Jesus seeks our friendship. Do we seek His? Friendship is truly a path we journey together.

Dear Lord, we know that praying is both talking and listening to You. We talk to You, dear Father, but how well do we listen? Help us to learn to communicate with You in such a way that we feel Your presence among us at all times. In the name of Jesus Christ, our Savior, we pray. Amen.

Savor Your Words Carefully

From the fruit of his mouth a man's stomach is filled; with the harvest from his lips he is satisfied (Proverbs. 18:20, *New International Version*).

Scripture: Proverbs 18:6-8, 19-21
Song: "Into My Heart"

Have you ever said anything you wished you hadn't said? If only you could take back those words which spilled out of your mouth. But it is too late.

The Pharisees came to Jesus and asked why His disciples disobeyed the traditions. He said to them, "Listen and understand. What goes into a man's mouth does not make him 'unclean,' but what comes out of his mouth, that is what makes him 'unclean'" (see Matthew 15:10, 11).

"Look before you leap" is an old wise saying that we have all heard on several occasions. An even wiser saying is "Think before you speak." Someone said, "engage your mind before you put your tongue in gear."

I have had the privilege of being a counselor for several years. It is important to be a good and patient listener. Someone called it, "Listening with the third ear." You listen to the words, but also, it is what is 'beneath' the words, what is in the soul that makes one tick.

You are looking for the truth. Only truth can set one free. As you carefully listen to the one who has sought your counsel he will reveal to you what are his/her deepest needs.

Almighty God and Father of all, You alone can help us to be pure in mind and spirit. Teach each of us to speak words of love and compassion to all of those around us. Help us to have a pure heart and mind so that only pure words and kindness may come forth from our lips. May nothing we say defile us. In the name of Jesus Christ, we pray. Amen.

There Is a Time to Be Silent

Do not say, "'I'll pay you back for this wrong!'" Wait for the Lord, and he will deliver you (Proverbs 20:22, *New International Version*).

Scripture: Proverbs 20:15-22
Song: "Take Time to Be Holy"

There is a wonderful passage in the 40th chapter of Isaiah in which he seems to be defending God. "How can you say the Lord doesn't see your troubles and isn't being fair? Don't you yet understand? Don't you know by now that the everlasting God, the Creator of the farthest parts of the earth, never grows faint or weary?" No one can fathom the depths of his understanding." "They that wait on the Lord shall renew their strength. They shall mount up with wings like eagles, they shall run and not be weary; they shall walk and not faint" (see Isaiah 40:27-31, *Living Bible*).

We are reminded that it was "in the fullness of time." He came at just the right time. Waiting, in this sense, is not simply doing nothing or being lazy. It is being absolutely certain that, though I can not put my finger on it, God is busy at this very moment accomplishing His ultimate will for all of us . . . and also looking after us. How can I be sure of this? God is faithful and keeps His promises. Paul poses a mighty question: "He who did not spare his own Son, but gave him up for us all—how will he not also, along with him, graciously give us all things?" (See Romans 8:32). God can be trusted to do what needs to be done!

O **God and everlasting Father**, we know that You can be trusted to always be right. You are the perfect one true and living God. In You we can put our trust. And only in You do we find the fullness of life. Our prayers this day are in the name of Jesus, our Lord and Savior. Amen.

Poor And Pleasing God

Better is the poor that walketh in his integrity, than he that is perverse in his lips, and is a fool (Proverbs 19:1).

Scripture: Proverbs 19:1-8
Song: " 'Tis So Sweet to Trust in Jesus."

Danny is a single young adult who strives to live for God. He always puts God first, even when His coworkers laugh at him. When his bills come due, he often has a difficult time paying them on time. His promotion at the office is long overdue, and yet he remains faithful to his belief that God will help him find a way to pay what he must pay. He is also aware that others who do not always follow the rules are being promoted. Many times being a Christian doesn't seem worth the effort, but Danny decides to follow Jesus.

The writer of Proverbs teaches us that an honest worker who is poor is better than a rich person who is dishonest before God. It is easy to be like everyone else, especially when we have a really good excuse like, "God knows I need the money." When we see corruption all around us, it is easy to justify our actions when we do the wrong thing, sometimes even to reward ourselves for our own faithfulness! This breaks the heart of God. We have to choose to please God and trust Him even when we are poor.

Almighty God and heavenly Father, teach us to worship and please You both in the good times and the bad times of our lives—especially when we are in need. When we fall short of money help us to believe that You are still our guide and heavenly source of provision. In the name of Jesus Christ, the Savior of the world, we pray. Amen.

August 19-25. **Dr. A. Koshy Muthalaly** is on the faculty at Southern Nazarene University, in Bethany, Oklahoma, in the department of Adult Studies.

He Is on the Side of The Poor

Rob not the poor, . . . for the LORD will plead their cause, and spoil the soul of those that spoiled them (Proverbs 22:22, 23).

Scripture: Proverbs 22:7-9, 16, 22, 23
Song: "When the Church of Jesus"

Mother Teresa spent most of her life working in the busy, crowded city of Calcutta, India. Teeming with people rushing to and fro, its streets are busy with the hum of daily activity. Amidst the crowded streets are the rich and the poor, all blended into the stream of society, each unaware and unconcerned for the other.

What strikes a visitor most about the city of Calcutta is the sense of religiosity displayed everywhere. In contrast, one cannot miss the large numbers of poor and dying on the streets. Often they have no one to care for them. They live from day to day, scavenging for their food, and are often exploited for cheap labor.

The book of Proverbs reminds us today that even though the poor are left unnoticed by their fellow men, God cares for them. He pleads their case and takes their side. He loves them, and they are special in His sight.

The Lord encourages us to know that He is our advocate and stands with us today. We are not forgotten in His mind. Each one of us is special in His eyes and as we trust Him, He shows us a way out of our need. When we call upon our Savior, Jesus Christ, to guide us and to fulfill our needs, we can see His presence at work in us.

Lord Jesus, we thank You for Your blessings on our lives. Help us to remember that You love the poor and we are to help care for them as You have cared for us. In Jesus' holy name, we pray. Amen.

God Blesses Those Who Help the Poor

He that giveth unto the poor shall not lack. (Proverbs 28:27a).

Scripture: Proverbs 28:20-27
Song: "Make Me a Blessing"

Old Mr. Welder was a farmer who had worked hard all of his life, and God had blessed his labors. He grew to be very wealthy. His farm had expanded as he had the funds to purchase more land. He even moved into a bigger home. But soon he forgot his very humble beginnings. He also ignored those who had helped him along the way. He was aware of the needs of several people in his church but turned a deaf ear to their situations, saying that they were just lazy and out to take advantage of hard working people like him.

What a sad state of affairs it is when we forget that it is God in His mercy who has brought us thus far. We can thank Him by responding in gratitude to the needs we see around us.

Jesus told His disciples once that they would always have the poor with them! If we keep our eyes and ears open, there is always someone near by who has a bigger need than we do. Christ has given us the opportunity to show His love to the world by helping the poor and helpless of this world.

Our text for today encourages us to bless others with the blessings that God has given us. Ultimately all blessings come from God alone. Shouldn't we share them?

All knowing God and Father of all, You have brought us a long way. Help us not to forget that we all have been in need in some way in our lives. May we recognize Your hand of blessing upon us. Teach us to share what we have been given with those who are less fortunate. In the name of our blessed Savior, Jesus Christ, we pray. Amen.

Give The Poor Their Rights

Open thy mouth, judge righteously, and plead the cause of the poor and needy (Proverbs 31:9).

Scripture: Proverbs 31:4-9
Song: "My Faith Looks Up to Thee"

Janice was in trouble, big trouble. She had forgotten to read the small print before she signed the contract, and now she had violated some of the terms unknowingly. She was nervous and afraid, especially of the financial consequences. She shared her fears with a friend of hers at work. Her friend agreed to talk with a lawyer friend who could advise her on the course of action that she should take.

The very next morning Janice had an appointment with the lawyer who was willing to straighten things out for her and to relieve her of a lot of anxiety. His expertise was exactly what she needed. More than that, she needed a friend to guide her to someone who would defend her in her helplessness.

In our text for today, we are encouraged to defend the rights of the poor. If God takes the side of the poor and defends them, shouldn't we be on God's side? He has given us the opportunity to help Him show compassion and love to the world. The passage tells us that even the poor have a right to justice, and we are to give it to them. In other words, we are not to take advantage of them just because they are poor. In Scripture, our God is often portrayed as our Advocate, the One who speaks on our behalf.

Almighty Father, when we find ourselves in a position to defend someone who is less fortunate than we are, give us the courage to do so. We want to be on Your side. In Jesus' precious name, we pray. Amen.

Do Not Withhold Good

Withhold not good . . . when it is in the power of thine hand to do it
(Proverbs 3:27).

Scripture: Proverbs 3:27-35
Song: "Jesu, Jesu, Fill Us with Your Love"

My homeland is a land where there are millions of poor people. They live their whole lives on the streets in poverty not thinking of tomorrow but just trying to survive today.

It is very easy for us who have more material things and money to buy food and clothes and a home to keep us out of the weather, to close our eyes to the needs of the poor. As Christians, we certainly must try to do what we can to help. It is often easy to excuse ourselves by saying that there are too many poor people in the world and we cannot do anything substantial to help. However, to relieve the hunger of one poor person is within the realm of possibility.

Hunger is something that knows no national or ethnic boundaries. It is universal, something that affects all human beings alike. We may not be able to feed the millions around us, but we can certainly take care of the hunger of one single person who happens to come to our door and ask for food. This is definitely something that can be done!

Our text today reminds us that when we have the power to do something good, we ought to be doing it. After all, tomorrow, you or I may be that person in need.

All knowing and everlasting God and Father of all mankind, keep us from being so wrapped up in ourselves and our wants that we forget others in need. Help us to count our blessings and share them with those who do not have enough to meet their daily needs. Keep our hearts sensitive to those around us. In Jesus' holy name, we pray. Amen.

God Blesses The Generous Heart

The liberal soul shall be made fat: and he that watereth shall be watered also himself (Proverbs 11:25).

Scripture: Proverbs 11:17, 18, 24-28
Song: "What Gift"

Bob is a factory worker. He works long hours and earns good wages. He came from small beginnings and has never forgotten how the Lord has blessed him. He thanks God daily for the opportunity for hard work and for the blessings that he enjoys because God gives him the blessing of work.

Bob is a very active Christian in his church community. He teaches Sunday school and loves the Lord dearly. He wants to see others love the Lord and His Word as much as he does. He wants to see others live godly lives in the community. He wants to let the world know that Christ is Lord of all.

Bob has a secret gift. He has a generous heart. Recognizing how God has used many people to bless him, he is very sensitive to the needs of others. He reaches out to his neighbors and church members alike and helps them. Sometimes he shovels the sidewalk for all the neighbors on his block! Many of them are senior citizens. They are grateful. He reaches out financially when he senses a genuine need. No one knows except the people whom he helps and the Lord. It is a silent commitment he has made to God in gratitude for what he has received. It is really no wonder that the Lord has blessed Bob and his family.

Father, help us all to remember that we wouldn't enjoy the blessings we have except for Your loving hand on our lives. Teach us to bless others with the same blessings we have received. Let others see Jesus through us today. In the name of Jesus, our Savior, we pray. Amen.

Happiness is Showing Kindness to the Poor

But he that hath mercy on the poor, happy is he (Proverbs 14:21b)

Scripture: Proverbs 14:20-22, 31-34
Song: "O Love That Will Not Let Me Go"

The face I saw haunted me. It was the smiling face of a little child. The child was being carried by her older sister—only three or four years older than she was. It was obvious that they had not eaten in days. Her tears had washed a little rivulet down her dirty, unwashed cheeks. Her eyes caught mine, and she smiled at me through her bony face. That smile gripped me, even though I was standing across the street.

I had just purchased a hamburger for lunch. But I couldn't eat without doing something first. I walked over and handed her the burger. She was grateful. She shared it with her sister. They smiled back at me. I walked away realizing how little it took to make another so happy. I wondered why she was poor and I rich. Her world was so different from mine.

In the blessings that God has given, He wants us to share those blessings with His creation who do not have what He has entrusted to us today.

God is faithful and we are called to show the same mercies to those who are poor around us. I went home happy the day I gave to those two small children. It had cost me so little to be merciful. God calls us to do just that!

Heavenly Father, open our eyes to those who need help today. They are all around us. Often it costs so little to share. Help us to care so that we can bless another life in some way. Help us to be merciful and kind. In Jesus' holy name, we pray. Amen.

Hark! The New King Calls

For the LORD hath chosen you to stand before him, to serve him, and that ye should minister unto him (2 Chronicles 29:11).

Scripture: 2 Chronicles 29:1-11
Song "Yield Not to Temptation"

The new king calls for a restoration of God's work guided by God's Word. This is the emphasis for this week. Verse 11 is the new 25-year-old king's call to Judah.

Our thoughts this week will be based on the New Living Bible Translation. Hezekiah was a good king. He served Judah for 29 years and was pleasing in the Lord's sight. He serves as a good example for Bible readers in America and around the world today.

Commitment and dedication to God's Word is refreshing anytime and any place. As we read more of the Bible text this week we will sense the joy in the hearts of God's followers, and we will be challenged to go and do likewise. The old hymn "Yield Not to Temptation" touches the need in Judah and challenges us today.

"My dear Levites, do not neglect your duties any longer! The Lord has chosen you to stand in His presence to minister to Him, in worship, and make offerings to Him" (verse 11).

Our **Father in Heaven**, we thank You for the good King Hezekiah and for Your service through him. Help us to keep this close contact with You today. We thank You for Christ, the life and source of eternal life for us. We thank You that the death of Christ on the cross led to victory over death. We thank You, Father, for Your abundant provisions for all of our needs. Help us always to wisely follow Christ. In His name, we pray. Amen

---

August 26-31. **Bill and Claudia McGilvrey** have ministered to churches in Virginia, Tennessee, North Carolina, and Illinois. They have five children, sixteen grandchildren, and two great-grandchildren.

The Temple Restored

Let the word of Christ dwell in you richly in all wisdom; teaching and admonishing one another in psalms and hymns and spiritual songs, singing with grace in your hearts to the Lord (Colossians 3:16).

Scripture: Chronicles 29:15-24
Song: "O Worship the King"

The new king led the Levites in music of praise. The leaders obeyed the king with their instruments and voices. They were in full tune with the temple worship. Hezekiah called for the offerings at the appropriate time. The joy of sharing was given to all and thus set an example for fellow worshipers. Our hymn today is an example of our innermost feelings as we sing the following:

"Thy bountiful care what tongue can recite? It breathes in the air; it shines in the light. It streams from the hills; it descends to the plain, and sweetly distills in the dew and the rain."

When we sing praises unto the Creator, we feel His presence. We worship God and know the joy of connecting to the divine power and presence of God in Christian worship.

"Let the words of Christ in all their richness live in your hearts and make you wise. Use His words to teach and counsel each other. Sing psalms and hymns and spiritual songs to God with thankful hearts. Whatever you do or say, let it be as a representative of the Lord Jesus Christ, all the while giving thanks through Him to God, the Father" (see Colossians 3:16-17).

Great God of the Universe, we marvel at Your wisdom and guidance, Thanks for Hezekiah and Your working through him in restoring the temple. Today help Christians in an all-out effort to restore the church as described in the New Testament. We pray in Jesus' name and for His sake. Amen.

Take Your Stand

They sang praises with gladness, and they bowed their heads and worshipped
(2 Chronicles 29:30).

Scripture: 2 Chronicles 29:25-30
Song: "Jesus is All the World to Me"

King Hezekiah stationed the Levites at the temple of the Lord with cymbals, harps and lyres. He obeyed all the commands that God had given to King David, the king's seer and the prophet Nathan. Then Hezekiah ordered that a burnt offering be placed on the altar and the entire assembly worshipped the Lord. The singers sang, and the trumpets blew until the burnt offering was consumed. Then the king and everyone with him bowed down to worship and give joyous praise to the Creator of the entire universe.

The happiest days in the life of a nation or of an individual are the times when one bows down to worship God and yields to Him giving the full right of way in life here on earth. This close contact with our heavenly Father makes a true impact on every phase of life.

Let us put forth our best effort to keep in contact with God. May we honestly strive to follow Christ. We can then have the true and living relationship that honors God. We then become workers for Christ Jesus, the Savior of the world, and in so doing, help to accomplish His eternal purpose here on earth.

So let us take our stand and stand firmly as long as our earthly life shall last. We will be glad and rejoice with all of God's family eternally.

God of all Wisdom, we thank You for a brief glimpse of glory with You and Christ. Help us to take our stand and do our part well that Christ and His bride, the church, will receive honor, glory and praise forever. Amen

Praise The Lord

"Praise ye the LORD, Sing unto the LORD a new song (Psalm 149:1).

Scripture: Psalm 149:1-9
Song: "Praise God from Whom All Blessings Flow"

The Lord delights in His people when they praise and honor Him. David the shepherd boy liked to sing. Many psalms and much singing appear in the Bible. The last two chapters in the book of Psalms are about praise.

"Praise the Lord and sing to the Lord a new song. The Lord delights in His people when they praise and honor Him."

We attended the funeral of a man whose son sang "Great is Thy Faithfulness" and nailed that praise in our memories. "Great is Thy faithfulness, O God, my Father, There is no shadow of turning with Thee; Thou changest not, Thy compassions they fail not; As Thou hast been Thou forever wilt be. Pardon for sin and a peace that endureth, Thy own dear presence to cheer and to guide; Strength for today and bright hope for tomorrow, Blessings all mine, with ten thousand beside! Great is Thy faithfulness! Great is Thy faithfulness!, Morning by morning new mercies I see; All I have needed—Thy hand hath provided—Great is Thy faithfulness, Lord, unto me!" We will never be able to give all the praise that God and Christ deserve for all His care and redemption at Calvary.

Faithful Father in Heaven, we marvel again and again at Your faithfulness! We try to understand Your wisdom recorded in the Bible. We yield to Your authority. We face the future with trust and confidence in Christ, all because of Calvary and the empty tomb. We pray in the name of Jesus Christ, our Lord and Savior. Amen.

It Can Be Done

So the Temple of the Lord was restored to service. And Hezekiah and all the people rejoiced greatly because of what God had done for the people, for everything had been accomplished so quickly (2 Chronicles 29:35-36, *New Living Translation*).

Scripture: 2 Chronicles 29:31-36
Song: "Work for the Night is Coming"

This section of Scripture with the sacrifices and offerings to the Lord is a picture of what God wanted from His people. The priests and the Levites were very busy with all this activity, and the Bible text summarizes it in these words—"so the temple of the Lord was restored to service" (*New Living Translation*).

This Bible story reminds me of the life of Thomas Campbell that extended through his son, Alexander Campbell. These men, along with many others, were involved in what became known as the Restoration Movement.

The *Christian Standard* and *The Lookout* have published special issues explaining the continuing effort to restore the church as it was during the first century—the New Testament times. Christians throughout history have given their lives to teach the work of the church as Christ taught.

Many Christians strive to worship and praise God today as the first century Christians did. When we stand together to worship the one true and living God, we see the strength in unity. Hezekiah is a real example of what can be done.

Almighty and everlasting Creator and God of our fathers, when we see and understand how Christians in other times have worshipped You, we marvel and sense the challenge to serve You. Help us to understand and do all that we can today for Christ and His church. In Jesus' holy name, we pray. Amen.·

Come, Celebrate!

"O people of Israel, return to the Lord, the God of Abraham, Isaac & Israel; so that He will return to the few of us who have survived the conquest of the Assyrian kings." (2 Chronicles 30:6, *New Living Translation*).

Scripture: 2 Chronicles 30:1-12
Song: "When I Survey the Wondrous Cross"

The king now sent an invitation to all Israel and Judah to come to Jerusalem and celebrate the Passover and the Festival of Unleavened Bread. Most of the people laughed and made fun of the messengers.

However, some humbled themselves and accepted the invitation. Evidently second thoughts guided those who laughed, and they decided to go to Jerusalem. We do well to think things over, to gain all views, which will help in keeping things in proper balance. The king was trying to help the people. The result was God's glory and honor.

Please note verse 13. "And so a huge crowd assembled at Jerusalem in midspring to celebrate Passover and the Festival of Unleavened Bread."

Today we need to be reminded to humble ourselves to do what our Lord Jesus Christ has asked us to do. Let us remember to observe the Lord's Supper on the first day of the week so that we will never forget that the Lamb of God died for us on Calvary's cross. Let us be reminded that He died that we might have eternal life. This is the center of Christian worship.

Forgiving Father in Heaven, we thank You for Your Word revealed to us in the Bible. Help us to share what we learn that more people will glorify and honor You. Thank You for the rich fellowship we share with other Christians worldwide. We ask in Jesus' holy name. Amen.

Devotions

September

photo by Chuck Perry

September 1

Great Joy In the City

"Then the Levitical Priests stood and blessed the people, and God heard them from His holy dwelling in Heaven"! (2 Chronicles 30: 27, *New Living Translation*).

Scripture: 2 Chronicles 30:21-17
Song: "Joyful, Joyful, We Adore Thee"

Having full assurance of God's response completes the circle. Our Bible text today gives emphasis for the second real reason for worship—sacrifices and offerings. Yes, the people doubled their week of worship. The king responded with generous gifts— 1,000 bulls and 7,000 sheep for offerings. The officials donated 1,000 bulls and 10,000 sheep (vs. 26 *New Living Translation*). There was great joy in the city, for Jerusalem had not seen such a celebration since the days of Solomon, King David's son.

Then the Levitical priests stood and blessed the people. God heard them from His holy dwelling place in Heaven. God is still listening and blessing as His people joyfully present their lives, their tithes and offerings to Him.

As the Christian world spreads the Word of God and takes the plan of salvation and the words of Christ's sacrifice on the cross to the world, we serve Him.

Christians have good news to report that will bring joy not only in the city but also in the whole world. Let us share the news!

Our **Father in Heaven**, we thank You for your Word revealed to us in the Bible. Help all of us spend some time every day reading and meditating on Your Word. Help us to hide Your ways in our heart and let Your word shine through our lives. In the name of Jesus Christ our Lord, we pray. Amen.

September 1. **Bill and Claudia McGilvrey** have ministered to churches in Virginia, Tennessee, North Carolina, and Illinois. They have five children, sixteen grandchildren, and two great-grandchildren.

Where Is The World Squeezing You To Conform?

And be not conformed to this world: but be ye transformed by the renewing of your mind, that ye may prove what is that good, and acceptable, and perfect will of God (Romans 12:2).

Scripture: 2 Chronicles 33:1-6
Song: "Turn Your Eyes Upon Jesus"

Sometimes we hear these statements: "Everybody is doing it." There is "safety in numbers."

What makes us do what we do? Most of us learn our behavior from our parents or from those around us. Friends, television, and newspapers, magazines, radio, and where we go for information and entertainment can also reinforce the world's social pressures. We must choose carefully our friends and how we spend our time. "Everyone else" might be wrong. Manasseh sinned by following the nations around him instead of his father.

God holds His children to a high standard. My parents held me to a different standard than the one to which they held other people's children. I was their son, and they loved me too much to let me get away with doing wrong.

When we find ourselves under conviction, let's not make excuses. "If we confess our sins, he is faithful and just to forgive us our sins" (1 John 1:9). Let us agree with God because He alone is holy.

Oh Lord, teach me Your ways. Show me where I have conformed to the world so I may repent. Lead me in righteousness, for Your Name's sake. I want to be holy, as You are holy. Transform me by the renewing of my mind. In the name of Jesus, our Savior, we pray. Amen.

September 2-8. G. **Allen Penton** is a writer living in Lilburn, Georgia with his wife and three sons.

Transformation Through Discipline

Wash me thoroughly from mine iniquity, and cleanse me from my sin
(Psalm 51:2).

Scripture: 2 Chronicles 33:7-13
Song: "Change My Heart O God"

Manasseh was an evil man. He did everything that God told His people not to do. When we sin and disobey, God has the ability to discipline us. He chastens everyone He loves. When God disciplines us, it is because He loves us. There are other reasons for suffering besides God's discipline, but when God disciplines us for sin, we suffer.

God used the violent King of Assyria to discipline Manesseh. Not only did Manasseh lose the kingdom, but he was physically brutalized as well. The result of God's discipline was that Manasseh repented. He agreed with God about the ugliness of his own sins, and he changed his heart and behavior.

Many people have an idea of how to change other people's bad behavior. God took Manasseh to the point where he was hopeless and helpless. From that vantage point Manasseh could see God and humble himself. When we see God for who He is, and see ourselves for who we are, we become humble, and God transforms us from the inside out. Then we become new in Christ Jesus. Manasseh did not fake it. He really became a worshiper of God.

Dear Father God and Lord of all, I want to humble myself and repent. I ask You for mercy. Show me any stubborn and rebellious ways in my heart that I might repent quickly. I do not want to go into captivity to recognize my sins. Transform me today, as You will. In the name of Jesus Christ our Lord, we pray. Amen.

Echoes of Prayer

Turn ye unto me, saith the Lord of hosts, and I will turn unto you, saith the Lord of hosts (Zechariah 1:3b).

Scripture: 2 Chronicles 6:36-42
Song: "Grace that is Greater than All Our Sin"

The Children of Israel are God's chosen people. They knew the Commandments of the Lord. But knowledge of the Commandments did not give them the ability to keep them. They knew what was sin, but were powerless to abstain.

Solomon understood this about God's people. He prayed that when the people sinned and God punished their sin that they would repent and return with their whole hearts and that God would restore them. We know God answered Solomon's prayer in the life of Manasseh.

But God did not answer Solomon's prayer just once. He also answered it today. When I was taken captive by sin and was unable to escape, I turned to God. God heard and restored me and allowed me to once again fellowship with Him. One reason why I love God as I do is that His love for me is greater than my sin.

Whenever we face the consequences of our sins, whenever we are taken captive to sin, we have a Father in Heaven who loves us and is able, ready and desiring to save and redeem us. His abiding love stirs in us a desire to bring Him honor and pleasure. His willingness to forgive fills us with desire to live holy lives before Him.

Lord, help us to see areas in our lives that need to be changed. Grant to us the willingness to repent and to walk in Your ways. Without Your help and power, we are unable to obey You, Lord. Thank You for Your love and direction. In the name of Jesus, our Savior, we pray. Amen.

God Will Restore

I will restore to you the years that the locust hath eaten, the cankerworm, and the caterpillar, and the palmerworm, my great army which I sent among you (Joel 2:25).

Scripture: 2 Chronicles 7:11-16
Song: "O God, Our Help in Ages Past"

We learn in school about laws of nature. We learn what makes rain and study animal behavior. We know about sicknesses and how germs spread. However what we learn in school about these things are secondary causes. They are effects of a greater cause.

God said "if I shut up the heavens . . ." and "if I command the locust . . ." and "if I send pestilence . . ." There may be other reasons God would send drought, insects or diseases, but we see here that one reason is our sin. When we sin, God may discipline us so we will return to godliness.

God puts the responsibility on His people. "If my people . . . " brings the burden of His judgment on us who are His people. Here we see God's focus is not on unbelievers to "clean up their act," rather on us who need to humble ourselves and seek His face. It is not just sinners that need to get their lives straight. God lays the burden at the feet of His people. He asks us to "turn from our wicked ways."

There is a reward. If we, God's people, call on His name and return to His ways, He will forgive us and He will heal our land.

Lord, thank You for Your promises of restoration. You have promised to restore both our land and us. We come to You in humility. We seek Your face. We ask You to heal our land and to heal us. We believe Your Word and put our trust in You. In Jesus' mighty name, we pray. Amen.

Pleasing God

Let the words of my mouth, and the meditation of my heart, be acceptable in thy sight, O Lord, my strength, and my redeemer (Psalm 19:14).

Scripture: 2 Chronicles 33:14-20
Song: "O for a Thousand Tongues to Sing"

I cannot hold onto my sin and still worship God. I have to choose one or the other. Manasseh returned to Jerusalem, but then he had a choice to make. Would he allow the idols that had once trapped him in sin?

It is easy for me to fall back into old patterns of life. It must have been a temptation to Manasseh to do the same. He had sinned, paid the price (sin always has a price) and now was free again in his own land.

What Manasseh wanted was to worship God. He no longer wanted the distractions of the idols. They may have been pretty and possibly even exciting, but Manasseh knew the true and living God. Having tasted the sweet gift of forgiveness, he did not want to do anything that would displease God.

Even when nobody was looking, Manasseh wanted to please God, who was looking.

Let's ask these questions and see what we must do to follow the one true and living God. What are the things in life that distract us from worship of God? What is God telling us to put away? The only way to maintain freedom is to destroy anything that comes between us and the Lord and Savior.

Heavenly Father, Help us O Lord, to destroy everything in our lives that would keep us from being totally focused on You in worship and adoration. We ask You to send Your pursing fire to burn up anything that would come between You and us. May we live lives that glorify You. In Jesus' name and for His sake, we pray. Amen.

Winning by Losing

He that findeth his life shall lose it: and he that loseth his life for my sake shall find it (Matthew 10:39).

Scripture: Luke 18:9-14
Song: "I Surrender All"

One of the greatest dangers in life is to compare us with others. We can always find others who are worse than we are in actions, attitudes or lifestyles. Sometimes we will then act proud and exalted—feeling better than they are. We can also find others who lead us into condemnation, competition, and striving.

God does not grade on a curve. His standards are absolute. The Holy Spirit convicts us when we sin and calls us to repentance. Our compassionate God always forgives when we ask for His forgiveness through Jesus Christ our Lord.

God blesses the person who is humble. It matters not if others are better or worse. It is before the audience of the Almighty, Omniscient God that we live our lives. How silly we are to try to impress Him with our rationalizations and excuses for our sins.

It is only when we confess our sins and seek His mercy through Jesus Christ that we receive forgiveness. When we bow at His feet in humility, He will lift us up. We know that only in the blood of Jesus can we have our sins washed away. It is in Him that we can come to the God of all creation. Let us celebrate our victory over sin in Christ.

Lord **Jesus Christ**, Son of God, be merciful to me, a sinner. We repent of comparing ourselves to others. We repent of making excuses for our sins. We seek Your mercy. Help us to walk in Your sight all the days of our lives. For Your name's sake, we pray. Amen.

The Sorry Paths

These things write we unto you, that your joy may be full (I John 1:4).

Scripture: 2 Corinthians 7:5-13a
Song: "Amazing Grace"

The difference in types of sorrow is difficult to see. Sometimes the only way to know the type is by the results.

I remember being sorry for many things and for many reasons. I remember being sorry I got caught doing something I should not have done. That sorrow made me more deceptive. I was sorry I hurt someone else. That could change my behavior by willpower for a little while, but there was no permanent change. Satan is good at making me feel inadequate and insufficient. That sorrow leads to depression.

Sometimes God draws my heart to godly sorrow. Suddenly I become aware of His holiness and my sin. I begin to get an understanding of His great, majestic, and self-sacrificial love for me and my unworthiness. My hard heart melts. I repent and do anything to please Him who loves me so. My desire for Him allows Him to create in me a clean heart, new desire and a fresh, deeper love for Him.

Does your sorrow lead to repentance? Does it lead to a change from the inside that is manifested on the outside? Does it make you love God more? Do you worship Him more fervently and adore Him more extravagantly? Let us ask these questions and answer them honestly.

Almighty God and Father in Heaven, we repent of sorrow that was not from You. We ask You to give us godly sorrow where we need it. We seek Your direction in all things, Your forgiveness and Your holiness. We pray this because of our position in Jesus Christ, the Savior of the world. In His holy name we pray. Amen.

Hide 'n Seek

"Seek the Lord . . . Seek righteousness, seek humility. It may be that you will be hidden in the day of the Lord's anger" (*Zephaniah 2:3, New King James Version*).

Scripture: Zephaniah 1:12-2:3
Song: "Rock of Ages"

The Greeks pictured the eccentric philosopher Diogenes as walking about the streets of Athens. He carried a lantern in broad daylight. His reason? He was looking for a wise man. He found none.

Zephaniah reveals that God will walk the streets of Jerusalem with a lamp looking for men who are indifferent to His holiness. He has no trouble finding the unwise men. The city is filled with those who are convinced He will not act.

However, God will act. His holiness and His love demand action. He will bring noise, bitterness, wrath, trouble, distress, desolation, darkness, gloominess, clouds, alarm, and anger. Whew! Zephaniah, by the Spirit, pours it on.

"The great day of the Lord is near" and it will be a "day of the Lord's anger." There will be no place to hide. His lamp illuminates every nook and cranny. His eye sees around and through the densest cover. His ear can detect the racing heart of fear; the stuttered breath of anxiety He will find.

What is the alternative? Seek the Lord. That is where the wise man will be found.

God of light, laugh not at our foolish games of hiding. Our sin shames us in Your presence. By Your Spirit give us the wisdom to seek righteousness and humility. By Your grace let us find You in Your Son. Amen.

September 9-15. **Ron Davis** is a Christian writer who lives with his wife, Ruth, in North College Hill, Ohio. They have two grown daughters and two granddaughters.

Every Morning

"Every morning doth he bring his judgment to light, he faileth not; but the unjust know no shame . . . . They rose early, and corrupted all their doings" (Zephaniah 3:5, 7b).

Scripture: Zephaniah 3:1-10
Song: "Morning Has Broken"

Few things are as certain as the sun rising each morning in the east. As the earth turns to face the sun, men rise, go about their day's work, and enter into the day's relationships. Most are like Judah: they rise with evil in their pocket planners. It may as well be written in. A lie at 9:15. A lust at 9:33. A leer at 9:44. Every hour. Every quarter hour. Every minute or two. Entry after entry, until the page is blotted out with ink, dark and mean.

Nothing is as certain as God every morning is. He brings His judgment and justice with the morning light. He is totally in contrast to Judah's judges; they are "evening wolves; they gnaw not the bones till the morrow." Their wickedness rests only when they are asleep. God does not sleep. His righteousness and holiness are ever present. "He faileth not."

Every morning the world awakes to find the horrific headlines of man's sin. Murder. Greed. Adultery. Cruelty. Every morning what the world needs to hear is that God's judgment and justice are sure, that God's love and mercy and grace are as open as the arms of Christ on the cross. What better way could one start the day?

Just and righteous Lord of Heaven, grant us the patience to wait for You. Give us the pure language of Your love in Christ. May all call upon Your name; may all serve You with one consent. Thy will be done on earth as it is in Heaven. In Jesus' holy name, we pray. Amen.

A One-Voice Choir

"He will rejoice over you with gladness, He will quiet you in His love, He will rejoice over you with singing" (Zephaniah 3:17b *New King James Version*).

Scripture: Zephaniah 3:11-20
Song: "Come, Christians, Join to Sing"

Great choirs rouse and inspire God's people. From the Mormon Tabernacle Choir of Utah to the Brooklyn Tabernacle Choir of New York, few sit unmoved in the presence of glorious, harmonious choral praise.

But God's voice in song is more magnificent, more soothing. God's lullaby of love will allow His people to "feed their flocks and lie down, And no one shall make them afraid." Grand pastoral symphonies will begin to sound like cacophonous rap music. When God lifts His voice, all will hush in reverent silence. When God booms with His earth-shattering vocal trumpet, all will be awed by His grandeur.

Imagine God using His voice to rejoice over us. Imagine the melodious smile of His pleasure. We will not be able to resist joining in. "Sing, O daughter of Zion! Shout, O Israel! Be glad and rejoice with all your heart, O daughter of Jerusalem!" (v. 14). What nobler reason to sing exists? What purer motive to join the choir than to honor the Choir Leader? In the words of Christian Bateman's marvelous hymn:

"Come, Christians, join to sing Alleluia! Amen! Loud praise to Christ, our King: Alleluia! Amen!" God will rejoice over us in singing as we rejoice in Him.

Mighty One who saves us, thank You for singing the song of Christ in our hearing. That song is a beautiful melody in our lives. Thank You for quieting us with Your lullaby of love. Rouse us with the stirring music of the cross. In Your precious name, we pray. Amen.

You Have Mail

"These are the words of the letter that Jeremiah the prophet sent from Jerusalem to . . . all the people whom Nebuchadnezzar had carried away captive" (Jeremiah 29: 1 *New King James Version*).

Scripture: Jeremiah 29:10-14
Song: "When We All Get to Heaven"

Credit card offers, magazine subscription promotions, bills—the daily mail brings much that is undesired and undesirable. But most of us rifle eagerly through all that for one most desirable envelope: a personal letter, especially a personal letter from a loved one far away. And, joy of joy, if that letter brings good news.

Jeremiah had the delightful pleasure of writing God's letter to the captive Jews in exile. He had delivered plenty of bad news on behalf of God. Now he gets to write good news, news of future hope. God's people will one day soon occupy the land God gave to their fathers.

John the apostle recorded on behalf of God, Jesus' word of future reunion and glory: "In my Father's house are many mansions: if it were not so, I would have told you. I go to prepare a place for you. And if I go and prepare a place for you, I will come again, and receive you unto myself; that where I am, there ye may be also" (John 14:2, 3).

Ignore the junk mail of ungodly greed and false hope. We have letters. Letters from God. Letters of hope of future reunion. Let the smiles commence.

Lord of the future, thank You for the good news You have sent to us. Words of hope of future reunion of Your family sustain us in the bad news that surrounds us. We eagerly anticipate moving into the mansion Your Son the Lord Jesus has prepared for us. In Jesus' name, we pray. Amen.

Buy the Truth

"The kingdom of heaven is like unto a merchantman seeking goodly pearls: who, when he had found one pearl of great price, went and sold all that he had, and bought it" (Matthew 13:45,46).

Scripture: Proverbs 23:15-23
Song: "Once to Every Man and Nation"

Buying the truth is not as easy as it once may have been. Newspapers and other news sources may have become more concerned with selling than with truth.

Yet, the proverb writer's admonition is still true: buy the truth (v. 23). Truth is invaluable. Increasingly so in a world that markets lies and falsehood. Lies will sell. Stand at the checkout lane of grocery stores and other marketers, and read the headlines before you: "Aliens Open Hole in the Ozone: Mankind at Risk of Incineration." Listen to political rhetoric: "Yes, friends and fellow citizens, we can have our cake and eat it, too. And it's free! I'll help see that you get your slice."

Lies sell. But they're absolutely worthless. Truth is so rare as to be priceless. Yet, God strongly recommends, "Buy the truth!" Jesus' parable of the pearl teaches the same lesson: truth is so valuable it is worth giving up anything and everything else.

For each person the decision for the future is stark and clear: to fritter away one's resources on the lies of the world or to invest those resources in truth, God's truth. Let us be wise and buy the truth!

God of truth and Father of the One Who said, "I am the truth," help us to love the truth so much that lying never enters our minds. Give us wisdom to invest our resources in that which is true, the gospel and the kingdom. In Jesus' holy name, we pray. Amen.

Tired of God?

"Thou hast been weary of me, O Israel . . . . thou hast wearied me with thine iniquities" (Isaiah 43:22b, 24).

Scripture: Isaiah 43:14-21
Song: "Great is Thy Faithfulness"

Tired of praying? Tired of going to church? Tired of doing good deeds? Of giving offerings? Are you tired of God?

Israel grew tired of God. He was just too demanding. Too expectant. Too holy. Too present. Too predictable. And God was tired of Israel's sins.

Israel looked at God's faithfulness, His sameness, and yawned. They wanted something new. Something different. Something exciting. Little did they realize that He was about to do something new. They would not yawn. There will be "a way in the wilderness, and rivers in the desert" (v. 19).

Deserts look lifeless. Barren dunes of sand rearrange themselves endlessly. Yet given a refreshing shower of rain, those same dunes will blossom like a horticulturist's pride.

Life sometimes looks lifeless. Barren days of sameness spin and recycle themselves into monotony. Yet given the redeeming shower of Living Water, those same lives blossom into a Savior's joy.

Feeling a little sluggish? Ennui pushing you into a dark closet? Remember this: "His compassions fail not. They are new every morning:" (Lamentations 3:22, 23).

Dear Lord God, Holy One, the Creator of Israel, our King, open our eyes to the newness of each day. Demonstrate the marvels of Your intricate creation. Help us to see in a way we have never seen before. Thank You for making us new in Christ Jesus, our Lord. In His holy and righteous name, we pray. Amen.

God Can Tally our Sins

"If thou, Lord, shouldest mark iniquities, O Lord, who shall stand? But there is forgiveness with thee" (Psalm 130:3, 4).

Scripture: Psalm 130:1-8
Song: "Our Hope Is in the Lord"

"**O**ne million, one, two, three . . . ." God is quite capable of keeping a tally of our personal sins. He can do it for billions of people at the same nanosecond. His is a Golden Penteteuchal processor, well beyond a measly Pentium(r) one.

The psalmist sees God's ability. He can "mark iniquities." He knows an iniquity when He sees one, for He is holy. He sees an iniquity when He knows one, for He is omniscient.

But the psalmist also knows three greater truths. "There is forgiveness with thee," O Lord (v. 4). "With the Lord there is mercy" (v. 7). "With him there is plenteous redemption"(v. 7).

If all we knew of God were that He keeps a tally of our sins, our lives would be a woeful mountain of anxiety and dread. Thanks be to Him, He is merciful, forgiving, and redemptive. He is no hard schoolmaster, writing our names on the board and chalking those condemning marks that mean detention, or worse, the rod. He is the loving Father who gives hope. The psalmist calls for us to "hope in the Lord" (v. 7).

Oh, yes, He can "mark iniquities," but "he shall redeem Israel from all his iniquities" (v. 8). That is our only hope. The hard pedagogue of the Law pointed us to the grace of a forgiving Savior. Our hope is in the Lord.

We cry out to You, O Lord, from the depths of our sinful despair. Our slate is filled with the ugly marks of sin. Erase it in the blood of Christ. He is our hope, our only expectancy hope. In Jesus' holy name, we pray. Amen.

Beaten into Powder

And he did that which was right in the sight of the LORD (2 Chronicles 34:2).

Scripture: 2 Chronicles 34:1-7
Song: "Whiter than Snow"

The old song pleads, "Break down every idol, cast out every foe." Young Josiah did just that. Not only did this boy king forbid the worship of idols, he broke and he cut and he beat them to powder. Such a passion for the one true God! Like the Ephesians who burnt their books of magic, like Zaccheus who gave back more than he had taken, Josiah meant business with the Lord.

A professor of mine once said that, as a young man, he was a great boxing fan. He kept a scrapbook filled with photographs of boxers, boxing statistics, and newspaper clippings. He loved anything having to do with the ring. His problem was, he said, that he loved boxing too much. He felt that his hobby had become idolatrous. One day, he burned his scrap-book. When some in the class heard this, they laughed. The professor, however, had meant business with God.

Have we allowed anything to get between God and us? Is anything hindering our true worship, robbing us of the time we need with Christ? What will we do about it? Josiah didn't try to crowd God in beside an idol; he got rid of the idol. He took action because he meant business. Let's mean business!

O God, there is no other God beside You. Forgive us for allowing ourselves to be carried away with lesser interests. Give us the desire and the strength to sweep these other gods away and serve You alone. In the name of Christ, our Savior and Lord, we pray. Amen.

September 16-22. **Gary Robinson** is the founding minister for a church in Kent, Ohio. He and his wife, Barbara, have two children, Ruth and Alexander.

Find the Book

Thy word have I hid in mine heart, that I might not sin against thee
(*Psalm* 119:11).

Scripture: 2 Chronicles 34:8-18
Song: "Holy Bible, Book Divine"

If Abraham Lincoln's Bible sat on a shelf at the beginning of his presidency, it didn't remain there. As the terrible weight of office settled onto his shoulders, as the Union dipped her sons in blood, Lincoln found himself reaching for the Scriptures. He once said to a skeptical friend, "Take all of this book upon reason that you can, and the balance on faith, and you will live and die a happier and a better man." In a time of national crisis, one man had found the Book.

So it was in King Josiah's time. The nation had split asunder. Enemies threatened on all sides. Religion, like the temple, had become a shambles. Then, in the dust of disrepair, Hilkiah the priest found the book of the Law of Moses. Likely, it was a scroll of Deuteronomy. Certainly it was the Word of God. It touched first the ears, then the heart of the king and caused a revolution.

Perhaps our Bibles sit dusty on some forgotten shelf. Maybe we carry the Book to church but the edges of its pages are white, too white to have been thumbed. Quickly now! A great treasure lies beneath its cover. Let's find the Book! Let's crack the Book! God is waiting for us there.

Heavenly Father and Lord of all creation, we know that Your Word is truth. It is light, it is life to us; sweeter than honey, more precious than gold. Help us to open our Bibles and see. Help us to pick the Book up, dust the Book off, read it up one side and down the other and so be blessed. In the name of Jesus Christ, our Lord, we pray. Amen.

Holy Sorrow

He mocks proud mockers but gives grace to the humble
(Proverbs 3:34, *New International Version*).

Scripture: 2 Chronicles 34:19-28
Song: "Dear Lord and Father of Mankind"

I believe it was Mark Twain who said, "It's not the things I don't understand in the Bible that bother me. It's the things I do." Someone once told me that he sometimes got angry at what he read in the Bible; so angry, in fact, that he tore out the offending pages!

It's true. God's Word bites us sometimes. When it does, we react in a variety of ways. When His Word addresses our sins we sometimes want to change what it says. We may tear out pages. We may stuff the Bible in the closet. We may try to soften hard passages, bending them to suit our choices. Or we may do something like King Josiah did—become sick at the thought of our disobedience. Far from tearing the Holy Scroll, Josiah tore his royal robes. He wept, not in anger, but in sorrow.

This isn't the thief's sorrow at being caught or the adulterer's pain at being found out. This is the awful realization of sin itself. The Word of God is a mirror that reflects our image distorted by sin, the true image of God. It takes a brave heart to look into such a mirror. It takes a humble heart to accept its verdict, but God promises to honor the humble.

Holy God, we confess that we stray from the path You have marked for us. We confess our rebellion and our inactivity. We accept Your verdict. Now, for Your Son's sake, forgive us and renew us in purpose and passion. In the nane of Jesus, our Savior, we pray. Amen.

September 19

Stand Firm!

The king stood by his pillar and renewed the covenant in the presence of the Lord (2 Chronicles 34:31a, *New International Version*).

Scripture: 2 Chronicles 34:29-33
Song: "I Am Resolved"

Josiah "stood by the pillar" (see 2 Kings 23:3) as he renewed God's covenant with His people. The pillar stood no straighter than this young king or firmer than his resolve to lead Judah back to God. Our situation is not much different from that which Josiah faced. "We live in a world of invertebrate theology, jellyfish morality, and seesaw religion," wrote R. G. Lee. Things can change, but only if we stand firmly for what is right.

Leadership like Josiah's is crucial in crisis. During national crises, great men have always stepped out of the shadows to lead. We call such men heroes, and with good reason. They stood for something and so stood taller than the rest. They took hold of their societies and shook them.

We may never have our names recorded in history. Few outside our families, our churches, our workplaces may remember what we said or did. But those few will feel the impact of what we believed. Our determination to follow Christ will touch people for years to come. They will remember for Whom we stood like a pillar, we pray, and stand for Him too.

Dear Lord and Father of us all, in those famous words, "I would be true, for there are those who trust me. I would be pure, for there are those who care. I would be strong, for there is much to suffer. I would be brave, for there is much to dare" teach us to live in such a way that others will see Your leadership in this world. In the name of Jesus Christ, we pray. Amen.

Doing The Word

Blessed are they that keep his testimonies, and that seek him with the whole heart (Psalm 119:2).

Scripture: 2 Chronicles 35:1 -10
Song: "How Firm a Foundation"

I keep a picture of my late father with me always. Though I never photographed him in this pose, I can always summon the image to mind. He's sitting on the couch in our living room. Casual and barefoot, reading glasses and his black Bible is open before him. He read the Book as much as he could. More importantly, he lived the Book as best he could.

Our Scripture text for today paints a similar picture. The details—Passover, Levites, and burnt offerings—may be foreign to us, but the devotion to the Word of God is unmistakable. Led by Josiah, who had recovered the Law, the people once again did what the Lord had commanded them through Moses. They read the Word, they obeyed the Word.

Beware of separating reading the Word and obeying the Word. To read or hear the Bible without doing what it says is like running a stop sign at a busy intersection. It's like telling someone, "I love you," then slapping his face. It's not only counter-productive, it's dangerous! The Bible is our map. We read, then heed. The Book is our Operator's Manual. If all else fails, could it be because we haven't read the instructions?

Almighty God and Father of all Truth, we come to You with open Bibles clasped to open hearts. Your Word is light—not just to see but to walk in. Give us the desire to read and do, hear and obey. Teach us Your ways, O God, that we may be seen by the world as Your voice. Help us to make Your Word alive in our lives. In Jesus' holy name, we pray. Amen.

No Greater King

Now unto the King eternal, immortal, invisible, the only wise God, be honor and glory forever and ever. Amen (1 Timothy 1: 17).

Scripture: 2 Kings 23:24-30
Song: "All Hail King Jesus"

When the Mister smugly told his Missus that he'd heard her refer to him as a "model" husband, she directed him to the dictionary. There the over-inflated spouse found this definition by the word "model": A small imitation of the real thing.

The same could be said of Josiah when we compare him to Jesus Christ. There are similarities. Both were kings, both were zealous for God from their youth, both died tragically. Yet Josiah, Judah's godliest king, remains a small imitation of the Real Thing. Humble though he was before God, Josiah could not make his people like himself. His reforms were thorough, but they never really changed the hearts of his countrymen. Jesus' work went much deeper. He didn't reform; he transformed. His followers didn't just turn over a new leaf; they came up with a new life. He died, not merely heroically, but according to the plan of God. Then the king came to life again to share His eternal kingdom with us all.

Jesus truly is the king unlike any before or since. He is King of kings and Lord of lords. He was there when the world was created. He is part of the Godhead. He is worthy of our hearts. Let us serve Him, let us praise Him, and let us love Him all our days.

Heavenly Father, You gave up Your crown for a cross. You died in mingled blood and spit for us. You are exalted. We exalt You. We thank You. We renew our pledge to love and our desire to serve You. In the name of Jesus Christ, our Savior and Lord, we pray. Amen.

The Difference He Makes

And that ye put on the new man, which after God is created in righteousness and true holiness (Ephesians 4:24).

Scripture: Ephesians 4:17-24
Song: "Since Jesus Came Into My Heart"

One winter afternoon, my neighbor and I happened to be shoveling our driveways at the same time. We struck up a conversation. Somewhere along the way, I invited the man to church. My neighbor had been standing fairly close to me. When I mentioned church, however, he began to back away slowly. He kept talking, but he also kept backing away—as though I had something catching. I guess I did!

That's the way it is when the "old" men meet the "new" men. The "old" are quick to realize a big difference, a great gap, which makes them uncomfortable around the "new." The difference is actually the presence of God—His righteousness, and His holiness. These are qualities some can't understand or enjoy—that is, until they come to know Christ.

When we are Christians, we can celebrate the difference Christ has made in us. More importantly, we can cultivate that difference. In so doing, we can help the world to see Christ. We are not to show arrogance, to distance ourselves from the suffering humanity, but simply to be more like Christ. This is what it means to be "in the world but not of the world."

Almighty God and our Father in Heaven, help us to be different from the world. Help us to be godly in our actions. Help us to be kind, not cruel. Calm, not angry. Loving, not lustful. At peace with men and with You. Help us to wear Jesus like a garment until He becomes like our skin. In His holy name, we pray. Amen.

Which Way is Up?

Thus saith the LORD, Stand ye in the ways, and see, and ask for the old paths, where is the good way, and walk therein, and ye shall find rest for your souls (Jeremiah 6:16).

Scripture: Jeremiah 6:16-21
Song: "Heavenly Sunlight"

God designed humans to "look up" to Him. The Greek word for "man" is *anthropos*, which means, "one's face turned up." When we turn to God with meekness, He makes known His perfect will with a clear invitation and a promise of "rest."

An unexpected rush of water may sometimes overcome a young swimmer in a heavy current. When his lungs are screaming for air and panic begins to set in, he needs to remember his father's patient instruction to, "Look up, son." As soon as he obeys and turns his face to the sky, he floats to the surface where his deliverance and his father await.

Our loving heavenly Father has also given us clear instructions for avoiding calamity. He is light, and in Him is no darkness at all. If we choose to live in darkness, we tie God's hands. The consequences of ignoring God's will and living in darkness are dire. God is very persuasive, but He has never forced anyone to obey Him. He has limited Himself to our free will. However, if we choose to "look up" and walk in the light, as He is light, our deliverance is sure. What a relief!

Gracious heavenly Father, we are so thankful to know Your heart of goodness to us. Thank You for giving us Your Word that we may know Your heart toward us. May we obey Your Word. We rejoice with You because of our deliverance. In the name of Jesus Christ, our Savior, we pray. Amen.

September 23-29. **Constance Darnell** is a Christian writer. She has been married for 25 years and is a mother of two children.

Pure as Silver

I have set thee for a tower and a fortress among my people, that thou mayest know and try their way . . . . Reprobate silver shall men call them, because the LORD *hath rejected them* (Jeremiah 6:27, 30).

Scripture: Jeremiah 6:22-30
Song: "Jesus, I Come"

God has always given His people the means and the opportunity to stand righteously before Him. Righteousness is your God-given ability to stand in the very presence of God without any sense of sin, guilt, or condemnation. That's purity.

On January 14, 1848, while excavating for a new sawmill, John Sutter's workers discovered gold. This discovery started the great California Gold Rush. Men and women from all over the country came to seek their fortune in the wild lands of California. Many an ignorant prospector excitedly loaded tons of the shiny golden rocks found along the streambeds in the Sacramento Valley and carried them with excitement to the assayer's office. There they learned they had discovered worthless iron pyrite, later to be called "fools' gold."

Only God knows our hearts. We are ill-advised to choose our senses' assessment or the instruction of men over the "precious metals" of God's Word. God has given us His pure Word so that we can face the challenges that each new day presents. Then, we wisely do His perfect will for our lives. He desires for our hearts to be "pure gold" and not "fools' gold" as we stand righteously before Him in love.

Our most gracious heavenly Father, thank You for giving us Your pure words that are as pure as silver tried in a furnace. Thank You for preserving and encouraging us through each day. In the name of Jesus Christ, our Savior and Lord, we pray. Amen.

Will Someone Please Turn on the Light?

*Amend your ways and your doings, and I will cause you to dwell in this place.
. . . in the land that I gave to your fathers, for ever and ever* (Jeremiah 7:3b, 7).

Scripture: Jeremiah 7:1-7
Song: "O Word of God Incarnate"

The introduction of light is the only thing that will ever dispel darkness. Dwelling on darkness does not make it go away. In fact, dwelling on darkness only makes it seem darker. God's warnings and promises have always been reliable and serious. Whenever the children of Israel hearkened unto Him rather than hardening their hearts, God immediately blessed them. He always keeps His word.

If a person walks into a windowless room and closes the door with the lights off, the blackness will be consuming. If he lights a single match in that darkness, the tiny light will be brilliant in the black room. All the darkness cannot extinguish the light, but the little light illuminates the room and chases the darkness from it.

So it is with our minds. Even when we are consumed with idolatry and our foolish hearts are darkened, God has made a way out. He has given us His Word so that we may know His perfect will and ignite His power in our lives. When we faithfully act on the Word of God, our deliverance is sure. The transformation to the renewed mind and the light of deliverance is only one thought away.

What are you thinking today?

Father, You know our hearts as no other, and You know our frames, that we are dust. We come before You and thank You for Your forgiveness for our broken fellowship with You and ask that You would guide us in the way we are to walk. In Jesus' holy name, we pray. Amen.

Disobedience Brings Disaster

But this thing commanded I them, saying, Obey my voice, and I will be your God, and ye shall be my people: and walk ye in all the ways that I have commanded you, that it may be well unto you. But they hearkened not, nor inclined their ear, but walked in the counsels and in the imagination of their evil heart, and went backward, and not forward (Jeremiah 7:23,24).

Scripture: Jeremiah 7:16-28
Song: "Trust and Obey"

There was a time when the nation of Israel had found rest. They obeyed God's Word and He gave them deliverance and peace. However, when later generations turned away from God's will and decided not to walk according to His will, they were denied the promised rest.

A beginning skier learns important instructions from the instructor. "Bend your knees! Face down the mountain! Point your skis in to stop!" If the skier obeys the instructions, he will be successful. Some skiers decide they know better than their teachers. They miss all the gorgeous scenery, injure themselves, endanger the lives of others, and even end up skiing backwards down the mountain! Students who disobey may end up stuck in the freezing snow crying, "Why me?"

God's Word was clear to Israel. They willfully disobeyed and chose to worship other gods. The consequences were disastrous. They chose evil rather than good and lost the promised rest. We, too, have choices to make each day. God clearly defines His Will for our lives. When we choose His way of life we allow God to give us rest.

Almighty God, **our heavenly Father,** we thank You for forgiveness for the times we have disobeyed Your will. We turn our hearts to You and thank You for deliverance from the disasters that disobedience brings. In the name of Jesus Christ, our Lord, we pray. Amen

A Key to Successful Living

In returning and rest shall ye be saved; in quietness and in confidence shall be your strength (Isaiah 30:15).

Scripture: Isaiah 30:15-19
Song: "Leaning on the Everlasting Arms"

One great key to victorious living is composure under pressure. When we trust God for deliverance in every situation, He is able to work in us "to will and to do of His good pleasure." The knowledge that God is working in us gives us great quietness on the inside and genuine confidence to deal with problems.

If you haven't noticed, there is a lot of sitting going on in the Bible. When God finished the creation in six days, on the seventh day He rested. When Jesus Christ had finished sacrificing himself for us, He ascended into Heaven and "sat down on the right hand of God." When the day of Pentecost was fully come, the gift of Holy Spirit "sat upon each of them" (the twelve apostles). God even designed one day per week to be given to rest.

All this sitting in the Bible should make us stop and reflect on how we are spending our lives. When a challenging task is completed, we need to rest in our heavenly Father's arms; then He can prepare us for the tasks ahead. When we trust in Him, God strengthens us to undertake our responsibilities with confidence and composure.

Dear gracious heavenly Father and Lord of all, we are so thankful that we can trust in You and Your power. In the midst of all the noisy demands of the world You have given us a haven of peace and quiet. We give You all the glory for every good thing in our lives. In the name of Jesus Christ, our Savior and Lord, we pray. Amen.

The Secret to Living Restfully

There remaineth therefore a rest to the people of God (Hebrews 4:9).

Scripture: Hebrews 4:1 -11
Song: "He Keeps Me Singing"

Our rest, as believers, is embodied within the finished work of Jesus Christ. We enter into that rest when we are born again of God's Spirit. At that moment we pass from death unto life. We were circumcised with Christ, baptized in Him, buried with Him, raised together with Him, and we ascended with Him to be seated at the right hand of God. As we learn more about what God accomplished for us by giving the world His Son, our perspective changes and our serenity deepens.

A mountain climber who finally reaches the summit after hours of difficult climbing feels exhilaration as he looks down at the path he has come. There may be memories of pain or loss on the trail as he scans the distance he has come. Those memories are swiftly overshadowed by the thrill of the victory on the mountaintop.

So it is with our position in Christ. We no longer need to be condemned, frustrated, or full of fear. When we apply God's Word, we are in Christ and He is in us. When we speak God's Word, we grow up into Him. As we believe God's Word, it comes into concretion. Jesus Christ has given us a new perspective. He paid for our seat at the right hand of God with His blood. It's the best seat in the house.

Dear **heavenly Father**, we believe Your Word is truth and we are so thankful for it. Thank You for giving to us such a simple way to know Your heart. Teach us to live each day in the joy of knowing You. In the name of Jesus, our Savior and Lord, we pray. Amen.

The Rest is His-story

Come unto me, all ye that labor and are heavy laden, and I will give you rest. Take my yoke upon you, and learn of me; for I am meek and lowly in heart: and ye shall find rest unto your souls. For my yoke is easy, and my burden is light (Matthew 11:28-30).

Scripture: Matthew 11:25-30
Song: "Constantly Abiding"

The believer's right to rest is a direct result of the finished work of Christ. Before he "gave up the ghost" on Calvary's tree, Jesus said, "It is finished" (John 19:30b). What was finished? Our redemption was finished.

A woman in the process of giving birth is doing some of the most challenging labor of her life. She is working hard; she is the only one who can accomplish the job. Once the process has begun, she may want to quit, but there is no turning back. All of her preparation, anticipation and excitement have been focused on one goal: new life. The woman draws courage and resolve from the knowledge that her baby will soon be in her arms. When the child is finally brought forth, the mother is happy and relieved. All the work was worth it.

Jesus knew what the Messiah must do to redeem mankind from the consequences of Adam's sin. He knew about the agony, the humiliation, the sickness and death He carried with Him to Calvary. Yet, He endured all of it, despising the shame, for one reason: new life for mankind. To Jesus, it was all worth it to have us safely in His arms.

Heavenly Father, we are thankful for the life and death and resurrection of Your Son, Jesus. Help us to follow His teachings in all that we do. In His precious name, we pray. Amen.

September 30

Sooner or Later

Be sure your sin will find you out (Numbers 32:23).

Scripture: Jeremiah 25:1-7
Song: "Cleanse Me"

Most of us can remember a time when we disobeyed the rule but didn't get caught. Maybe it happened not long ago. The traffic light was yellow, you were running late, so you sped through the intersection just as the light turned red. But no policeman saw you, and you drove away without a ticket.

Maybe you were a child. Mom said no dessert 'til after dinner. But she was out of the house, the cookie jar was full, and your stomach felt empty. You grabbed a treat and downed it without leaving a crumb. Mom never knew the difference.

There's a problem with not getting caught. You may think you can ignore the rule again—and again—and that no one will ever know. Sooner or later, a policeman will see you break the traffic law. Sooner or later Mom will know you disobeyed. Sooner or later, "your sin will find you out."

Maybe you can remember a time when you disobeyed God, and nothing happened. The sky didn't fall. You didn't lose your job. No one knew—except God. Today's Scripture reminds us that He is patient. He may not punish us after just one sin, but He will not, He cannot ignore a pattern of stubborn disobedience. When punishment comes to a person who has lived this way, he has no one to blame but himself.

Thank You, God, for forgiving my sin. Help me, God, to resist the lure of sin today. Help me to make myself more yours today than I was yesterday.

Mark A. Taylor has served Standard Publishing as vice-president and publisher.

My Prayer Notes

Devotions

October

photo by Chuck Perry

October 1

Always a Rulebook

Go and make disciples . . . , teaching them to obey everything I have commanded you (Matthew 28:19, 20, New International Version).

Scripture: Jeremiah 26:1-6
Song: "Thy Word Have I Hid in My Heart"

After dinner with some friends, we decided to play a game. Our family had enjoyed it for years, but our friends had never played it.

We tried to explain the rules ourselves, but eventually we decided simply to read the directions. The game maker had described every play clearly, without confusion. Every possible circumstance was covered. Throughout the evening we referred to the instruction book again and again, not only to help the new players, but also to remind us of the rule.

This simple story illustrates a principle of life. The rule book—and our willingness to obey it—always makes the game possible.

The tendency to ignore the rules has been with humankind for many centuries. It was the central problem addressed by Jeremiah in today's passage. It reminds us that God has written the rules, and He expects us to follow them.

We are grateful, God, that you have clearly told us exactly how to live. Forgive us for our tendency to rewrite the rules to suit ourselves. Help us to be more willing to obey You today. In the name of the Savior, we pray. Amen.

October 1—6. **Mark A. Taylor** is vice-president and publisher at Standard Publishing. He and his wife, Evelyn, have two grown children.

Stung by the Truth

As soon as Jeremiah finished telling all the people everything the Lord had commanded him to say, the priests, the prophets and all the people seized him and said, "You must die!" (Jeremiah 26:8, New International Version).

Scripture: Jeremiah 26:7-13
Song: "Thy Word"

The path to popularity is not paved with principle. Refuse to go along with the group's bad decision, and the group will call you names. Turn away from the dirty joke, stay sober, keep clean, and the muddied masses will wonder out loud why you're so weird. When one person chooses the right, the wrongdoers around him feel exposed by his goodness.

Sometimes the crowd will crucify you for what you say. Oppose wrong. Your audience will probably not stop to consider whether you're right or wrong. They'll just pounce on you for daring to disagree.

This is exactly what happened to Jeremiah in the incident described by today's Scripture. The wicked people of Judah were stung by his prophecy; its purity and truth illuminated their paganism and error. Instead of considering the message, they attacked the messenger.

Have courage! Be as willing as Jeremiah to speak the truth, even when no one wants to hear it.

Help us today, our Father, to love the truth, to live by the truth, and to speak the truth, even when the truth is a threat to those who hear it. May we stay close to You and Your Word so that we may reflect Your will. In Christ we pray. Amen.

Our Little Suffering

They were stoned; they were sawed in two; they were put to death by the sword. They went about in sheepskins and goatskins, destitute, persecuted and mistreated—the world was not worthy of them (Hebrews 11:37, 38, New International Version).

Scripture: Jeremiah 26:14-19
Song: "In the Hour of Trial"

You have to admire Jeremiah. God gave him a message he knew would be unpopular. Yet he boldly proclaimed it to the priests, the prophets, and all the people (Jeremiah 26:7). When they called for his death, Jeremiah didn't waver (v. 14). "Do what you want with me," he responded. "God's way will prevail."

His resolve in the face of persecution reminds us of Shadrach, Meshach, and Abednego (Daniel 3) or Stephen (Acts 7) or any one of the martyrs since then (see Hebrews 11:32-38). When confronted with adversaries committed to killing them for their faith, they did not flinch.

While we may not face death, we can at least submit to being uncomfortable for our faith. We can give an extra gift to a Christian cause, even when we want that money for ourselves. We can resist temptation. We can praise God in the midst of sickness or setbacks.

In such small portions of suffering, we can at least imitate the sacrifice of the martyrs. We can demonstrate some portion of the faith that motivated men and women like Jeremiah.

Heavenly Father, help us to trust You, so that we may be prepared to suffer for You in the calamities of tomorrow. In the name of Christ, we pray. Amen.

Not Even One Step

Do not swerve to the right or the left; keep your foot from evil
(Proverbs 4:27, New International Version).

Scripture: Proverbs 4:20-27
Song: "True-Hearted, Whole-Hearted"

An error of just a few degrees in a space launch will cause the rocket to miss its mark by thousands of miles. Forgetting just a few months' savings as a young adult can mean thousands of dollars less at retirement time. Just one wrong turn can cause hours of delay.

These everyday illustrations underline the truth that King Solomon had discovered. In today's Scripture, he urges us to guard our hearts, focus our vision, and walk only in the center of the pathway. An idle thought, a sideways glance, one step off the path can lead eventually to our ruin.

One minister was distracted by an adult bookstore located near his drycleaner. So he found a different drycleaner.

An alcoholic explains that he avoids the beer aisle of the grocery store, and he eats only at coffee shops or fast food restaurants that don't serve alcohol. He refuses to take even one step back toward his addiction. Instead of toying with temptation, we can keep our eyes on God.

Instead of toying with temptation, we can keep our eyes on God. Instead of wondering "how far can I go?" we can keep our feet in the center of His will.

Help me today, Lord, to stay as close to you as I can. Sound a warning signal in my spirit when I'm tempted to take even one step away from You. Amen.

An Unfailing Father

I am God, and there is no other; I am God, and there is none like me
(Isaiah 46:9, New International Version).

Scripture: Isaiah 46:8-13
Song: "God Is So Good"

Children test their parents' will by asserting their own. Parents do their job by showing their children who is in control. Those sentences roughly summarize the relationship of kids with their parents until the children become adults.

For many, the struggle begins before the child is two. The toddler edges close to a forbidden bauble, all the while keeping her eye on Mom. "No, no," Mom tells her, and the child looks closely to see if Mom really means what she says.

Sometimes those confrontations convince the child that Mom will get her way. But usually the tests continue. The grade schooler may refuse to do his homework. The young teen may run with friends his parents don't approve. The high schooler may try activities that violate parental boundaries.

All of this is a picture of how we relate to God. We disobey Him and then wince at the consequences. We break the boundaries that He has set, and sooner or later we will suffer the effect. We chase after other gods, but time after time He reminds us, "I am God, and there is no other."

Heavenly Father, forgive me for my waywardness; forgive me for forgetting that You alone are God. Help me to relate to you as my God as well as my Father. Help me to accept the boundaries of Your will. In the name of Jesus, we pray. Amen.

Hearing and Understanding

Blessed are the pure in heart, for they shall see God (Matthew 5:8).

Scripture: Matthew 13:10-16
Song: "Open Our Eyes, Lord"

What a challenge to try teaching English to my Japanese neighbor! He is an executive, well-educated and intelligent. He studied English for many years as a young person in Japan. Though he knows much about English grammar and understands many English words, still our language baffles him.

Hardest of all are the idioms and figures of speech.

Why does "fed up" have nothing to do with a meal? How can you visit the grocery and avoid "sour grapes"? When is "for the time being"? What kind of arithmetic gives you "six of one and a half-dozen of the other"? How fast must you run to "keep up with the Joneses"?

My friend perfectly comprehends each of these words. But put together, their meaning escapes him. "Seeing, he doesn't see. Hearing, he doesn't understand." Nothing in his experience has equipped him to decipher these expressions.

In the same way, a person who has not experienced spiritual reality may reject spiritual ideas. A person consumed with himself may not fathom talk about God. We who know Him are prepared to understand even more about Him. And we receive the benefit Jesus promised: "Blessed are your eyes, for they see: and your ears, for they hear" (v. 16).

As I study Your Word and seek Your will, My Lord, help me to understand your ways. As I walk by Your light, give me understanding to walk farther. In the name of Jesus, we pray. Amen.

October 7

How May I Help You?

Thus saith the Lord: Execute ye judgment and righteousness, and deliver the spoiled out of the hand of the oppressor: and do no wrong, do no violence to the stranger, the fatherless, nor the widow, neither shed innocent blood in this place (Jeremiah 22:3).

Scripture: Jeremiah 22:1-9
Song: "Take My Life, and Let It Be"

The alien, the fatherless and the widow represent any that are disadvantaged. God always cares about those who cannot help themselves, no matter what the reason. And because His Spirit prompts us to action, we care too. We reach out through prison ministries, food banks, and neighborhood centers. We feel good when we send checks of aid to those who lost their homes in floods. We carry the gospel around the world to those downtrodden in sin. It's the right thing to do.

However we can also reach out to the alien, fatherless, and widows among us. We can slip a few dollars into the hand of a single mother struggling to make ends meet. We can go fishing with the child of divorce. We can invite a widow to dine with us instead of always entertaining couples.

The kings of Judah enjoyed a privileged position that also carried responsibility. We too are in a privileged position; we are saved by grace. And we too carry a responsibility to be fair and to support the less fortunate, not because of an outward law but because of an inward Spirit.

Lord, thank You for motivating me to pass on Your grace to others by a word, a deed, or a smile. You created the world for us, and Your Son died for our sins. The least we can do is show others Your wonderful grace. In Jesus' name, we pray. Amen.

October 7-13. **Shirley Brosius** is a Christian education specialist and freelance writer from Millersburg, Pennsylvania. She and her husband, Bill have two sons and three grandchildren.

Might Doesn't Make Right

Woe unto him that buildeth his house by unrighteousness, and his chambers by wrong; that useth his neighbor's service without wages, and giveth him not for his work (Jeremiah 22:13).

Scripture: Jeremiah 22:13-23
Song: "O to Be Like Thee!"

We were quite excited when a pair of bluebirds moved into a backyard birdhouse. We watched them build their nest with bits of grass and lint. Then one day as my husband mowed the lawn he noticed two blue eggs smashed on the grass below the nest. We couldn't imagine what had happened until we noticed a sparrow, which looked like he was wearing a black mask, perched on the birdhouse. He had evicted our bluebirds and taken over their nest.

Fortunately, the bluebirds simply moved into another birdhouse and raised a family there. The sparrow, however, never did show any signs of raising a family, and about a week later he disappeared. His selfish methods had come to naught.

Jeremiah warned Jehoiakim that his greed and dishonesty would cost him dearly. According to the prophet, even Jehoiakim's death would not be mourned. But the king felt secure in his prosperity and ignored the prophet.

No matter how expedient it may seem to gain something for ourselves at someone else's expense, such action is wrong. God has the final say. And the judgment he decrees falls on kings and common people alike.

Lord, forgive us for times we may have profited at someone else's expense. Help us to hear Your Word and listen to Your Spirit so that we will treat others as we want to be treated. Help us to remember our relationship with You is more important than prosperity. In Jesus' name, we pray. Amen.

Kneel to Stand for Truth

"Woe be unto the pastors that destroy and scatter the sheep of my pasture!" **Saith the Lord** *(Jeremiah 23:1).*

Scripture: Jeremiah 23:1-6
Song: "We've a Story to Tell to the Nations"

As we read newspapers we see signs of the same types of problems faced by the nation of Israel. From national presidents to local councilmen, leaders who lack respect for God's Word may accept bribes, commit adultery, and look the other way at wrongdoing if such activities personally benefit them. Unfortunately, their behavior affects not only themselves, but also cities and nations.

The nation of Israel found itself in troubled waters when government leaders no longer led with integrity. As rulers slipped away from God, rejected morality, and pandered to the ungodly; the country faced ruin.

We can fight political corruption and nourish a spirit of hope by working to build the kingdom of God. As leaders are brought to repentance, they discover the Spirit's power to govern with integrity. As they come to Christ, they learn to rely on His wisdom to govern.

Our nation's leaders need our support to reject ungodly counsel, resist evil pressures, and to keep personal ambition in check. The battle for a strong and righteous nation begins in homes where Christians kneel to pray for the men and women whom God has placed in leadership.

Lord, we know Your ways are best. May Your Spirit work in the hearts of our nation's leaders so that they will follow Your ways. May You bring peace and righteousness to our land. And may we do our part to nurture a nation that honors You. In Jesus' name, we pray. Amen.

You are Responsible

He hath showed thee, O man, what is good, and what doth the Lord require of thee, but to do justly, and to love mercy, and to walk humbly with thy God?
(Micah 6. 8).

Scripture: Micah 6:3-8
Song: "I Would Be True"

When my son and his family moved into a new apartment seven months ago, a large blind that should have covered a sliding patio door was missing. In spite of repeated phone calls to the building superintendent, no blind has been provided. Rent has increased substantially since they moved in, but still no blind. Finally I hung some old green-figured draperies, which cover only part of the window and clash with the blue couch. While this helps somewhat to shield my son's family from the bright sunlight by day and provides some measure of privacy by night, it is still not the proper solution to the problem that the owners should have provided.

While desk clerks may have hidden behind "management" when called to account, the decision to purchase a blind lies with an individual. And in this case that person does not seem to care about inconveniencing tenants.

Micah, by using the singular pronoun "man," reminds us that while the Lord was telling the nation of Israel to do what was right, He was also speaking to individuals. After all, a nation is made up of individuals. As we individually heed God's commands, the groups we compose—churches, nations, and even corporations—will end up doing the right thing.

Lord, sometimes we feel helpless to fight injustice. Remind us to do our part to change hearts by pointing people to You. For only as individuals come to You will the right thing be done for the right reason—love and respect for a Holy God. In the name of Jesus, we pray. Amen.

Trust God!

Therefore I will look unto the Lord; I will wait for the God of my salvation: my God will hear me (Micah 7:7).

Scripture: Micah 7:1-7
Song: "Great Is Thy Faithfulness"

In our region fruit farmers keep a keen eye on the weather and try to ward off late frosts by turning on sprinklers. This year, in spite of their best efforts, peach blossoms were nipped. As a result peaches have been in short supply. But the farmers continue to be faithful in pruning and caring for their trees. They hope for a better harvest next year.

Sometimes fruit of the Spirit also seems to be in short supply. Even within churches conflicts may arise. Individuals with gifts of the Spirit such as mercy and administration, may seem to be at odds. Personalities may clash.

But just as a fruit farmer looks to God because he knows the weather is in His hands, so individuals may look to Him to find peaceful solutions where none seem to exist. Sometimes God asks us to wait patiently as He works in hearts. Sometimes He calls us to forgive and forget. Each individual is responsible to listen and respond to that still small voice. His mercies are new every morning.

Perhaps a friend or family member has betrayed a confidence or in some way disappointed you. Don't despair. Trust in God. Even when the fruit of the Spirit seems to have been nipped in the bud, great is His faithfulness.

Lord, as we look around we sometimes become discouraged because dissension abounds. Thank You for the message of the prophets that reminds us of the hope we have in You. We know You will act on our behalf as we live in joyful obedience. In the name of Christ, we pray. Amen.

God, Our Advocate

Arise, O Lord, in thine anger, lift up thyself because of the rage of mine enemies: and awake for me to the judgment that thou hast commanded (Psalm 7:6).

Scripture: Psalm 7:1-11
Song: "0 God, Our Help in Ages Past"

Newspapers recently carried an account of a man who was wrongly imprisoned for 18 years. DNA tests, based on an individual's genetic blueprint, were used to clear him of the conviction. Although he had maintained his innocence and was never identified by the victim, someone had testified that he had been in the area of the crime. Eighteen years is a very long time to wait for justice.

This man must have experienced the same emotions David expressed in today's text—anger, frustration, and fear. We too may experience injustices from an earthly perspective. Perhaps we, or someone close to us, have been crippled by the careless act of another. Or maybe we feel anger toward someone who has spoken maliciously against us. Perhaps someone at work has taken credit for our ideas. We may want to get even with one who has wronged us.

But, like David, we may leave judgment to God. He wants us to know the joy of a life well lived, even when we feel wronged. Someday evil will be exposed. Someday God will take us to Heaven because of what Jesus Christ has done for us. And Heaven will more than make up for any injustices that have occurred here on earth.

Lord, as I reflect on the hurts of life, I am saddened. Many times justice seems elusive. The wrong does seem to prevail. Help me to be steadfast and to keep my eyes on You, the advocate for every victim. Thank You for Your magnificent loving care. Amen.

We are Family

Behold, what manner of love the Father hath bestowed upon us, that we should be called the sons of God: therefore the world knoweth us not, because it knew him not (1 John 3:1).

Scripture: 1 John 2:28–3:7
Song: "Blest Be the Tie That Binds"

My four older brothers and sisters and their families came home to visit our farm on Sunday afternoons when I was a child. We had great fun playing board games, chopping ice from a stream to make homemade ice cream, or just sitting on the big front porch talking.

Although our parents and a sister are now with the Lord, we continue to get together a few times each year. We are a family and will always be a family, in spite of occasional squabbles. My brothers have the receding hairlines of my father. I have the straight coarse hair of my mother.

As children of God, we also form a family. Gatherings in this family are just as much fun as we rejoice in the Lord and enjoy fellowship in teaching and worship. In God's family we are marked by spiritual characteristics of our Father, such as love, kindness, and self-control.

While we know our righteousness comes from Christ, we try to put off sin and lead holy lives so people will see in us His "image" and His "likeness." Someday, when we see Him, we shall be like Him and our family resemblance to our heavenly Father will be complete.

Lord, thank You for my earthly family, which has brought such joy to my life. And thank You for my spiritual family, which has also supported me in the joys and sorrows of life. I pray that those of us who are physically related may also be spiritually related. In Jesus' name, I pray. Amen.

God's Family Tree

"Ye shall be my people, and I will be your God" *(Jeremiah 30:22).*

Scripture: Jeremiah 30:18-22
Song: "The Family of God"

While doing research on the Internet, I discovered some cousins who were previously unknown to me. That helped me understand how searching out the family tree has become a compelling hobby for many. Some find a greater sense of belonging, a feeling of personal pride and identity through the discovery of their heritage.

Who are we? Where do we come from? At what point in time did our ancestors migrate here? What circumstances compelled them to leave their homeland? How exciting this wealth of information can be!

Researching our spiritual heritage can be even more exciting! God repeatedly tells us we have a special sense of identity that transcends our flesh and blood relationships: "You will be my people and I will be your God."

What a privilege to be one of His people; to be able to enjoy an intimate, personal relationship with our Creator. We will one day enjoy the ultimate family reunion, the reconciliation of God's people to God himself. In the meantime there are many "cousins" we have yet to meet. I'm so glad I'm a part of the family of God. Aren't you?

Father, we thank You for the gift of our human families. We recognize that we are also part of Your family. What a joy to be able to come before You, whatever our need, as we would a loving earthly father. Thank You for all the blessings we receive as Your children! In Jesus' name, we pray. Amen.

October 14-20. **Dan Nicksich** is the Senior Minister of First Christian Church of Somerset, Pennsylvania and a member of the Greater Johnstown Christian Writer's Guild.

Great Prosperity / Great Gratitude

Otherwise, I may have too much and disown you and say, "Who is the Lord?"
(Proverbs 30:9a, New International Version).

Scripture: Jeremiah 31:1-6
Song: "Praise God, From Whom All Blessings Flow"

Due to last year's lengthy drought, our county was asked to encourage voluntary water restrictions in each household. An everyday commodity we usually take for granted became something quite precious.

What do those experiencing warfare desire? Peace. What do those living through dry conditions pray for? Rain. What does the patient farmer look forward to? Harvest.

Rest from war and abundant harvest were God's promises to Israel. To a war-torn country and to those living through times of scarcity, such blessings were joyously received. The music and dancing mentioned in our Bible text were obvious expressions of their thanksgiving.

God's "everlasting love" has also blessed us abundantly. A generation of Americans has known a peaceful homeland and abundant material goods.

Our response to long-term prosperity is sometimes to take God's blessings for granted. In fact this year's abundant rainfall has brought a curious lament that some crops are not doing so well. How easy it can be to overlook God's blessings of peace and prosperity. Don't fail to give Him the glory and praise He is due. Have you given thanks recently for those things we sometimes take for granted?

Lord, it's easy to look around and see many things for which we should give You thanks. Forgive us for taking so many things for granted. Help us to be more appreciative of all You do for us. In Jesus' name, we pray. Amen.

No Rest For The Wicked

Upon this I awakened and beheld; and my sleep was sweet unto me
(Jeremiah 31:26).

Scripture: Jeremiah 31:23-30
Song: "Wonderful Peace"

In 1811, the U.S. Treasury Dept. created a "conscience fund" for those who had cheated the government and later repented. To avoid further scrutiny, many choose to repay their debt anonymously. One letter, accompanying such a cash repayment, provides a rich commentary on human nature: "Enclosed is $6,000 I owe in back taxes. I haven't been able to sleep nights. If I still can't sleep, I'll send the rest."

We can smile at this story of incomplete repentance, but Isaiah tells us there is no rest for the wicked (Isaiah 57:21). A troubled conscience can bring on sleepless nights. Not so with the righteous. The Lord's blessing for those with clear consciences is refreshing and satisfying sleep.

If a weary business traveler longs for a good night's sleep in his own bed, just imagine Judah's longing to return home. The prophet's words assured them that a return to their native land was more than just a dream.

As God's people we live in anticipation of His many blessings. The Lord watches over us in bad times as well as good. Through it all, He who richly provides all things keeps us safe and secure. No matter what trials and stresses you face, may His presence grant you refreshing and satisfying rest in anticipation of His promises.

Lord, grant us the satisfaction that comes from knowing You. Forgive us of sins we have committed against You that we may have clear consciences. Help us serve You faithfully throughout this day. In Jesus' name, we pray. Amen.

Intentionally Forgetting

"I will forgive their iniquity, and I will remember their sin no more"
(Jeremiah 31:34b).

Scripture: Jeremiah 31:31-37
Song: "Grace Greater Than Our Sin"

So you're having trouble with your memory. You mislaid your keys along with your glasses. Not to worry. They're both in our "Lost and Found" along with your umbrella, your Bible and that favorite sweater. It's not surprising that we occasionally find such items. What's beginning to bother us is that the owners of these wayward pieces never seem to think the church is the place they misplaced them. Have they forgotten they were ever here?

One speaker compared memory to a drawer in a filing cabinet. After many years of wonderful experiences, our "memory drawer" is packed full. Hence, the difficulty we have in remembering the names of new acquaintances or in remembering just where we placed our keys.

How could a perfect God forget? How could He "remember our sins no more?" With God, we speak not of amnesia or loss of memory. God has chosen to deliberately forgive our sins, to remember them no more. It's not so much forgetting, as it is an act of the will on His part. It takes a deliberate act of the will to forgive those who have sinned against us. We have few opportunities to demonstrate the grace of God so completely, and in doing so you will be blessed and will be a blessing to the one you forgive.

Lord, I don't like to forgive others. I do, however, want to be like You. Help me to forgive when I am given the opportunity that I might bear testimony to Your grace within me. In Your Son's name I pray. Amen.

Healthy At One Hundred!

Nevertheless, I will bring health and healing to it; I will heal my people and will let them enjoy abundant peace and security (Jeremiah 33:6, New International Version).

Scripture: Jeremiah 33:1-13
Song: "Count Your Blessings"

My grandmother has something in common with the Queen's mother (the Queen of England, of course). They both turned 100 in the year 2000. The media may not have noticed our family's gathering of more than 100 people, but what a great day of rejoicing we enjoyed. Grandma is still mentally alert and was physically well enough to walk about and visit with many of her guests.

Grandma's unusually good health was brought home to me today as I visited three church members in various stages of recovery. None of these three have even reached their 50th birthday. The first had just been moved from intensive care into a regular room. The second had just been released from the hospital, and the third was recently able to put away her cane since her broken foot had sufficiently healed to allow her to resume walking normally. All of them praised the Lord for their healing to this point. How uplifting to be around those who rejoice despite accidents or illness.

Despite their years of unfaithfulness, God promised the people of Judah they would again enjoy His healing touch, His peace, and His security. Health, peace, security — Let's thank God for these blessings from His hand.

God, we recognize that our health is a fragile thing. Let us rejoice while we enjoy good days and look to You for strength when ill. In all things, help us to trust in Your promises and to enjoy those blessings You so graciously bestow. In Jesus' name, we pray. Amen.

Strengthened by the Storm

Let patience have her perfect work, that ye may be perfect and entire,
wanting nothing (James 1:4).

Scripture: Psalm 119:49-56
Song: "Have Thine Own Way, Lord"

The tale is told of an old violin maker who was the envy of the other craftsmen for the superiority of the instruments he produced. His surprising secret was this: while others cut their wood from trees in nearby valleys, he made the difficult journey up the side of a mountain to secure the wood of trees which had been beaten and twisted by the storms.

From those weather-beaten trees came the wood that produced the deep, rich tones for which his creations were known. The trial of exposure to mountain gales had caused these trees to produce the strong, tough fibers so necessary for the master's finished product.

And so it is with us. There are those who seek the comfort of God's promises while suffering. They persevere. There are those who stand strong in the face of mockers and critics. They grow even stronger.

Most of us crave the easy road, the journey of comfort. What we sometimes fail to realize is that it is in the storms of life that we are most suitably strengthened and equipped. Were it not for the difficult times we face, we could never be the select instruments of service chosen by our Master and finely tuned for His purpose.

Use me, dear Lord, in Your service. Remind me during the difficult days that these too can be part of Your refining process. May hardship and persecution not make me bitter, but better suited for service to You. In Your precious name, I pray. Amen.

Grace In Life and Death

Yea, though I walk through the valley of the shadow of death, I will fear no evil: for thou art with me; thy rod and thy staff they comfort me (Psalm 23:4).

Scripture: Titus 2:11-15
Song: "He Leadeth Me"

Woody Allen has been quoted as saying that he doesn't fear death. He just doesn't want to be there when it happens.

We have to smile at such a statement. On the other hand, there are those who face death in the calmest, most optimistic manner. What a powerful testimony they provide us.

A six-year-old girl dying from leukemia tells her parents, "I'm going to see Jesus soon. Any messages?"

A student at Columbine High School affirms her newly-discovered belief in God even though she knows it may cost her life, and it does!

A Civil War soldier, dying from a horrible wound, asks a chaplain to give thanks for the faith he received as a child at his mother's knee.

It is usually the time of death that makes the hope of Christ so precious. But the grace of God is also a mentor, urging us to refuse the temptations of this world.

Will our final words prove to be inspiring to those around us? Will we face death with such serenity and faith? It is of critical importance that we know the grace of God in daily living since those who know the grace of God in life are those who manifest the grace of God when dying.

Heavenly Father, we know that Your grace brings strength that we might avoid the path of unrighteousness. Thank You for the power You give us that we might live for Him who died for all, Jesus, our Savior, in whose name we offer this prayer. Amen.

God's Great Works

"O Lord, I have heard tell of thy deeds; I have seen, O Lord, thy work."
(Habakkuk 3:2, New English Bible).

Scripture: Habakkuk 3:2-6
Song: "How Great Thou Art"

I had heard so often that I just *had* to see the Grand Canyon, that when I finally visited it several years ago, it was more with a sense of duty than expectation. I was not prepared to behold a grandeur that would change my life. It was a perfect October morning, and looking down into the immense chasm left me speechless with wonderment. What an incredible variety of pastel colors, what massive and majestic rock formations! My amazement grew as I walked along the path near the edge of the canyon. Every few feet the scene changed—almost like gazing into a kaleidoscope. Each twist and turn revealed unique patterns. Even the same scene changed before my eyes, as clouds drifting overhead cast shadows, and intense colors faded and then brightened. Everywhere I looked, I was overwhelmed with a sense of reverence. "I have seen, O Lord, thy work!"

I use memories of that visit now as a touchstone. Life sometimes seems overwhelming, and difficulties higher, deeper, wider than any hope for solution. But then I get my bearings. I remind myself, "Remember. The Lord God made the Grand Canyon. He can do anything."

Dearest Lord, thank You for all of creation, which reminds us everywhere we look how great Thou art. Nothing is impossible for You. We bow before You in awe and gratitude and thanksgiving. In Jesus' name, we pray. Amen.

October 21-27. **Maria Anne Tolar** is a Christian writer who lives in Portland, Oregon.

Faithfulness in Hard Times

Though the fig tree does not bud and there are no grapes on the vines . . . yet I will rejoice in the Lord, I will be joyful in God my Savior (Habakkuk 3:17a, 18, New International Version).

Scripture: Habakkuk 3:8-19
Song: "Oh, For a Faith That Will Not Shrink"

Years ago a friend described the season his cherry tree produced one cherry. Then as he was mournfully studying the one lone cherry, a bird swooped down and ate it. His story was amusing. But real adversity is anything but funny.

Have you ever had a season like the one Habakkuk describes in this passage of Scripture: Your trees don't bloom. Your vines are fruitless. Olive crop fails. Orchards yield nothing. No cattle in the stalls. In a modern paraphrase, no job. No prospects. No money. No groceries. No insurance. His conclusion seems paradoxical: "Yet I will rejoice in the Lord. . . . The Sovereign Lord is my strength; he makes my feet like the feet of a deer, he enables me to go on the heights."

Several years ago I read about some business "success stories." Almost without exception, the people who achieve great prosperity credit the lessons and insights they learned from early adversity and failure for their ultimate success. Hardship teaches profound lessons of the necessity of perseverance and faith.

Heartaches and adversities occur to us all. But when we rejoice in the Lord, He helps us overcome. Those blighted orchards can produce fruit for eternity.

Dear Lord, You are greater than any problem, any sorrow. Let us rejoice in You always, in all circumstances, because joy in You is our strength. In the name of Jesus, we pray. Amen.

Heart After God

The Lord is my strength and my shield; my heart trusts in him, and I am helped. My heart leaps for joy (Psalm 28:7, New International Version).

Scripture: Psalm 28:1-9
Song: "The Solid Rock"

When we think of David, we think of his passionate heart for God. He was a greatly beloved and righteous king of Israel. But David was also a man who was surrounded by enemies his entire life.

As a boy tending his father's flocks, he fought off lions and bears when they attacked the fold. He alone went into battle against Goliath, whom he saw as an enemy of all Israel, defying the army of the living God. The jealous King Saul became his mortal enemy. Saul's daughter Michal was so humiliated and appalled by King David's unabashed and intense worship of God as he accompanied the Ark into Jerusalem, that she despised him in her heart.

But David never wavered in his love of God, never became lukewarm to please others. God was his fortress and shield and protection. His enemies were powerful, but no match for David's zealous faith and trust in God.

Would that our enemies were the wild beasts that attack the sheep of our father's fold. Would that we could be despised for loving the Lord with every fiber of our being. Would that we could become as great as David, not for who we are but for Whom we love.

Dearest Lord Jesus, thank You for being my shield and strength and Savior. For every problem and worry, no matter how huge or how small, let me look to You for the answer. In Your holy name, I pray. Amen.

Springs of Deliverance

So you shall draw water with joy from the springs of deliverance
(Isaiah 12:3, New English Bible).

Scripture: Isaiah 12:1-6
Song: "Joyful, Joyful, We Adore Thee"

On my grandfather's farm in Idaho when I was growing up, there was no indoor plumbing. Water for family use came from a spring, down in a grove of willows a long trek from the house. The family saying was that the house only had running water if you ran after it.

But what water! Delicious and refreshing, crystal clear, icy cold, pure, and perfect; it was the most wonderful water in the whole world. One small natural spring had provided for the needs of a family of ten, and later for an army of grandchildren. There was more than enough for a huge bucket of ice-cold drinking water always kept right inside the back porch, plus water for doing dishes, and for taking baths and scrubbing floors and watering the flower garden. That one spring seemed to offer a supernatural supply: no matter how many buckets were drawn out, the spring always seemed to hold the same amount of water. Not until water was piped into the house years later did the spring gradually disappear. Its important job was finally done.

In like manner what a joy it is to draw living water from God's springs of deliverance, water that is never depleted by the daily needs of the whole world.

Dearest Lord, how grateful we are that You are our God, that You are our provider, and that You are good and kind and merciful. Let us be bold to proclaim to a lost world that You are the deliverer for everyone who calls on You for the water of life. In Jesus' name, we pray. Amen.

Keeping Faith

Open the gates to let a righteous nation in, a nation that keeps faith
(Isaiah 26:2, New English Bible).

Scripture: Isaiah 26:1-6
Song: "Who Is on the Lord's Side?"

My husband recently made a trip to a South African country. As he toured one large village, he was dumbfounded by the poverty he observed, shaken by how unbelievably hard some people's lives are. He was moved to tears when he visited one dump. It is literally home for dozens of people, including many orphans, who eke out a living sifting through garbage in hope of finding cast-off clothing and food that others have thrown out.

In that same village, he visited the local grade school. The students were shepherded out to sing for the visitors. He was captivated by these beautiful and joyful children with their amazing voices. And he was utterly astonished by what they sang about—there in the schoolyard, school children praising Jesus, proclaiming God's goodness.

Afterwards, he explained to a teacher that such songs are not permitted to be sung in the schools of his own country, that God cannot even be mentioned, that prayer must be silent. They were dumbfounded, stunned. Not to be able to sing about Jesus! They were moved to tears for such a country.

We have so much, and so little. We have such blessings, but not the freedom to boast of the One who gave them.

Lord, give us the compassion to help others live better lives, and the humility to see how desperately we need help ourselves. Help us to long for a righteous nation, one that keeps faith with You and is thus worthy to reach out to the world with the Gospel of Jesus Christ. In the name of Jesus, we pray. Amen.

The Way, the Truth, and the Life

The path of the righteous is level, and thou markest out the right way for the upright (Isaiah 26:7b, New English Bible).

Scripture: Isaiah 26:7-13
Song: "Higher Ground"

A friend once told me how practical and basically easy Christianity is. You simply have to refuse to compromise just once. He'd started out in a business where it is common for even well-established, well-respected colleagues to occasionally request special favors, to ask that the regulations be bent in their favor just a little, just this once. "No," only had to be said once, and he was never asked again. But those who said "Yes," opened a can of worms. The person who is granted a questionable favor the first time always wants an even bigger favor the next time. Once they find you will compromise your principles in a small matter, they push to see how far you will go.

Sometimes it doesn't seem easy taking the straight and narrow path of the righteous, "the King's highway." But who needs the scenic route or the detours or the side roads when the goal is to go to Heaven?

Reading Scripture is the surest, fastest, safest way of finding the path. God's word teaches us His will and His mind. As we bring our thoughts into alignment with His, as we will to do His will, we are set on the path of life. Forsaking all other ways and roads and shortcuts is not just the fastest way home. It is the only way home.

Dearest heavenly Father, thank You for Your Word, for the miracle of the Bible, for the privilege of hearing from You directly. Thank You for giving us the opportunity to learn about You. In the name of Jesus, we pray. Amen.

Obeying Our Orders

I charge you to obey your orders irreproachably and without fault until our Lord Jesus Christ appears (I Timothy 6:14, New English Bible).

Scripture: 1 Timothy 6:11-16
Song: "Trust and Obey"

Military personnel in basic training learn to obey their superiors without question and without delay. Many of us learned the same lesson from our earthly parents. Some moms and dads operate on the basis of the slogan, "*Slow* obedience is *No* obedience." A certain amount of this kind of speedy compliance to rules is essential to the successful operation of an army or of a family.

If it is important for us to be quick to obey humans who have authority over us, how much more important it is to comply quickly and joyfully with the commandments of the Lord. After all, we don't serve a cruel taskmaster, an unfair or fallible tyrant who has set up pointless rules just to make our lives miserable and hard. He is a great and good God, a God of compassion and holiness, who loved us so dearly He sent His only Son to help us run the great race of faith and take hold of eternal life.

Paul told Timothy to obey His orders "irreproachably and without fault." And so must we. The truth is, the more we obey and serve God, the more exciting and meaningful and joyful our lives become.

Dear Lord, what an awesome privilege and delight to be part of Your kingdom. Thank You for loving us enough to show us the path to You. Our heart's desire is to obey You and to bring honor to the name of Jesus. Amen.

Do The Crime, Pay The Time

They mocked God's messengers, despised his words and scoffed at his prophets until the wrath of the Lord was aroused against his people and there was no remedy (2 Chronicles 36:16, New International Version).

Scripture: 2 Chronicles 36:9-16
Song: "Create in Me a Clean Heart"

A recent public service announcement on TV showed a man behind bars. His cell door closed with a loud clang, and a caption read, "Do the Crime, Pay the Time." It demonstrates the result of breaking the law.

Under the leadership of bad kings, the people of Judah did not heed God's prophets or God's message and suffered the consequences—their nation fell.

How many of us tell little white lies which our children overhear and think, "If it's okay for Mom and Dad to lie, then it must be all right for me." A recent survey revealed that two of three kids raised in Christian homes in the United States and Canada ages eleven to eighteen had recently lied to a parent, teacher, or other adult.

How many of us break laws we think are insignificant like driving over the speed limit? Or when we attend an event, we say our child is younger than he or she really is to get into the event for less money? How long will we continue to do wrong and not suffer the consequences of our actions?

Our faithful God, we praise You for being One who loves and wants only good for Your children. May we continue to seek Your will, read Your Word, listen to Your message, and live lives that will make You proud. Help us to be examples of doing right. In Jesus' name, we pray. Amen.

October 28—31. **B. J. Bassett** is a writer, conference presenter, and Christian education director. She and her husband have four children and two grandsons.

October 29

The Winter of My Life

The land enjoyed its sabbath rests . . . until the seventy years were completed
(2 Chronicles 36:21b, New International Version).

Scripture: 2 Chronicles 36:17-21
Song: "Come, Ye Disconsolate"

Have you lost a loved one? A job? Are you financially destitute? Emotionally devastated? Do you feel abandoned? Lonely? If you are going through tough times, you are going through a winter of your life.

In the course of time God's children experience the seasons of life. They are much like the seasons of the year. Spring promises hope with newness and birth—trees budding and flowers blooming. Summer follows spring with lots of sunshine, growth, and fun in the sun. Then comes fall, or harvest time. It's a time to store the fruits of our labor and provide for long winters. Fall is followed by winter that is desolate and barren. The winters of our lives can be dismal and lonely. Yet it is not a time to forsake God's plan of needed rest and worship. Winter never lasts forever. It is followed by spring and the promise of new life and hope.

Just as the Scripture reading for today tells of a bleak time in Judah's history, many of us will experience lots of winters during our lifetimes. They are tough times. Yet, we need to remember that God wants us to rest and to worship Him during all of the seasons of our lives.

Holy Father, thank You for Your perfect plan of the seasons of our lives. We don't always want to go through the long and desolate winters, but no matter what the season, let us never forget to set aside time to spend in prayer, meditation, and study of Your Word. May we welcome the rest You provide and worship You joyfully from our hearts. In Christ' name, we pray. Amen.

Blessed Are Those Who Mourn

Blessed are those who mourn, for they will be comforted (Matthew 5:4, New International Version).

Scripture: Psalm 137:1-6
Song: "No One Understands Like Jesus"

Several weeks ago I wrote in my journal, "Daddy died today." Since that time I've experienced some very sad times, and I'm moody.

One day I told my husband that I had been sad all day. He asked, "Did you think about your dad today?" I answered curtly, "Only all day."

During our family vacation I isolated myself from the rest of the family. At work I found it difficult to focus. I read every book on grief I could get my hands on, and I cried. There was no doubt that I was grieving.

The musicians wept over their loss and remembrance of Jerusalem. Jesus wept over His friend Lazarus. We weep over our losses whether they be the loss of a job, an empty nest, homesickness, bankruptcy, or the loss of a loved one.

God created us as living and feeling human beings. He wants us to feel and to remember. So let the hurt hurt and give yourself time. "Blessed are those who mourn, for they will be comforted."

Like the musicians who wept over Jerusalem, we too need to weep over our losses and be comforted by God.

Heavenly Father and Creator, even though life is sometimes difficult, thank You for Your love and plan. Thank You for creating us as living and feeling people. Thank You for Your comfort in difficult times. Thank You for the example of Your Son Jesus, for the comfort of Your Word, and for the encouragement that comes through others. In Jesus' name, we pray. Amen.

Help Me, 0 Lord

We . . . will praise you forever; from generation to generation we will recount your praise (Psalm 79:13b, New International Version).

Scripture: Psalm 79:5-13
Song: "Sweet Hour of Prayer"

In 1959 my husband and I celebrated our first wedding anniversary and his college graduation. Now, we wanted to start a family. We prayed and waited. The months grew into years. We followed all of the doctor's advice and instructions. Still no baby. Many nights I called out to God and begged for a baby, then cried myself to sleep.

Maybe it was a selfish prayer. I had always loved children and wanted one of my own. I don't remember if I bargained with God as the psalmist did, or if I pledged to give Him all of the glory. I also don't remember if I asked that His will be done and not my will. I do know that God always answers our prayers, Sometimes His answer is "Yes," sometimes it's "No," and at other times it is "Wait."

After five years of marriage, God blessed us with the adoption of a baby girl. Over the next few years God blessed us with three more babies. Our family has grown to include a son-in-law and grandsons. From generation to generation we give thanks and praise to God.

Perhaps there are things in your life you have wanted for a long, long time but have never received. Maybe the time is right now. Pray to God, and don't forget to give Him thanks.

Heavenly Father, thank You that You always hear and answer our prayers. Help us not to pray selfish prayers, beg, or bargain with You, but seek Your will. May we always give You the glory and praise You so richly deserve. And may all our generations praise You. In Jesus' name, we pray. Amen.

Devotions

November

photo by Chuck Perry

Yield To The Master Potter's Hands

We are the clay, you are the potter; we are all the work of your hand
(Isaiah 64:8b, New International Version).

Scripture: Isaiah 64:6-12
Song: "Have Thine Own Way, Lord!"

Like the people of Isaiah's time we have been corrupted and polluted by sin. Guilt makes us feel like dirty rags. When we read the Bible and see what God wants us to be, we get some inkling of how far short of our potential we have fallen. Is it time for us to take hold of God in prayer, repent, and ask our Creator to form us anew? We do that by yielding to the Master Potter's hands.

We are nothing but a blob of clay until the Master Potter molds us into what He desires. First we are worked and kneaded by the experiences of life until we are ready to yield and become completely pliable in the Master's hand.

Then we are flopped onto the Potter's wheel. As we spin around and around we are stretched and flexed as the Potter smoothes us with His fingers and thumbs. After He has shaped us into what He wants us to be, we are popped into the oven of hardships and baked. Some of us are thick and rough, others are smooth like fine china.

Are we willing to yield to the Master Potter? Will we be still and trust God to mold us into His renewed creation—the person He desires us to be?

Father, I am nothing but a glob of clay without the touch of Your hands. Help me put my trust in You—to yield to Your hands, to be molded into what You desire me to be. Mold me, Lord, shape me, put me into the fire. Amen.

November 1-3. **B.J. Bassett** is a writer, conference presenter, and Christian education director. She and her husband have four children and two grandsons.

Teach Me to Pray, Lord

He was praying in a certain place, and when he ceased, one of his disciples said to him, "Lord, teach us to pray. . . . . "(Luke 11:1, Revised Standard Version).

Scripture: Daniel 9: 1-10
Song: "Teach Me to Pray"

When my children were young, I'd go to my bedroom, close the door, and spend time with God. Recently my daughter said, "We knew what you were doing in your room with the door closed, Mom." During those times I was not only spending time with my Lord, I was also showing my children the importance of prayer.

Each of us needs to find a quiet place to commune with God. It is also important to find a time that best suits our schedules. Some people meet God in the morning; others meet Him in the evening. Some begin their day with a short prayer thanking God for the new day.

God's Word gives us many examples of prayers. Two very instructive samples include Daniel's prayer found in today's Scripture and the example Jesus gave His disciples in Matthew 6:9-15, often called "The Lord's Prayer."

My quiet time consists of reading a short devotion and a related chapter of Scripture. Then I write my prayers in a book using the A C T S idea. "A" is for adoration—a personal worship of God. "C" is for confession. "T" represents thanksgiving. And "S" is for supplication—asking God to intervene in other people's lives and in my life.

Father, holy, forgiving, merciful, and powerful—worthy of praise. Search me and show me the sin I need to confess. Thank You for Your Word which instructs me, and I pray for others to find their prayer closets and to be drawn near to You in prayer. In the name of Jesus, I pray. Amen.

That's Enough

All Israel have transgressed thy law, even by departing, that they might not obey thy voice (Daniel 9:11).

Scripture: Daniel 9:11-19
Song: "Where He Leads Me"

Our family was vacationing at beautiful Lake Tahoe. It was the sixth day we had relaxed on the beach. Our four-year-old grandson, Brock, said, "I'm hungry." We had not brought any food with us. I thought I'd save the day by offering suckers to him and his older brother, Ben. As I held my hands behind my back, I let Ben choose first, and he picked a green sucker. The other one was orange. That did it! Brock, usually a happy obedient child, wanted the green sucker and he began to cry. He cried, and cried, and cried. His mother put him down for a nap. Still he wailed. Then his father tried to console him, but with no success.

Finally we packed up and trudged to the car with Brock still crying. My husband looked into Brock's face and said, "That's enough." With his big, tear-filled eyes he looked up at his grandfather and stopped crying.

Later that day Brock came over to where we were sitting, and in his little repentant four-year-old voice said, "Grandma and Grandpa, I'm sorry I was bad."

Concerning our disobedience and sin, I can imagine our Heavenly Father looking down from Heaven into our faces and saying, "That's enough."

Heavenly Father, You created us and know us. Keep us ever in line and obedient to You. Make us aware of any wrong we do. Concerning sin, Lord, we pray that You will never have to look into our faces and say, "That's enough." In Jesus' name, we pray. Amen.

Run to the God of Comfort

As one whom his mother comforteth, so will I comfort you (Isaiah 66:13).

Scripture: Lamentations 1:12-16
Song: "A Shelter in the Time of Storm"

It was an especially cold winter, even for Ohio, and yet my young son Kent wanted to play in the freshly fallen foot of snow. Though he was bundled from head to toe, I knew that before long he would return to me with rosy cheeks and nearly-frozen ears.

He soon came running back into the house and into my outstretched arms. He received a hug and comforting kisses on his cold cheeks and red nose. His mittens were warmed on the heating vent. Then he was ready to go again into that white world of adventure.

Years later, this same son experienced a tremendously painful time in his adult life. He felt that God was far away. Then I received an e-mail saying he had attended church and that it felt like God "hugged" him.

We sometimes feel discouraged by the elements in our world that blow bitterly cold winds against our spirits. We want to cry and run into God's presence for comfort.

Our Lord is always there to give us a hug when life seems unbearable. He will bring the comfort we need and encourage us to again face the difficult challenges of our lives.

My heavenly Father, I run to You today for comfort and encouragement. Hold me in Your loving arms. Let me feel Your warm embrace. Then I'll climb down from Your lap and back into the cold world to share that comfort and encouragement with others. In Jesus' loving name, amen.

November 4-10. **Phyllis Qualls Freeman** is a freelance writer and a secretary at a medical facility. She and her husband, Bill, have three children and four grandchildren.

I Have Hope Because of His Faithfulness

Thy faithfulness is unto all generations: thou hast established the earth, and it abideth (Psalm 119:90).

Scripture: Lamentations 3:18-24
Song: "We shall see the King Some Day"

Can you remember a special event you earnestly wanted to attend? You were invited to a birthday party, a family reunion, or to go on a vacation. These events spark hope and expectation. Each day brings you closer to what you will experience when the special day arrives.

However, if each expected event turns into a disappointment, then you would eventually learn not to hope.

What makes the difference? When the one who gives us promises has proven to be dependable time after time, we expect their future promises to be fulfilled. But if someone is continually unreliable, we have little hope they will keep future promises.

God is reliable! We can trust His Word. Whatever God promises will come to pass. Jesus' return is one of the events for which we have hope. Even more immediate are the promises of comfort, strength, and peace that we can expect to receive from Him daily as we lean on Him.

Yes, He is a promise keeper. He is a faithful God. Even though difficulties may come, He will work on our behalf and will bring joy with the fulfillment of His provision. I find hope in the fact that one day I will see the King of Kings.

O faithful One, our hearts rejoice in the hope of Your promises and of Your expected return. You were reliable in the past and we know that we can trust You for our futures. When everything looks hopeless, help us to remember that You are faithful. In the name of the Jesus, we pray. Amen.

God Will Have Compassion

Though he cause grief, yet will he have compassion (Lamentations 3:32).

Scripture: Lamentations 3:25-33
Song: "Love Divine, All Loves Excelling"

Kyle didn't enjoy baseball or other team sports as did his older brother. So when he wanted to take karate lessons, my husband and I encouraged him to do it. The discipline of the sport helped him learn concentration, and his school studies improved. At 16 years old he earned his black belt in karate. As part of a demonstration he once gave to a group of 200 Christian campers, Kyle broke boards with his feet and split a cinder block with his hand.

Though so powerful, Kyle also has a gentler side. I once witnessed this powerful young man catch a house fly in his cupped hands and let it out of the door rather than smash it as his mom would have done. He was compassionate toward a helpless little creature.

It is apparent that God has awesome power. We see this power demonstrated from time to time in nature as lightening strikes, hurricanes tear through houses, floods ravage the countryside, and earthquakes topple great cities.

Yet, because of God's tender mercies, He holds you and me safely in the palm of His hands. He has made a way for us to escape from eternal death.

Through Jesus, His Son, the all-powerful God tenderly extends us a chance to live forever.

Thank You Father, for sending Jesus to die on the cross in our place. We thank You that we can accept His sacrifice and live. Each day You show compassion by giving us a fresh chance to experience Your mercies, for which we are grateful. In the holy name of Jesus, we pray. Amen.

I Lift My Heart Toward Heaven

Hear the voice of my supplications, when I cry unto thee, when I lift up my hands toward thy holy oracle (Psalms 28:2).

Scripture: Lamentations 3:34-41
Song: "I Surrender All"

In 1974 a sixteen-year-old slammed his car into my green Chevrolet and I sustained lower back and neck injuries. After suffering for three years, I attended a church where special prayer was offered for the sick. Later that night, after I received prayer, I discarded the back brace I had worn for eight months and my body began a progressive healing.

One of the painful movements for my arms and shoulders had been to lift clothing out of a closet or use my arms in any type of lifting above my shoulder level.

I now felt that I was supposed to lift my hands in praise to the Lord during the singing of praise choruses or in prayer at my church. Previously, shyness had prevented me from any outward demonstration of worship.

I wanted to offer praise to the Lord in this way, so I raised my hands slightly during worship times. The more I did this, the less pain I experienced. After a few weeks I felt a new freedom in worship and no pain at all. I came into a new realm of submissive worship.

Does God ever impress upon you to lift your thoughts or your heart or your hands to Him? We should love Him so completely that we worship Him with our whole being!

Lord, I lift my heart to You and meditate on Your goodness. I lift my head toward Heaven with a heart full of love. I lift up my hands in symbolic surrender of my will to Yours. I will ever praise You, Father, in the most holy name of Jesus, Your Son. Amen.

Hear My Cry, O Lord

I sought the Lord, and he heard me, and delivered me from all my fears
(Psalms 34:4).

Scripture: Lamentations 3:49-57
Song: "O God, Our Help in Ages Past"

Often my young son, Kyle got into unusual predicaments. Once he climbed onto a window sill from his crib.

After hearing a small whimpering voice, I discovered a bulge in the window shade which was my infant son waiting for me to rescue him.

A couple of years later a small voice called out from the fenced back yard, and I searched to find the source. It seemed to come from the small doghouse with the doorway half boarded over to accommodate our little dog. Once more I found Kyle in a place from which he needed to be rescued.

How often do we as adults get into life situations that are frightening or from which it seems impossible to escape? The most natural response in the world for Christians is for us to cry out, "Help me, Father. I'm lost, I'm in a jam, I can't get myself out of this one." He hears and will answer.

As time went on, my son learned which places were dangerous and which were safe, and I was needed to rescue him less and less frequently.

God is willing to hear our cry and rescue us, and yet He longs for us to mature in Christ so that we will recognize the dangers around us and avoid them.

Loving Father, thank You for hearing our pleas for help and responding as a mother would to the cry of her child. Help us to grow up and please You with our maturity and wisdom. Then enable us to reach out a helping hand to others. We pray in Jesus' holy name. Amen.

November 9

Revive Us That We May Rejoice

Wilt thou not revive us again: that thy people may rejoice in thee?
(Psalm 85:6).

Scripture: Lamentations 5:15-22
Song: "Revive Us Again"

This past year my strength seemed to ebb away. Silently, I thought that my age was catching up with me.

One day at work my co-workers, who are registered nurses, recognized the symptoms of a possible heart attack and escorted me to the emergency room for evaluation.

Three days and many tests and procedures later I realized that the fatigue I felt was related to an artery that was about 70% blocked.

After a "balloon and stent" procedure and a period of recuperation and rehabilitation, I am amazed by my renewed strength. What joy to feel good again!

I sense that there is "gunk" which gathers in our spirit not unlike the harmful plaque that had blocked my arteries to reduce the flow of blood to my heart. Worry, anger, and the cares of life sometimes block our spirit's relationship to God and sap our spiritual vigor.

My surgeon had the wisdom and skill to open my blocked artery so that blood could flow unhindered to my heart. Through our vigilant prayer and reading of the Word, God can unclog any hindrances in our spirit. Then His power and love can revitalize us and bring renewed life.

Lord, we thank You for physicians who can skillfully open blocked arteries and rejuvenate our physical lives. We praise You for being the Great Physician, and we ask You to unclog those areas which hinder the flow of Your spirit through our lives. Allow Your love to flow through us and out to others. Revive us again. We pray in Jesus' holy name. Amen.

Liquid Prayer Brings Joy

Make a joyful noise unto the Lord, all the earth: make a loud noise, and rejoice, and sing praise (Psalms 98:4).

Scripture: Psalm 126:1-6
Song: "Since Jesus Came Into My Heart"

Vivid memories are etched in my mind of my mother weeping behind closed doors. Her prayers were not the "lay me down to sleep" kind. She was travailing in prayer for the needs of her family and of others. Prayer in travail eventually brings deliverance and responses of joy.

Through a myriad of prayers and tears God brought back the captivity of Judah. Then came laughter and singing.

Travailing prayer issues from a spirit of brokenness with purpose; it is a ministry of tears that Charles H. Spurgeon once defined as "liquid prayer." Earnest prayer touches the heart of God. There will be rejoicing in the harvest from seeds planted in weeping and prayer.

When Mom developed Alzheimer's disease we were devastated, and we prayed that God's grace would be seen through her in her closing years. This was answered when we discovered that the workers at the nursing home where she resides stop by Eva's chair for their hug and kiss from a face beaming with joy. She has no verbal communication skills now but is full of laughter and joy. God's love is deep in her heart and shines clearly on her face.

Almighty God, You are the deliverer from all our captivities. We ask in travailing prayer for daily grace and ultimately for deliverance. Help us to recognize every glimpse of freedom and victory and to respond with rejoicing. May Your joy shine on our faces to reveal You to others who do not yet know You. In the name of Jesus, we pray. Amen.

Society Tells Me So

"What do you people mean?" (Ezekiel 18:2a, New International Version).

Scripture: Ezekiel 18:1-9
Song: "Living for Jesus"

A church-going parent provided alcoholic beverages at her son's high school graduation party even though the state's legal drinking age is twenty-one.

"Everybody we invited agreed to give me their car keys," she said to me, "so they couldn't drive after drinking. I can't see anything wrong with this. No one got caught."

She appealed to a popular, but faulty, social proverb: breaking laws is acceptable as long as you're not caught.

People of Judah in Babylonian captivity also repeated a popular, but faulty, proverb to justify themselves. In essence, Ezekiel asked them, "What do you people mean? God holds each individual responsible for his own actions."

Still today, people who try to squirm away from personal accountability create havoc in homes, schools, and work places, adversely affecting communities and nations.

God's laws and principles are gracious and merciful. He developed them so we'd have guidelines to live successfully. If we practice God's principles instead of living by what is merely socially acceptable, the world will be better off. If we live personally accountable to God, He'll help us grow healthy families and secure communities.

Gracious God, help us to follow Christ's example and biblical principles. Your ways give us happiness and stability. In Christ's name, we pray. Amen.

November 11-17. **Lucinda Norman** is a writer and a high school substitute teacher. She and her husband, Ron, have one adult son, Rich.

Move Beyond Poetic Justice

The righteousness of the righteous man will be credited to him, and the wickedness of the wicked will be charged against him (Ezekiel 18:20c, New International Version).

Scripture: Ezekiel 18:19-24
Song: "There's a Wideness in God's Mercy"

Part of why I like mystery novels is that they often demonstrate poetic justice. After minor victories, the villain gets caught and punished. Despite setbacks, the detective makes good overcome evil. Characters get what they deserve by the story's end. Ultimately individual responsibility and justice are satisfied.

In Babylonian captivity, some of the people of Judah mistakenly complained that their captivity was God punishing them for their parents' sins.

In essence, Ezekiel told them to take responsibility for their individual actions. They weren't victims of their parents' sin. They had enough sin of their own.

When we examine ourselves, we too discover that we sin. Like Judah's complainers, we sometimes blame our parents, someone else, or something else for our sins. If God gave us justice, we, like those captives, would deserve punishment.

But part of what I love so much about God is that He has satisfied the demands of justice through the death of His Son Jesus Christ on the cross.

If we accept Jesus as our personal Savior, God washes us with forgiveness and wraps us in mercy and love.

Loving God, Your actions and attitude toward us make it possible for us to be honest with You and to confess our sins to You. How can we thank You enough for Your mercy and forgiveness You've given us through Christ? We pray in His holy name. Amen.

November 13
God Knows You and Love You Anyway

Repent! Turn away from all your offenses; then sin will not be your downfall.
Rid yourselves of all the offenses you have committed, and get a new heart
and a new spirit (Ezekiel 18:30b-31a, New International Version)

Scripture: Ezekiel 18:25-32
Song: "Just As I Am"

I had Mrs. Breakey as my teacher for first and second grades. If she stood me in the corner for talking during lessons, my mother knew before I got home.

Could mom somehow see me wherever I was? Years later I learned Mrs. Breakey and she were cousins.

After those experiences, God's omnipresence and omniscience seemed natural. For as long as I can remember, I've sensed God knew me, observed my right and wrong actions and motives, and loved the real me.

Ezekiel 18 verifies what I sensed as a child. God knows us personally. He doesn't charge us for our parent's behavior, but considers our personal right or wrong actions.

The best part is that, although God knows our darker sinful side, He urges us to confess our wrongdoing and enables us to turn away from it.

God knows we can't keep sin from being our downfall. He gave us His Son Jesus Christ to save us and to direct us. When we turn to Christ, He gives us a new heart and new spirit. These align us with God's perspective. Only then can we live lives pleasing to the God who loves us.

Caring God, where would we be without You? Although You know us better than even our parents could, You love us. Help us admit we have a darker side and to turn from it toward Christ. Renew our hearts and spirits so we're free to wholeheartedly love and please You. In Jesus' name we pray. Amen.

Watchmen for Our World

Son of man, I have made you a watchman for the house of Israel; so hear the word I speak and give them warning from me (Ezekiel 33:7, New International Version).

Scripture: Ezekiel 33:7-11
Song: "Let the Lower Lights Be Burning"

Along Lake Erie's shore in Barcelona, New York, is an intriguing stone lighthouse. Built in 1828, it's very unusual in that it is lighted by natural gas.

Lighthouses are stone or wooden watchmen, alerting sailors to their location so they won't be lost and warning of their shoreline's unique dangers.

Just as God considered Ezekiel a watchman for his era, we're God's twenty-first century watchmen, God's flesh-and-blood lighthouses. We highlight God's Word as well as expose moral and spiritual dangers to those around us.

Each of us is commissioned to fulfill God's purpose. God had a purpose for Ezekiel's captivity in Babylon. Not too long after Ezekiel's exile, God gave him a special call to be the captive nation's prophet.

Likewise, God gives purpose to Marlene's being a librarian, Megan's being a restaurant salad maker, Rich's being a firefighter paramedic, Ron's being a public school teacher, and to you in your situation.

Paraphrased, God's Word to us is, "Be my watchman where you are. Speak my words and warning to lost people where you are. I love them, too."

Our watchful God, sometimes we can't believe You choose us to tell others about Your holiness and love. Help us to be brave watchmen unafraid to share ourselves and our faith with those whose lives intersect ours. Grow our faith to be as sturdy as a stone lighthouse. In Christ name, we pray. Amen.

How Could We Not Know?

Since the creation of the world God's invisible qualities—his eternal power and divine nature—have been clearly seen, being understood from what has been made, so that men are without excuse (Romans 1:20, New International Version).

Scripture: Romans 1:16-25
Song: "The Spacious Firmament on High"

When we go to Lake Erie, I find an isolated spot on the stony beach to appreciate nature. If all I ever knew about God came from these experiences, it would be enough for me to sense His existence, to love Him, and to worship Him.

The power of the water and wind mirror God's strength. The consistency of the sun's, moon's, and water's daily cycles demonstrate His intelligence. The seemingly endless, expansive sky hints of eternity and of the almighty God's never-beginning and never-ending existence.

The majesty and variety of the blues or the depth of the cloudy grays, the clarity of gull calls, the rhythmic beat of the waves, the clean, moist scent of the air reveal God's artistic flair and care for detail. They also suggest that God, who created us, understands and then provides the nuances our senses take pleasure in.

Sometimes, as the scene fills my senses, I feel insignificant. On other occasions, I feel gigantic because I know and sense that God, who created all of this beauty and power, created and loves me.

How could any thinking person help but know the Creator exists and worship Him?

Our Creator God, You've revealed Yourself to us in a multitude of ways. May we always acknowledge the Creator behind the creations. May we be intelligent enough to worship You. In Jesus' name, we pray. Amen.

Be More Than Fair

You who pass judgment do the same things
(Romans 2:1c, New International Version).

Scripture: Romans 2:1-9
Song: "Grace Greater Than Our Sin"

How many times have you thought this or heard someone say, "Give me a break!"?

Psychologists tell us that the characteristics that annoy us about others are ironically the very things that irk us about ourselves. Sometimes we can control and improve ourselves to a limit. Rarely can we make others do as we please.

Only God can make a person be willing to change. Only God can change a person's heart. So the Bible wisely counsels restraint when we're quick to condemn others.

This doesn't mean we should avoid judging whether actions are moral or immoral by biblical standards. Rather, it's a challenge to Christians to practice grace, leniency, and mercy toward others, even when they do wrong.

After all, even as forgiven Christians, we're not perfect. Christ died because everyone sins. Further, we're unable to determine others' motivations. God knows these.

God gave us Christians a break. We can afford to give others a break. God asks us to turn the other cheek, to walk the extra mile, to be more than fair—for His sake and ours.

If someone fails to greet you today, give him a break. Take the initiative by giving him a friendly greeting first. Let's assume the best about others and treat them accordingly.

Gracious God, sometimes, I think Christ's dying was because of my wrongdoing. Thanks for sparing me from what I deserve. Open my heart to extend such grace to others. In the name of Jesus our Savior, I pray. Amen.

God Transforms Us

Whoever lives by the truth comes into the light, so that it may be seen plainly that what he has done has been done through God (John 3:21, New International Version).

Scripture: John 3:16-21
Song: "More Like the Master"

Every morning when Sylvia, my mom, boarded the school bus, she greeted and fluttered her eyelashes at Bill Chamberlin, a bashful farm boy. She thought it was funny to see the red creep up his neck and engulf his ears and face. Seven years later, they married.

Our quiet father figured he'd farm the rest of his life. God had other plans, God called him to the ministry. His siblings and we children couldn't imagine Dad talking before a congregation. Frankly, he couldn't imagine it either.

Dad changed from a shy farmer to a soft-spoken, yet dynamic preacher. He never minced words when it came to explaining that Jesus is God's Son and that anyone who wants a relationship with God has to believe Jesus died to take the punishment we deserve for our sins. God enabled Dad to speak boldly the spiritual truth he knew.

Could Dad have made that transformation himself? Unlikely. Family, friends, and neighbors plainly witnessed God reshaping him. Thirty years later, Dad still lives and speaks the truth, giving God the credit.

When the spotlight is on *our* lives, will people see what God has done to transform us?

God, grant us the will to let You mold us into the persons You created us to be. We want You to be proud of us. And when others examine our lives, we want them to see Your impression on us. We pray in the name of Jesus, the One who saves and can transform us. Amen.

Homecoming

You, O mountains of Israel, will produce branches and fruit, for my people Israel, for they will soon come home (Ezekiel 36:8, New International Version).

Scripture: Ezekiel 36:8-12
Song: "Lord, I'm Coming Home"

Do you love homecomings? Whether it be a family or a church reunion, people enjoy spending time with loved ones.

For a people that had been in captivity for years, having God make the declaration, "they will soon come home" was exciting. In our homecomings, feasting is a main attraction. And so God called on the land of Israel to prepare for Israel's coming home with abundant produce.

This homecoming of Israel reminds us of the homecoming the Christian is looking forward to—Heaven. My son, Andrew, wrote these lyrics to a song.

> *I've been thinkin' about my home*
> *I've never been but I will, I know*
> *Meadow green and the river wide*
> *Valley deep and the mountain high*
> *The saints of old are singing now*
> *My ears are ringing with the sound*
> *But greater still, as clear as day*
> *I can hear my Savior saying,*
> *"Come home, come home and rest a while."*

Precious Lord, thank You for sending Your Son so that we can follow Him home. Thank You for Your invitation to come home. We are excited about what You have prepared for "all those who love Your appearing." In the name of Jesus, we pray. Amen.

November 18-24. **Arthur O. Peterson, II** and his wife, Janis, live in Florida. He ministers with First Christian Church in Lake Butler.

Be Holy!

Just as he who called you is holy, so be holy in all you do; for it is written: "Be holy, because I am holy" (1 Peter 1:15,16 , New International Version).

Scripture: Ezekiel 36:16-23
Song: "Holy, Holy, Holy"

It has been said that the best argument for the cause of Christ is the life of a Christian. When a Christian demonstrates before a watching world the lifestyle and attitudes of his Master, the world is affected in a positive way. It has also been said that the worst argument for the cause of Christ is the life of a Christian. When a Christian's life before a watching world is careless and unholy and hypocritical, then the world is turned off by the message of Christianity. Then reproach is brought upon our Lord and His church.

Israel was God's representative before the eyes of the ancient world. Israel had become corrupt and had profaned God's name and reputation. As their tenure of punishment was coming to a close, God, through Ezekiel, reminded them that they had the responsibility to represent their God in a holy manner. God wanted to show a watching world His holiness and righteousness.

We are called today to that same purpose — to live for God in a fallen world, to demonstrate through our lives the redemptive nature of God. We are to let the unsaved see Jesus in us, and hopefully they will be drawn to His holiness and His righteousness.

Lord, today we want to show the world what You are like. Help us to let Jesus, Your Son, show through our weaknesses and limitations. Keep us ever mindful of the fact that others will learn about You when they look at Your followers. In Jesus' holy name, we pray. Amen.

Good News for Bad Hearts

Create in me a pure heart, O God, and renew a steadfast spirit within me
(Psalm 51:10, New International Version).

Scripture: Ezekiel 36:24-28
Song: "Give Me Thy Heart"

Open-heart surgery has become a routine procedure for cardiac problems in the human body. What was once a dreaded, last-resort surgery has now become a common practice, with the recovery time greatly speeded up. In today's Scripture reading, the people of Israel, who were now in Babylonian captivity because of their "heart disease," needed radical surgery. God says that He will "give them a new heart." He will take away their stubborn heart of stone and put in its place His Spirit. That transplant will help them willingly to keep God's Word and to live His lifestyle.

The New Testament also has many references to the importance of our "spiritual hearts." "Blessed are the pure in heart for they will see God" (Matthew 5:8); "Christ may dwell in your hearts by faith" (Ephesians 3:17); "Let the peace of Christ rule in your hearts" (Colossians 3:15); "Do not harden your hearts" (Hebrews 3:8); "Love the Lord your God with all your heart" (Matthew 22:37).

How is your heart today? Perhaps you need a spiritual EKG. Why not give your heart to the Great Physician for His examination and let Him perform whatever procedures He needs to in order for your heart to be right with Him?

Heavenly Father, we surrender to You our hard, "stony" hearts. We want You to make them new, to make them whole, to make them pure. We submit ourselves completely to You and Your divine will. Make us what You would have us to be. Through Christ, our Lord, we pray. Amen.

Coming Clean

Though your sins are like scarlet, they shall be as white as snow;
though they are red as crimson, they shall be like wool
(Isaiah 1:18, New International Version).

Scripture: Ezekiel 36:29-33
Song: "Whiter Than Snow"

We are constantly bombarded by advertisements of detergent companies and their claims, such as: "whiter white," "it gets all the dirt out," "it's sparkling clean," "it's Borax clean," and on and on. Most of us make a valiant effort to clean up and get rid of the dirt in our environments. We also take relaxing hot showers to clean our bodies.

There are, however, dirty spots on our souls that no man-made soap can clean. There are moral smudges that no manufactured detergent can touch. There are sin stains that no earthly cleanser can get rid of. These are the spiritual stains caused by disobedience and rebellion against God. Israel knew about this kind of dirt. They needed to be cleaned up if they were to continue to be God's covenant people.

In the Scripture reading for today, God is telling the people of Judah that there is only One who can clean them up and make them acceptable to a Holy God. That One is God Himself. Israel must yield to His cleansing agent, His Spirit. There is still only one way to really become morally clean and spiritually pure. That is through contact with the precious, saving blood of Jesus, the "Lamb of God that takes away the sin of the world" (John 1:29).

Dear God, we ask You to cleanse our sins through the blood of Your Son, the Lord Jesus Christ. We are not worthy of Your forgiveness, but we ask that You cleanse us so that our attitudes and actions will not bring reproach upon You. In Jesus' name, we pray. Amen.

God's Beautiful Garden

They will say, "This land that was laid waste has become like the garden of Eden" (Ezekiel 36:35, New International Version).

Scripture: Ezekiel 36:34-38
Song: "Come, Ye Thankful People, Come"

Everywhere we have lived during our thirty-three years of ministry my wife has found a place to plant flowers, trees, and a garden. She has a "green thumb" for making things grow. I can look at a spot and see only a place to mow. She looks at the same spot and envisions a beautiful flowerbed.

When people look at a flowerbed or a vegetable garden, there is no doubt that someone was responsible for the beauty or the produce. Someone had to clear the soil of rocks and weeds. Someone had to till the soil and plant the seeds. Someone had to care for it. The beauty of the flowerbed and the fruit of the vegetable garden testifies to the skillful, attentive care of the gardener.

In our text for today, surrounding heathen nations see the miraculous renewal of the land of Israel. The effect of God's rejuvenation of the productivity of the land was so wonderful that Judah's neighbors would exclaim, "This land that was laid waste has become like the garden of Eden" (verse 35). They are not only awed by the new life, but they also give credit where credit is due. They "will know that I the Lord have rebuilt what was destroyed and have replanted what was desolate" (verse 36). The final result is "Then they will know that I am the Lord" (verse 38).

Dear Lord, we want to become "good soil" so that Your seed, Your Word, can take root in our hearts and produce an abundant crop that will help others see You at work in us and glorify your name. Amen.

Can These Bones Live?

Wake up, O sleeper, rise from the dead, and Christ will shine on you
(Ephesians 5:14, New International Version).

Scripture: Ezekiel 37:1-6
Song: "Revive Thy Work"

I have always been intrigued by the questions that God asks in the Bible. "But the Lord God called to the man, 'Where are you?'" (Genesis 3:9). "What is that in your hand?" (Exodus 4:2). There are over fifty questions that God asks Job in chapters 38 and 39! But the question God asked Ezekiel in this passage is most intriguing: "Can these bones live?"

There is nothing deader than a skeleton (or maybe a doorknob!). When God asked this question of Ezekiel, He had just shown him a vision of a valley that was full of bones and not just bones—very dry bones. That meant that they had been there for a long time and were now bleached by the sun. Why would God ask His prophet such a question?

Obviously, God wanted to use the dry bones in this vision to illustrate to Ezekiel the spectacular nature of the work of His power and His grace to bring the nation of Israel back to life again (See Ezekiel 37:11-14).

In similar manner we may sometimes wonder today, "Can this church survive?" or "Can this person who is beaten and battered, discouraged, and defeated live again?" "Can this marriage be saved?" God's answer is, "Yes!" By His power and creative ability He can put life into skeletons and "hair on doorknobs" (if He wants to!).

Thank You, O God, for the life — the abundant life that is ours through Jesus Christ! Help us yield to Your power so that we can truly live victoriously. In Jesus' name, we pray. Amen.

God's Spirit Gives Life

I will put my Spirit in you and you will live
(Ezekiel 37:14a, New International Version).

Scripture: Ezekiel 37:7-14
Song: "Spirit of the Living God"

The Spirit of God was at work early in history. In Genesis chapter one, God's spirit is "hovering over the waters." In chapter 2, God created man and "breathed into his nostrils the breath [or spirit] of life."

In this visionary valley where God has brought Ezekiel, He now speaks hope to a despairing nation. They are saying, "Our bones are dried up and our hope is gone; we are cut off" (Ezekiel 37:11). But God responds, "I will put my Spirit in you and you will live" (Ezekiel 37:14).

The answer to the spiritual problem of the Old Testament people of God was a renewal of God's Spirit within them. The answer to the spiritual problems of God's people in today's world is a renewal of God's Spirit within us.

The Apostle Paul in the eighth chapter of Romans made this clear. "If anyone does not have the Spirit of Christ, he does not belong to Christ" (Romans 8:9). And, "Those who are led by the Spirit of God are sons of God" (Romans 8:14). And, "The Spirit himself testifies with our spirit that we are God's children" (Romans 8:16).

Perhaps you have felt that your spiritual "bones are dried up" and your "hope is gone." Open your heart to a renewal of God's Spirit through reading His Word and prayer.

Dear God, we pray that You will help us live more passionately for You. May Your Holy Spirit lead us to do Your will. Thank You for life. In Jesus name, we pray. Amen.

November 25
Zechariah's Angelic Visitation

They were both righteous before God, walking in all the commandments and ordinances of the Lord blameless (Luke 1:6).

Scripture: Luke 1:5-13
Song: "Tell It to Jesus"

Zechariah was a righteous man, a devout servant of God who served in the office of priest. Likewise was his wife Elisabeth a righteous woman who walked in obedience to God. Their walking before God *blameless* was the premise of God's honoring them with this awesome angelic visitation and promise of a son. How wonderful it must have been that before all the other priests and such a great multitude of people in the temple that God would send His angel to announce the birth of John the Baptist.

The angel of the Lord made it very clear that his appearance was a result of Zechariah's prayers being heard. Zechariah spent many years serving in the temple, praying to God for his needs as well as the needs of the people, believing God would answer his prayers. His belief in God brought such powerful results that Zechariah experienced great fear that was necessarily calmed by the angel. Then there was the great announcement, "thy wife Elisabeth shall bear thee a son, and thou shalt call his name John."

God will do powerful works in our lives if we will continue in devout, faithful obedience to Him.

Father, we thank You for Your faithfulness to us. May we learn great lessons from Zechariah and Elisabeth's experience — that You will do great works for us if we trust You and serve You. In Jesus' name, we pray. Amen.

November 25-30. **Sallie J. Breaux** ministers with the radio and television ministries of The Hope of Glory Lighthouse in Lafayette, Louisiana.

To Believe Or Not To Believe

Then Abraham fell upon his face, and laughed, and said in his heart, "Shall a child be born unto him that is a hundred years old? and shall Sarah, that is ninety years old, bear?" (Genesis 17:17).

Scripture: Luke 1:14-20
Song: "Trusting Jesus"

God works marvelously in the lives of those who love Him and who are dedicated in serving Him. Some of His marvelous works are so incredible and so miraculous that recipients of His blessings often find them unbelievable.

As we examine the experience of Zechariah and Elisabeth, we see similarities to the experience of Abraham and Sarah, to whom God also promised a son in their old age. Though Zechariah did not laugh outwardly as Abraham did, the incredible message from the angel of the Lord did stir up questions of unbelief on Zechariah's part. What a terrible mistake to question God's message.

God's people often set themselves up for negative consequences or strong chastisement because of lack of faith in God's promises. Zechariah became mute and was not allowed to speak until God's promise was fulfilled.

Let us be determined to walk with strong faith in God's promises, no matter how incredible they may seem to our finite minds. God is always faithful to keep His promises and will fulfill His prophecies regardless of our response. But it is with so much more delight that we can praise God for His wondrous works when we believe Him implicitly.

Heavenly Father, we thank You for Your tolerance even in our seasons of disbelief. Strengthen us to walk in faith, in obedience, and in diligent service to You. In Jesus' name, we pray. Amen.

God's Promise Removes The Reproach

Thus hath the Lord dealt with me in the days wherein he looked on me, to take away my reproach among men (Luke 1:25).

Scripture: Luke 1:21-25
Song: "God Can Do Anything"

Have you ever been in a situation that caused you to think perhaps your unsaved friends were more fortunate than you? Have you even felt embarrassed in your witness of the love of Christ when those to whom you witness seem to have much more going for them or more worldly goods?

If your answer is "yes," rest assured you are not alone. Many other Christians answer "yes" with you. The Bible is full of examples of believers who were in the same predicament. However, in every case we see God proving Himself faithful on behalf of the believer. God never changes and is continuously proving Himself faithful to those who love Him and walk in obedience to Him. The people who awaited Zechariah's exit from the temple saw evidence of His encounter with the messenger of God. Later they also witnessed the testimony of Elisabeth that God had taken away her "reproach" of barrenness.

Regardless of our situations, we can be assured that God is faithful. He will keep His promises and will ultimately remove every reproach from our lives. He loves us and will not let us down—only trust Him!

Precious Father, we are so grateful You never change and You are faithful to us. We know that You often stretch us far beyond our comfort zones to help us grow and to serve You better. But we also trust that You will not require us to go through unnecessary hardships or suffering. Thank You for Your goodness to us. Through Jesus' name, we pray. Amen.

Call His Name John

The angel said unto him, "Fear not, Zechariah: for thy prayer is heard; and thy wife Elisabeth shall bear thee a son, and thou shalt call his name John"
(Luke 1:13).

Scripture: Luke 1:57-66
Song: "Waiting on the Lord"

The arrival of the newborn is always an exciting time in the life of a family. The parents, grandparents, siblings, uncles, aunts, cousins, friends all await the new arrival. One of the first questions asked usually is, "What is the name?" It is particularly exciting when a couple who expected not to conceive are blessed to become parents.

There was much joy surrounding the birth of John. God had promised through His angelic message to Zechariah a son in spite of his and Elisabeth's old age. The angel said the baby's name was to be John. Elisabeth waited in excitement and in praise from the women of the community, who acknowledged the miraculous work of God in her body. Zechariah could not speak, but surely the men applauded him for this gift of old age. Perhaps other couples of Zechariah and Elisabeth's age had adult children and grandchildren. But Zechariah and Elisabeth committed themselves to God in service and prayer year after year, awaiting an answer to prayer.

God, who is always true to His Word, in due season presented to Zechariah and Elisabeth and to the world the long-awaited answer to prayer.

Thank you, Lord, for the life of John the Baptist, the forerunner of our Savior, Jesus Christ. Thank You for the encouragement we receive in this Scripture to wait in faith for Your answers to our prayers. Help us to be contentedly patient. We realize that You can see the big picture, and Your timing is perfect. In Jesus' name, we pray. Amen.

A Special Son

I say unto you, Among those that are born of women there is not a greater prophet than John the Baptist (Luke 7:28).

Scripture: Luke 1:67-75
Song: "The Heavenly Vision"

The Bible tells us in our Scripture text that, under the guidance of the Holy Ghost, the father of John uttered powerful words of prophecy concerning John and the coming of Jesus Christ. We know John as the forerunner of Jesus Christ; we know him as the one crying in the wilderness preaching repentance. We know John as the evangelist baptizing in the Jordan River and as the baptizer of Jesus Christ. Based on our biblical record of John's life, we are sure these are all part of the depth of Zechariah's prophecy.

It is obvious from the Bible that John realized his primary purpose was to introduce Jesus Christ to the world as Savior. John was faithful in ministry and loyal to his purpose. He gave his life to the ministry, preaching the need to repent and accept Jesus Christ as Lord of Lords and King of Kings. He faced great opposition, but refused to compromise. For this he lost his life. God was able to use John effectively because of his commitment. Jesus testified of John that there was and will never be a greater prophet than John the Baptist.

God desires to use each of us to His glory. Propose in your heart to reach the destiny God has for your life, and to allow His blessedness to flow through you.

Dear God, it is our desire to please You and to have the sense of commitment John the Baptist had in presenting Jesus to the world. Help us to yield ourselves willingly to serve You in the best possible way. In Jesus' holy name, we pray. Amen.

To Prepare His Way

This is he, of whom it is written, "Behold, I send my messenger before thy face, which shall prepare thy way before thee" (Matthew 11:10).

Scripture: Luke 1:76-80
Song: "Come, Thou Long-Expected Jesus"

It was through the Holy Spirit that Zechariah prophesied concerning John. Zechariah had fathered the one chosen to prepare the way for the coming of the Lord Jesus. In his joy, Zechariah spoke declaring John's prophetic ministry and his being the forerunner, saying, "And thou, child, shalt be called the prophet of the Highest: for thou shalt go before the face of the Lord to prepare his ways." What an awesome honor was bestowed upon John and upon his parents.

John was not the long-awaited Messiah. "He was not that Light, but was sent to bear witness of that Light" (John 1:8). John did not have the leading part in God's great drama of salvation, but he did have a very important supporting role. Many people cannot tolerate having anything but top billing. They consider anything else to be beneath them—to play second fiddle. But both Zechariah and John knew the role he was to have in man's redemption and were proud of it.

We too have the privilege of introducing the world to Jesus Christ. People lost in sin still need to know there is salvation available to those who will accept Jesus. In our witness of Him, we are privileged to prepare the way for Christ to enter the hearts of those yet living in darkness.

Lord Jesus, thank You for coming to us as light in darkness. You are the only true light, the only hope we have out of sin. Help us to see the urgency to introduce You to those lost in sin, thus preparing the way for Your entrance into their hearts. In Your name, we pray. Amen.

My Prayer Notes

Devotions

December

photo by Chuck Perry

December 1

Make Room For The Word

The grass withereth, the flower fadeth: but the word of our God shall stand for ever (Isaiah 40:8).

Scripture: Isaiah 40:3-11
Song: "Have You Any Room For Jesus"

It appears a difficult matter for people to make room in their hearts for Jesus. It seems so easy for individuals to make room for all else the world has to offer and leave Jesus out. Some will accept Him initially but seem to limit Him to just a small corner of their lives. If only men would come to the knowledge of what is ours in Jesus Christ. In our accepting Jesus Christ we receive life eternal, in which is enveloped much more than we can describe in words for this earthly life and beyond. Salvation from the penalty of sin, deliverance from yokes of bondage, joy, peace, love, answered prayers, fulfillment—just a glimpse of what is ours when we make room for Jesus. He cares for us and is concerned for every facet of our lives. The Scripture says of His care: "He shall feed his flock like a shepherd: he shall gather the lambs with his arm, and carry them in his bosom, and shall gently lead those that are with young" (Isaiah 40:11).

Let us who have not made room for Jesus do so today. Then let us share Jesus Christ, so the lost will have a way prepared to receive Him as Lord and Savior.

I express gratitude, dear God, for Your sending Your Son, Jesus Christ to die for my sins. Father, I commit to make room for Jesus in my heart. I further commit to prepare the way for Christ to enter the hearts of others by sharing my witness of Him. In Jesus' name, we pray. Amen.

December 1. **Sallie J. Breaux** serves with the radio and television ministries of The Hope of Glory Lighthouse in Lafayette, Louisiana.

Obeying Without Understanding

Then Joseph, being raised from sleep, did as the angel of the Lord had bidden him, and took unto him his wife (Matthew 1:24).

Scripture: Matthew 1: 18-25
Song: "When We Walk With the Lord"

The class discussion that Sunday was on child discipline. "I think you should give your children a reason when you say no," I commented.

"At times I have a 'feeling' they shouldn't do something," one mother said. "So I just tell them, 'Because I said so.'"

"That doesn't seem right," I argued.

Then came the familiar statement: "When you have children, you'll understand." I eventually discovered she was right. Many times when my children would ask, "Why can't I?" I had no answer except, "Because I said so."

Often God kept me from doing something I wanted to do. When I questioned why, He said, in so many words, "Because I said so." And though I didn't understand, I obeyed.

Abraham did not understand when told to offer Isaac for a sacrifice, but he obeyed and experienced God's provision.

Noah did not understand when God told him to build an ark, but he obeyed, and his family was saved from the flood.

And Joseph did not understand when an angel told him to take Mary as his wife, but he obeyed, and became the earthly father of the Messiah.

Lord, You may ask us today to do something that we do not understand. Help us not to question the reason why but simply to obey—because You said so. In Jesus' name, we pray. Amen.

December 2-8. **Donna Clark Goodrich** is a wife, mother, grandmother, freelance writer, editor, proofreader, and seminar leader from Mesa, Arizona.

December 3
The Star Doesn't Leave at Christmas

We have seen his star in the east, and are come to worship him (Matthew 2:2).

Scripture: Matthew 2:1-12
Song: "0 Worship the King"

There's a sense of wonder in the air as Christmas nears. Decorations and carols fill the busy malls. Twinkling lights adorn snow-covered houses. People smile, give to charities, visit nursing homes. And the children are on their best behavior. Then in a few minutes it's over. Wrapping paper covers the carpet. Toys are strewn all over the house, and in the stores, sales people hurry to remove Christmas cards and replace them with Valentines. The nativity set is packed away, and the Christ Child forgotten until next year.

Let's look at the first Christmas. A chorus of angels appeared to shepherds who left their flocks and came to worship the Infant in the stable. The Bible doesn't say, but it's possible that other visitors also came to the manger. It was a night of reverent celebration.

Did it end that day? No, sometime later, theologians have suggested as much as two years later, wise men from the east saw the star and came to bow down before Jesus and to bring Him gifts suitable for a king.

And so it should be today. Whether a day after Christmas, a week, a month, or six months, we should still be seeking Jesus. Let the star shine on!

Lord, don't let Christmas be only a day on the calendar to us. And help us not let it become merely a commercial event — a high-sales season or just another vacation from work or nothing more than a party to be celebrated with drunkenness and revelry. Let it be a Christ-like attitude of our hearts that continues all through the year. In the name of Jesus we pray. Amen.

Arise and Go

One thing I do: Forgetting what is behind . . . I press on (Philippians 3:13, 14, *New International Version*).

Scripture: Matthew 2:13-18
Song: "I'll Go Where You Want Me to Go"

It's hard to let go of familiar places we like. Some people never do. They continue to live in the past, remembering how it was "where we used to live."

For a long time after moving to Arizona, I continued to take my hometown paper. I compared everything in our new state to how it used to be at home—weather, prices, schools, churches. It took almost 24 years for me to let go.

I had a special attachment to a place where our children were born, so I can imagine Mary's feeling when Joseph woke her up, saying, "Get packed. We're moving to Egypt."

"Egypt! Why Egypt?"

"Well, an angel told me to in a dream to go to Egypt."

It would have been easy for Mary to complain, "Jesus was born here. We have friends here. It's too difficult to travel such a long distance with a baby. It's too far from our families." Or Joseph might have argued with the angel, "I have work here. I've built up a good carpentry business."

But he didn't—and Mary didn't. They were obedient to God's messengers and, in so doing, they helped save Baby Jesus from Herod's slaughter.

What if God calls you to go across the world, across town, across the street, to tell others about Christ?

Lord, wherever You're calling me to today, I may not understand. I may not even want to go there. But help me to let go of these things and places that are behind and press forward. In Jesus' name, we pray. Amen.

December 5

God Speaks; Will You Obey?

An angel of the Lord appeareth in a dream to Joseph in Egypt, saying, Arise, and take the young child and his mother, and go into the land of Israel: for they are dead which sought the young child's life (Matthew 2:19, 20).

Scripture: Matthew 2:19-23
Song: "O Master, Let Me Walk With Thee"

A person could read this Scripture and begin to put stock in dreams. He or she could observe: An angel came to Joseph in a dream and told him to take Mary as his wife; the wise men were warned of God in a dream not to return to Herod after they found Jesus; an angel appeared to Joseph in a dream and told him to arise, take the young child and his mother, and flee into Egypt; and in today's passage, an angel told Joseph to take Mary and Jesus and "go into the land of Israel."

God often spoke to His children through dreams in biblical times. However, we would be remiss to put the emphasis on the dreams themselves.

In the four passages above, it's not important that Joseph and the wise men received warnings and instructions in dreams. The point is that God was the source of these messages, and the recipients faithfully obeyed.

So, whether God seems to be speaking to you through a dream, through a sign, through circumstances, or through one of His servants, we know He speaks to us through the Bible, His written Word. Check to be sure any other seeming communication from God is in harmony with the Scriptures. Then the question is: Will you obey?

Lord, let us be doers of the Word and not hearers only. Let us be still before You that we may hear Your voice. Then help us to be willing to obey. In the name of Jesus, we pray. Amen.

Turning Complaint into Praise

Giving thanks always for all things unto God and the Father in the name of our Lord Jesus Christ (Ephesians 5:20).

Scripture: Proverbs 15:1-9
Song: "For the Beauty of the Earth"

As I answered the telephone, my friend asked, "How are you doing?"

"Lousy," I complained. "Our car won't start, and I've got a bunch of errands to run."

To my surprise, she began to pray, "Lord, we thank You that Donna's car is broken. Maybe there is an accident on a street she'd be on," she added, "or maybe someone needs her help, and You're keeping her home near the phone."

I'll admit I had never before looked at my problems from that angle. And since that day, when going through rough situations, I've tried to find the bright side. During the past eleven months when eight members of our family were hospitalized—four with surgeries—I've praised God for good health insurance and for relatives and friends who prayed and brought food to us.

Instead of complaining about our neighbors' loud music, I began thanking God for my unusually good hearing.

And rather than getting mad at the truck driver who ran the red light last weekend, I thanked God for helping me stop in time, and for His protection over us.

It makes a big difference in my day and my family's day when I praise instead of pout!

Lord, it's so easy to complain about what we don't have, to gripe about what we're going through. But help us to concentrate instead on how good You are to us and how much You have given to us. In Jesus' name, we pray. Amen.

God Doesn't Always Pay on Fridays

These men of faith I have mentioned died without ever receiving all that God had promised them; but they saw it all awaiting them on ahead and were glad (Hebrews 11: 13, Living Bible).

Scripture: Psalms 1:1-6
Song: "It Pays to Serve Jesus"

One of my pet peeves is to see someone do something wrong and not get caught. A student who cheated on a test then got a better grade than I did and a co-worker who made a mistake and blamed it on me are cases in point.

Whenever I complained about such people, my mother always replied, "God doesn't always pay on Fridays." She told me, "It may seem like they are getting away with it, but God sees all and He has His own payday."

One day I realized that this saying works both ways. Just as there are people who will someday get the punishment they deserve, there are good people who will be rewarded later.

My mother experienced many hard times—emotionally and financially—when my father, after years of marriage, left her to raise three children alone. But she remained faithful and her "payday" came much later when God brought my stepdad into her life.

Her final "payday" came twenty years ago today December 7, 1982, when God said, "Welcome home, thou good and faithful servant." No, God doesn't always pay on Friday, but He does always pay.

Lord, we wonder why bad things happen to good people, why those who serve You so faithfully go through so many trials. Help us to realize that, as the writer of Hebrews says, wonderful things are waiting for them ahead and they will be glad. In the name of Jesus, our Savior, we pray. Amen.

Linking the Old to the New

THE ROYAL LINE of David will be cut off, chopped down like a tree; but from the stump will grow a Shoot—yes, a new Branch from the old root
(Isaiah 11:1, Living Bible).

Scripture: Isaiah 11:1-5
Song: "Thou Didst Leave thy Throne"

The devotions this week have come full circle, from Joseph taking Mary as his wife, leading to the birth of Jesus in Bethlehem, to today's passage describing the new Branch from the old root. It is exciting how this verse links the Old Testament with the New, as do other verses:

Micah 5:2 says that out of Bethlehem shall come one who will rule in Israel, so it wasn't a coincidence that Joseph and Mary were in that town the night Jesus was born.

Isaiah writes that the Messiah when He comes will be called the Prince of Peace (9:6). Jesus says in John 14:27, "My peace I give unto you."

Isaiah goes on to foretell that the Messiah would be a man who was "wounded for our transgressions . . . [and] bruised for our iniquities" (53:5). This certainly corresponds to the beatings, mocking, and crucifixion the New Testament describes Jesus receiving.

If our heavenly Father so inspired the writers of the Old Testament to prophesy hundreds of years ahead of time what was going to happen in the New Testament, then we know He also has the ability to look centuries ahead of our time and knows what will take place in our future.

Lord, thank You that Your Word not only links together the Old and New Testaments, but that You provide a plan to link earth to Heaven and man to God. If You see the sparrow fall and know the very hairs of our head, then we know You also care for us. Thank You. In Jesus' name, we pray. Amen.

Chasing Away Fear

The angel said to her, "Do not be afraid, Mary, You have found favor with God" (Luke 1:30, New American Standard Version).

Scripture: Luke 1:26-33
Song: "Blessed Assurance"

Angels, those awe-inspiring special messengers of God, must be a spectacular sight to behold. In almost every biblical account where an angel appears to someone, he has to reassure the person by saying, "Fear not!" This was true of Mary in the scene described in today's Scripture reading. We do not know much about Mary, but we do know that she was a young lady of sterling character with a strong faith in God and a ready willingness to submit her life to God's will.

Today, we can take hope that, just as Mary found favor with God, we too can find favor with God. We can do that in the same way as Mary—by trusting Him and joyfully submitting our lives to His will. When we know we are on God's side, then we realize we have nothing to fear. We can rest in the truth of Romans 8:28 that says, "In all things God works for the good of those who love him, who have been called according to his purpose."

While there are things that make people afraid, as believers we know that God himself has all things under His control. As a result, we have no need to fear. Whatever may happen to us, good or bad, if we have accepted Jesus as our Savior we are children of God and we have found favor with Him.

Dear Father, we thank You for giving us favor and kindness, along with a place with You in eternity. We raise our hearts and hands to praise Your goodness and glory. In the name of Jesus, our Savior, we pray. Amen.

Doing the Impossible

Nothing is impossible with God (Luke 1: 37, New International Version).

Scripture: Luke 1:34-38
Song: "All Hail the Power of Jesus' Name"

For a virgin to have a child, and for that child to be the Son of God, must have been beyond anything Mary could have comprehended. It certainly was not physically possible and must have seemed very unlikely to this young Jewish woman. From a human standpoint, even the idea of her offspring becoming the ruler of the House of David must have seemed unlikely. Mary was afraid, but she did believe God and was willing to have Him do the impossible through her.

Today there are things that may seem impossible to us as believers. Many things are impossible for us to accomplish in our own strength. Instead of becoming discouraged, we should realize that God has never said that we should be able to do the impossible on our own. He has only said that we should trust in Him and that He would do the impossible in order to achieve His purposes.

We are finite and small beings in a very large world. However, our God is very big. While many things are impossible for us, nothing is impossible for God. It could be that the seemingly impossible things we face in life are opportunities for God to do the "impossible" through us. As we read the Bible, let us look for challenging new ways God may want us to serve Him!

Lord we ask You to forgive us for not believing in Your greatness and that You can accomplish anything. Lord, help us to remember Your marvelous works from the beginning of time and to have greater faith so that we may see You work miracles in our lives. In the name of Jesus, we pray. Amen.

Believing Is Seeing

Blessed is she who has believed that what the Lord has said to her will be accomplished! (Luke 1:45, New International Version).

Scripture: Luke 1:39-45
Song: "Faith Is the Victory"

God has always wanted us to believe Him and His words. Believing is accepting the things God has said as though they were absolutely true even though you have no evidence to prove them. It is saying that what God has spoken is true, regardless of what most people may think about it. It is catching a glimpse of the future reality in our minds, even though it has not yet happened.

This does not mean that we will have all our dreams come true, but it does mean that we will receive God's promises if we believe them.

When we believe what God has said, exciting things happen, both in the spiritual world and the physical. In the spiritual world, our spirits grow as our faith grows. There is fellowship on the spiritual level with our heavenly Father when we believe in Him and in His precious promises. On the physical level, when we believe, we have hope. Hope in God does not leave one disappointed.

We will not be shaken by our circumstances because we have the promises of God. When we have faith, we see things God has promised as if they have already happened, even if they are not yet actually taking place.

Lord, we thank You that You have given us many promises, and that we have seen many of them accomplished in our lives. Thank You, Father, for using Mary to bring Your Son into the world so that we all might receive Your many gifts. In the name of Christ, our Savior, we pray. Amen.

Serve God With Joy!

I will rejoice in the Lord, I will be joyful in God my Savior (Habakkuk 3:18, New
International Version).

Scripture: Luke 1:46-56
Song: "Praise God, From Whom All Blessings Flow"

We are all accustomed to musicals in which the characters
break into exuberant song to express themselves. Few of us
practice this kind of expression in our day-to-day lives.
However, there are some extraordinary experiences that are so
moving that we do gesture wildly, cheer, yell, or jump up and
down. Perhaps you celebrate victories of your favorite ball
team this way. Doubtless, you have seen many game show
winners behave this way.

In the Scripture readings for yesterday and today we have
encountered two extraordinary monologues, one by Elisabeth,
the mother-to-be of John the Baptist, the other by Mary,
chosen to be the mother of the Messiah. The poem or song
uttered by Mary has been recognized for many centuries as an
exceptional tribute of praise to God. It has long been known as
the "Magnificat" from the Latin word meaning "to magnify."

The exuberance of Elisabeth and Mary was not occasioned
by some trivial happening such as a sports event or a financial
windfall. They were elated that they were being honored by the
Lord to perform key roles in His plan for the redemption, not
just of Israel, but of the whole world. It had been the dream of
every serious Jewish woman for centuries to become the
mother of the Messiah, or of the new Elijah!

Dear Father, we thank You for Elizabeth and Zechariah, and Mary and
Joseph. Help us to serve Your plan of salvation for the world. We thank You for
opportunities to serve You. In the name of Jesus, we pray. Amen.

December 13

Our Refuge in the Storm

Though you have made me see troubles, many and bitter, you will restore my life again; from the depths of the earth You will again bring me up. You will increase my honor and comfort me once again (Psalms 71:20, 21, New International Version).

Scripture: Psalms 71:15-21
Song: "Under His Wings"

There are bad things that happen in our lives and in the lives of those close to us. Often we can feel despair as we suffer through the hardships of life. As children of God, we have not been promised that we will be spared from life's difficulties. Jesus said rain falls on the just and the unjust, meaning that some things happen in the world regardless of whether people are righteous or not. Some have tried to blame every misfortune on the personal sins of those to whom the misfortune has happened, but there is no biblical basis for such an idea. This was the mistake of Job's friends.

Even though we are not always protected from the bad things that can happen in our lives, we do have a really good reason to be optimistic about the future. We have an inheritance that we shall receive one day. In John 14, Jesus said there are many rooms prepared for us in Heaven, and that He will return to escort us to them some day.

As Christians, we have this blessed hope. We know that one day we will live with Him in Glory. We know that even if we die God will raise us up on the last day. Let us focus on this truth: no matter what happens, God will lift us up and comfort us in His time.

Dear Father, we have seen trouble in our lives. We thank You that You are by our side every step of the way, protecting and comforting us. You alone are the great healer of all our wounds. In the name of Christ, we pray. Amen.

God's Calling Cards

He has caused his wonders to be remembered; the Lord is gracious and compassionate (Psalms 111:4, New International Version).

Scripture: Psalms 111:1-6
Song: "A Mighty Fortress Is Our God"

Science has made tremendous advances in its understanding of the natural world, which Christians hold to be the creation of God. Many scientists do not believe in God, yet they continually study the works and wonders of God. They still delight in studying His handiwork. Through scientific research, we have learned much about how the natural world works. Through diligent study of plants, animals, and human bodies we have found many medications that save countless lives. Through the study of chemistry and physics man has developed technology to make life much more comfortable than it previously was.

In Romans 1:20, Paul writes that God has revealed Himself through the natural world. Part of the reason for this is that God is compassionate towards His creation. Though people may not believe in God, they have the evidence before them. God wants us to all believe. His Spirit calls to all of us, even those who thus far have refused to believe. God is gracious and loving. He wants all of us to believe and be saved so that we may enjoy fellowship with Him forever. God's compassion for us draws Him to make His wonders remembered. Even in His creation of the natural world, God calls to man because God wants us to know Him.

Lord, You are a compassionate and gracious God. We thank You that You have given us Your works as signs so that we may know to believe in You and Your goodness to us. In the name of Christ, our Savior, we pray. Amen.

An Honest Deal

I sought the Lord, and he answered me; he delivered me from all my fears
(Psalms 34:4).

Scripture: Psalms 34:1-5
Song: "Leaning on the Everlasting Arms"

Advertising companies offer to rescue us from debt if we will just sign up for their credit cards. Others offer us freedom from financial worry if we will just buy their secret to gaining wealth. They promise to change our lives and to deliver us from any concern we might have. This is playing on people's fear that they will not be able to do what they need to do to provide for themselves and their families.

There are countless other gimmicks that play on our fears in a society that is based on materialism. However, God offers us a quite different deal. His plan is quiet, yet radical, calling on us to seek Him instead of seeking worldly wealth.

He does not promise that we will not have financial difficulty, but He does promise us a way to have spiritual security that will last forever. In Matthew chapter six, Jesus tells us to not store up treasures on earth but to seek heavenly treasure. Earthly treasure can be lost, stolen, or otherwise rendered useless. Furthermore, what the world considers treasure does not satisfy our deepest longings.

The treasure we get from God is eternal and satisfies our most basic needs. It will last us our entire earthly lives and throughout eternity. To get this treasure, we need only seek God's kingdom and His righteousness with our whole hearts.

Lord, You are the one who rescues us. We need not lean on worldly understanding or solutions. You are the ultimate answer. Help us not to be deceived by the answers the world offers. In the name of Jesus, we pray. Amen.

God Works Through Our Weakness

She gave birth to her firstborn, a son. She wrapped him in cloths and placed him in a manger, because there was no room for them in the inn.
(Luke 2:7, New International Version).

Scripture: Luke 2:1-7
Song: "O Little Town of Bethlehem"

It must have been a hard three-day journey for Mary from Nazareth to Bethlehem. The roads were dusty, uneven, and rocky. She must have felt every bump as the little donkey on which she rode jostled her from side to side. It was not an easy trip for a woman who was nine months pregnant! And what is even worse, once they finally arrived in Bethlehem, there was no place to stay. Tired, homeless, and pregnant, Mary must have been confused and frightened. Why would God bring her to this place so far from home to deliver her first baby? Why would He bring her to such a crowded place with nowhere to stay but an area near a stable?

Sooner or later, life takes us all to Bethlehem. Unexpected circumstances spin out of our control, and we find ourselves confused and afraid. Jesus was born into her life when Mary was at her lowest: tired, hurting, and in a barn away from home. When we have nothing left to give, that is the time when Jesus wants to be born in us. His strength shows best when we are weak (2 Corinthians 12:9). Do you need His strength? Let His life be born in you today!

Lord Jesus, there are times when we don't understand where You are leading us. We get confused. Please forgive us when we fear. Help us to open our hearts to You. In Your holy name, we pray. Amen.

December 16-22. **Susan Petropulos** is a writer and serves as a ministry associate at her church in Wexford, Pennslyvania.

Unlikely Messengers

Glory to God in the highest, and on earth peace to men on whom his favor rests (Luke 2:14, New International Version).

Scripture: Luke 2:8-14
Song: "Angels, From the Realms of Glory"

Living out in the fields with sheep was a pretty rough and dirty business. Shepherds were the most ordinary of the ordinary men who lived on the outskirts of society, men who were for the most part forgotten. It was into just such a group of common workingmen that God sent His first announcement of the greatest event ever to happen to mankind. Imagine their terror and awe as the angels revealed God's most important plan to these most unimportant of men.

If you were God, would you have chosen to trust such an important announcement to a group of dirty, itinerant shepherds? What do you suppose that God saw in these men that others did not? God sent His Son as a sign of His love for all men. Had He sent His message to the rich, the religious, or the powerful; men such as these shepherds might never have believed that Jesus came for them too.

God sent His message to the very ones we would never have chosen because He wanted the world to know that no one is unimportant to Him! Each of us should be encouraged by the story of the angels and the shepherds. Though there are times when all feel unloved and insignificant, this beautiful story assures us we are loved and valued by God.

Father God, thank You for the gift of life freely given to us through Jesus. Your love for us is beyond our understanding. Help us to see others as You see them, through Your eyes of love. Help us take the message of Jesus to them. In the name of our Savior, we pray. Amen.

A Growing Faith

Mary treasured up all these things and pondered them in her heart
(*Luke 2:19, New International Version*).

Scripture: Luke 2:15-20
Song: "While Shepherds Watched Their Flocks"

Mary knew beyond a shadow of a doubt that the baby peacefully sleeping in the manger beside her was the Son of God. She knew that God was in control. But do you suppose that anything was happening as she had expected? After the long, grueling trip to Bethlehem the only place they could find for shelter was a smelly stable. As if things weren't bad enough, the time came for the baby to be born there. Now, just a short time later, the baby, the Messiah, received His first visitors, rough, smelly shepherds from the fields outside Bethlehem. Surely Mary was a bit surprised! After all, this was hardly the way most kings entered the world.

It is difficult sometimes to digest and assimilate the things that happen around us as the events are unfolding. The circumstances of our lives sometimes seem to make little sense when unexpected things happen in rapid succession. Mary took time to "ponder" about the things happening around her. When the picture was too big for her to understand, she took time to bring her confusion and concerns to the One who could help her sort it all out. We too need to take time to quietly reflect before God. He alone is the One who can end our confusion and show us His way.

Lord **Jesus,** life is so very complex, and we often get confused. Help us to remember that You are always there, waiting for us to come to You. Forgive us for the times when we have tried to figure things out on our own. In Jesus' name, we pray. Amen.

December 19

From the Manger to the Cross

A sword will pierce your own soul too (Luke 2:35, New International Version).

Scripture: Luke 2:21-35
Song: "O Come, All Ye Faithful"

The birth of a baby is always a thrilling time. In each little bundle of new life lies the promise of hopes and dreams yet to be fulfilled. Surely when Jesus was born to Mary, she and Joseph must have dreamed of what it would be like to raise such a wonderful and special child. This was, after all, the long-awaited Messiah, the very Son of God, and God must have great plans for Him.

Imagine their surprise as they stood in the temple with Simeon, a man known for his devotion and righteousness, a man known to hear from God. Instead of words describing Jesus' glory, Simeon spoke of Jesus as a man of pain. Pain that would not just pierce a nation but that would pierce them as well. Yes, this child was indeed the Promised One of God. But He did not come to rule in the manner of earthly monarchs; He came to be the sacrificial "Lamb of God, who takes away the sin of the world." Jesus came to die!

As we think this Christmas season about the star, the angels, the shepherds, and the wise men, we must also think about the cross. For this child given to us by God was given as a sacrifice for you and for me. The manger can hold no glory unless it leads to the cross. For it is at the cross that God's promise was fulfilled. "O come let us adore Him!"

Father God, the love that gave such a sacrifice is beyond our understanding. Help us to live with the cross ever before us as an example and inspiration so that our lives might be living sacrifices to You. In the name of Jesus, we pray. Amen.

Anticipating Jesus

Coming up to them at that very moment, she gave thanks to God and spoke about the child to all who were looking forward to the redemption of Jerusalem (Luke 2: 38, New International Version).

Scripture: Luke 2:36-40
Song: "Will Jesus Find Us Watching?"

When our daughter was four years old she loved to see her Pap-Pap come for visits. His visits were usually infrequent and unannounced, but whenever any car pulled into the driveway she would run to the door expecting to see his familiar green Subaru. When Pap-Pap finally would come, my daughter's response was always the same.

"Pap-Pap's here! See, I TOLD you he was coming!"

Anna expected Jesus. For years she practically lived at the temple, fasting and praying, waiting expectantly for the Messiah. When Jesus came, Anna was not surprised. She told everyone she met about the wonderful gift of God! Just like my little daughter watched for her Pap-Pap, Anna was watching for the Savior!

Life is full of distractions as life surely was in the days of Anna. There are appointments to keep, errands to run, and meetings to attend. With clubs and sports, hobbies and crafts, our days are filled to the brim with activity. It is easy to forget to watch when our lives are so full. But Jesus is coming again. When He comes for us in the clouds of glory, will we be watching?

Lord Jesus, forgive us when we get so caught up in our busyness that we forget to watch for You. Help us to see You today. Help us keep our priorities straight so we are not caught up in fascination with trivial earthly events. Teach us how to watch for You. In the name of Jesus, we pray. Amen.

Buried Treasure

His mother treasured all these things in her heart
(Luke 2:51, New International Version).

Scripture: Luke 2:41-51
Song: "Thou Didst Leave Thy Throne"

It had been twelve years since that time in the stable in Bethlehem. There was the mysterious visit of the wise men, the hurried flight to Egypt, and their anxiety-filled return to their old hometown of Nazareth.

There were twelve years of growing, playing, learning and loving for Jesus and Mary and Joseph. And now He was finally on the brink of manhood. Mary and Joseph knew that a time would come when they would have to release Jesus to the destiny set before Him. But as they stood in the temple courts and listened to the words He spoke both to the teachers and to them, Mary and Joseph began to see that this child was becoming much more than an ordinary man.

Mary sensed that the words spoken by her son were important. She wasn't sure how or why, but she listened, even to what she did not understand, and she kept those words in her heart. Keeping God's words in our hearts is one way in which we can come to know Him more. As we read and reflect on His Word, whether or not we understand, God begins to speak, giving life to the written page and to the heart where it is stored. Jesus is the Living Word. He came to give us life. Mary knew the wisdom of keeping His words in her heart. Do we?

Father God, Your Word is a lamp for our feet, a light for our paths. Thank You for the Living Word, Jesus. Help us to let Your light shine in us today. In the name of Your Son, we pray. Amen.

Back to the Future

For to us a child is born, to us a son is given, and the government will be on his shoulders. And he will be called Wonderful Counselor, Mighty God, Everlasting Father, Prince of Peace (Isaiah 9:6, New International Version).

Scripture: Isaiah 9:1-7
Song: "I Know Who Holds Tomorrow"

Who can really know the future? It looms out there before us, big and empty and sometimes rather menacing. We long to know what lies ahead, and yet, at the same time, we fear it. What a comfort it is to realize that God knows exactly what the future holds. Hundreds of years before Jesus came to earth as a baby in a manger in Bethlehem, God had a plan. And he commissioned Isaiah to announce it. His plan was not just for that time 2000 years ago in Israel. His plan is still unfolding, day by day, week by week, and year by year. The shepherds, the magi, Anna, Simeon, and others had crucial roles in God's plan for the birth of the Savior. Maybe God has important roles for us to play in the latter part of His plan! Let's keep ourselves ready and available to Him.

As we look toward the end of this year and on into the next, God knows what each one of us will face. No matter what comes, He will be there to face it with us. Jesus came to redeem us. Now His Spirit lives in us and gives us the courage to face the future. He went before us to the cross, and He goes before us now. What a comfort to know that as we head into the future He is already there!

Our Awesome God, how can we praise and thank You enough for who You are and what You have done and are doing for us! O Lord, help us to live our lives today, tomorrow, and always so that they glorify You! In the name of Jesus we pray. Amen.

True Repentance

Produce fruit in keeping with repentance
(Matthew 3: 8, New International Version).

Scripture: Matthew 3:1-10
Song: "How Firm a Foundation"

Ben Hogan was a notorious gambler and saloonkeeper in the oil-boom towns of western Pennsylvania in the late 1800s. The story is told that on a visit to New York City he entered a building where a preaching service was going on to mock and scoff. Instead, the Spirit of God convicted him of his sins, moved him to repentance, and impelled Ben Hogan to cry out to God for forgiveness.

Later, Hogan met the famed evangelist Dwight L. Moody, who advised him to return to the oil region from which he had come and to set right what he could of his evil deeds. Hogan was at first received with suspicion, but his actions showed better than words that his repentance was genuine.

John the Baptist did not welcome many of the religious leaders who came to where he was preaching and baptizing. Their lives did not show evidence of true repentance.

It is not enough simply to tell God, "I'm sorry" in words. True repentance involves a change in behavior and thinking. The goal of life will be to please God, not one's self. The change true repentance makes in daily living will be evident; it will speak much more loudly than words.

Dear God, only You have power to forgive sin and change hearts. Father, cleanse us through Your Word and Holy Spirit so our lives will show evidence of true repentance. May our attitudes, our words, and our daily behavior testify that we have truly made You the Lord of our lives. Amen.

December 23-29. **Beverly Bittner** is a Christian writer and tutor living in Corry, Pennsylvania.

Because It Is Right

Jesus replied, "Let it be so now; it is proper for us to do this . . ."
(Matthew 3:15a, New International Version).

Scripture: Matthew 3:11-17
Song: "Christ Is King"

Four-year-old Beth's favorite question seemed to be, "Why, Mommy? Why?" The tired and exasperated mother finally said, "Because I say so, that's why!"

How like Beth we are with God. We want all the answers, and we want them right now.

John the Baptist was clear about his mission. He was to preach repentance to help prepare men's hearts to receive the Messiah. When Jesus came to John and asked to be baptized, John, recognizing the Messiah, could only ask, "Why should You come to me to be baptized for repentance?" He knew the Holy One was without sin.

No lengthy explanations were offered. "Because it is the right thing to do," was sufficient. The act of obedience was noted in Heaven. Like a lightning bolt the heavens opened and the Holy Spirit came down. As if that were not enough, God himself spoke words of approval that sounded to some like crashes of thunder. This direct testimony of the Heavenly Father established without a doubt the identity of the baby whose birth we celebrate at this Christmas season.

John's actions remind us that we too must be obedient to God's word. We can trust Him to reveal all that we need to know "in the fullness of time."

Father God, help us accept the truths we find in Your Word without doubts and questions, knowing that You will reveal all we need to know at the proper time. In the holy name of Jesus, our redeemer, we pray. Amen.

December 25

Jesus the Creator—Redeemer

The Sun of righteousness [shall] arise with healing in his wings (Malachi 4:2b).

Scripture: John 1:1-15
Song: "Come, Thou Long-Expected Jesus"

Many will celebrate Jesus today as a charming baby in a manger, an enchanting figure who will make no real demands upon their lives. Is it possible that this tiny Babe holds the secret to eternal life in His little hands? Charles Wesley expressed something of this mystery in his hymn for today.

"Born Thy people to deliver, Born a child and yet a King; Israel's Strength and Consolation, Hope of all the earth Thou art; Dear Desire of every nation, Joy of every longing heart."

Jesus, the Son of God, is as important to spiritual life as the sun is to physical life. The connection between the baby of Christmas and the savior spoken of in today's key verse is more than a play on two English words that happen to sound alike. Without the light and heat of the sun, all plant, animal, and human life would die. Until God moved, the earth was a barren and desolate place, dark and cold without the light and warmth of the sun.

Pain and loss, disappointment and grief, can make our lives seem dark, cold, and without hope. Jesus, the "Sun of righteousness," came to offer healing to all who will accept Him as the Great Physician. The great Creator of the universe, the perfect Sustainer of life became our Redeemer in that Bethlehem stable two millennia ago.

Lord Jesus, You are to be praised and lifted up. From the manger to the cross, You loved Your people, and You love us still. Accept our gratitude on this special day when we honor Your birth. Help us to convey to others the true significance of Christmas today. Amen.

All Glory to God!

Now unto the King eternal, immortal, invisible, the only wise God, be honor and glory for ever and ever. Amen (1 Timothy 1: 17).

Scripture: John 1:19-28
Song: "All Glory, Laud and Honor"

A popular singer was coming to our town for a concert. The morning the tickets went on sale, every phone line was jammed with fans demanding seats. In two hours the concert was sold out, and life returned to normal. But for those two hours, the ticket sellers seemed to be more important than the star himself. All attention was on those who were promoting the rock star and who were able to provide access to the star and his musical performance.

The popular John the Baptist was gaining prominence as he called for people to repent, be baptized, and prepare for the coming Messiah. In the excitement, confusion reigned. Was John the Promised One, or not? "Who are You?" the religious leaders demanded. Over and over, John explained, "I am not the Messiah, I am only God's messenger."

For a time, John was the center of attention. He could have bragged on himself. He could have become full of self importance at being chosen for the task of announcing the Messiah. But John remained humble. He properly gave recognition to Jesus as his superior.

As Christians we may be tempted to give ourselves credit for what we do for Him. But all honor, and glory belongs to God, and we should always give Him credit.

Dear God, help us be faithful in the work You have for us to do. May we always remember to give You honor and praise. You alone are worthy In Jesus' name we pray. Amen.

Credit Where It's Due

Among them that are born of women there hath not risen a greater than John the Baptist (Matthew 11:11a).

Scripture: Matthew 11:2-15
Song: "What a Wonderful Savior!"

There is an ungodly tendency among mankind to try to puff ourselves up, to "put on airs," to try to appear to be more important than everyone else. This tendency even existed back in Jesus' day. He referred to those who liked to wear fancy robes and be addressed by titles of honor.

By contrast, John the Baptist refused to exalt himself in any way. John knew exactly what role God had assigned him, and he was honored by it and content with his ministry. Even though there were those who were willing to consider John the Messiah, he would have none of it. This proper attitude of John's was not unnoticed by the Messiah. Jesus gave John proper credit. "Among them that are born of women," Jesus said, "there is none greater than John the Baptist." Certainly Jesus' words gave more credibility to John's ministry than any John could have given himself.

Do you ever feel that you don't get proper credit for what you do for the Lord? Are you ever tempted to say or do things to call attention to your good works? Nothing done for Jesus goes unnoticed in Heaven. If rewards are due us, they will be given at the proper time. We don't have to brag on ourselves. Rather, we should serve Jesus joyfully and humbly.

Father God, thank You for giving us a role to perform in Your kingdom. We are honored to be allowed to serve You. Help us never become proud or vain. But may we hear You say to us one day, "Well done, thou good and faithful servant." Through Jesus' name we pray. Amen.

Not Forgotten

God is not unjust; he will not forget your work and the love you have shown him (Hebrews 6:10a, New International Version).

Scripture: Matthew 14:1-12
Song: "Near to the Heart of God"

A highlight of the summer for me was a week at adult history camp. I was even asked to contribute some books I have written on history to the museum sponsoring the camp. Campers were also invited to contribute an appropriate item to a time capsule that will be opened in 2059.

Fifty years from now, few people outside of my family and close friends may remember the books I have written or the circumstances of my life and death. I could be sad about that, except that I have Jesus' assurance of a home in Heaven.

In our Scripture for today, we read about the death of John the Baptist. After a brilliant career as an influential prophet of God, John died an ignominious death at the whim of a profane, adulterous couple. Could not Jesus have intervened and saved the one who had been so faithful to Him? Had God turned His back on this loyal young servant who was only in his early thirties? No, for the important measure of our lives is not length but the extent to which we have fulfilled God's plan for us. Neither Jesus nor His Father cancelled His appointment at the cross because that was a part of the Father's plan for the salvation of the world.

Though you may experience hardship and feel that God has forgotten you, "He will not forget your work!"

Father God, help us to follow the examples of John and of the Lord Jesus Christ, who were faithful until the end. May we look forward to eternal life with You. In Jesus' name we pray. Amen.

December 29

Serving God From the Heart

John came unto you in the way of righteousness (Matthew 21:32a).

Scripture: Matthew 21:23-32
Song: "I Would Be Like Jesus"

Jesus reserved His most scathing condemnation for those who pretended to be righteous, but whose hearts were not dedicated to God. In today's Scripture the chief priests and elders challenged the authority of Jesus. He in turn asked them what they thought about the authority of John the Baptist. "Was it from heaven, or of men?" While they didn't believe in John, they were too cowardly to say so.

Jesus went on to liken the priests and elders to a son whose father asked him to work in the vineyard. The son gave an outward appearance of complying with his father's wish, even addressing him politely as "Sir." But he didn't actually go to work. He was a hypocrite like the priests and elders.

Jesus added that the publicans and harlots who had made no pretense of being righteous, but were converted, would enter God's kingdom ahead of the priests and elders!

John the Baptist, however, represented a third category of persons. John came "in the way of righteousness" never having lived a life of debauchery, nor having lived a hypocritical life of pretended righteousness. John said "Yes" to the call of his Heavenly Father and then carried through by faithfully doing what he was asked.

Let's serve God with integrity, not just play church!

Gracious God, thank You for the invitation to come to You. May we worship and serve You in spirit and in truth. Help us always to be humble and genuine in our relationship to You and to each other. May we faithfully carry through with the commitment we have made to You. In Jesus' name we pray. Amen.

The Look of Love

"Jesus looked at him and loved him" (Mark 10:21, New International Version).

Scripture: Mark 10:17-22
Song: "Jesus Loves Me"

The "rich young ruler" may be a familiar story to us as we read today's Scripture passage. But let's take a closer look. What do we see here? We see a young man searching for something he could do to seal his destination for eternal life. We see a man confessing his spiritual checklist—he has been striving to be a faithful Jew by obeying the law since he was a boy. We see a man trying to earn God's approval. It would have been better to have asked "What must I be?" rather than "What must I do?"

Jesus saw the folly of the young man's thinking, and yet He "looked at him and loved him."

Jesus sees our hearts as well. He knows the times when our actions are motivated by our desire to earn His approval. He looks at us and the folly of our thinking. Yet He loves us!

Jesus has said that we do not *earn* eternal life. Heaven is a gift we receive. Our righteous acts flow as a response to this gift, as our praise for God's goodness, as a gift back to the Giver. Jesus' blood has covered any spiritual checklists we have made. Our price has been paid because God looked at His creation, and He loved us.

O Father, we thank You for looking at us and loving us despite the errors of our thinking. We thank You for reminding us through Your Word that Jesus has already made a way for us to reach Heaven. We accept Your gift. In His name we pray. Amen.

December 30, 31. **Kelly Carr** is an editor and Christian writer living in Cincinnati, Ohio, with her husband, Steve.

Riches, Camels, and Jesus

It is easier for a camel to go through the eye of a needle than for a rich man to enter the kingdom of God" (Mark 10:25, New International Version).

Scripture: Mark 10:23-31
Song: "He Is Exalted"

Such humorous images come to mind when we read about a camel fitting through the eye of a needle. But let's read the verse again, this time focusing on the last half: "than for a rich man to enter the kingdom of God."

Wealth was holding this particular rich man back. From what? we ask. Not from *what,* but from *whom*? The love of money stood between the rich young man and Jesus. But don't we all have things in our lives that hold us back from Jesus? We could all insert ourselves into the verse: "It is easier for a camel to go through the eye of a needle than for *me* to enter the kingdom of God."

The truth is, none of us can enter God's kingdom on our own. We would never meet the requirements. But praise God that He sent One to walk with us! We do not have to be enough on our own. We do not have to dwell on the temptations that hold us back from God.

We only have to trust in Jesus and accept Him as our personal Savior. Let's turn loose of the things that bring us glory and reach out to take His nail-pierced hands. Then someday, when we see our unworthy selves accepted with open arms by the King of all creation, we can smile and think, *The camel just got through*!

Most holy Father, we thank You for loving us. We thank You for reaching out to us and inviting us home to Heaven. We come before You through the blood of Jesus. In His name we pray. Amen.